TIBETAN BUDDHISM

Tibetan Buddhism

A Guide to Contemplation, Meditation, and Transforming Your Mind

Khenpo Sodargye

EDITED AND TRANSLATED BY
The Wisdom and Compassion Translation Group

SHAMBHALA

Shambhala Publications, Inc.
2129 13th Street
Boulder, Colorado 80302
www.shambhala.com

Cover art: Courtesy of Robert Beer
Cover design: Daniel Urban-Brown

First Edition
Printed in the United States of America

Shambhala Publications makes every effort to print on acid-free, recycled paper.
Shambhala Publications is distributed worldwide by Penguin Random House, Inc.,
and its subsidiaries.

LIBRARY OF CONGRESS CATALOGING-IN-PUBLICATION DATA
Names: Suodaji, Kanbu, 1962– author.
Title: Tibetan Buddhism: a guide to contemplation, meditation, and transforming your mind /
Khenpo Sodargye; edited and translated by The Wisdom and Compassion Translation Group.
Description: Boulder: Shambhala, 2024. | Includes bibliographical references. | Identifiers:
LCCN 2023011375 | ISBN 9781645472247 (trade paperback)
Subjects: LCSH: Buddhism—Doctrines. | Buddhism—China—Tibet Autonomous Region. |
Buddhism—Tibet Region.
Classification: LCC BQ7604 .S86 2024 | DDC 294.3/42—dc23/eng/20230509
LC record available at https://lccn.loc.gov/2023011375

CONTENTS

Translators' Note

SINCE THE EARLY 2000s, many laypeople have embarked on the journey of systematically studying and practicing the Dharma under the guidance of Khenpo Sodargye Rinpoche, a chief master at Larung Gar Five Sciences Buddhist Academy, one of the largest and most influential Tibetan Buddhist academies in the world. These lay practitioners started their lifelong spiritual journeys by studying Khenpo Sodargye Rinpoche's teaching series on several must-know subjects, upon which this English book is based.

These beginning lay practitioners normally formed study groups on their own and attended weekly three-hour group study sessions, supported by Khenpo Sodargye Rinpoche's oral teaching videos, and were tutored by a more advanced Dharma peer. Through this process they would first complete in-depth study of the teaching series over two months.

For the next four months, they would study Khenpo Sodargye Rinpoche's commentaries on classical short texts on subjects including how to be an ethically good person (the prelude to becoming a good Buddhist),[1] how to become a bodhisattva,[2] and how to advance on the path to enlightenment.[3]

This half-year study program was intended to establish a solid foundation for learning Tibetan Buddhism.

After this foundation was established, many practitioners proceeded to study Patrul Rinpoche's *The Words of My Perfect Teacher* with Khenpo Sodargye Rinpoche's commentary and, most importantly, learn how to put the teachings into practice. Staying with the weekly rhythm, lay practitioners would complete intensive study of the text within three and a half years. In parallel, these practitioners would also complete at least one entire cycle of preliminary practices (*ngöndro*).

While keeping the preliminary practices in their routine for the rest of their lives, many practitioners further advance to the practice of the Great

Perfection (Dzogchen)—the pinnacle of the Nyingma tradition—with Khenpo Sodargye Rinpoche as their *vajra* guru.

Advanced lay practitioners, like their monastic counterparts at Larung Gar, can also study texts by Buddhist masters including Shantideva, Asanga, Chandrakirti, Nagarjuna, Dharmakirti, Longchenpa, and Mipham Rinpoche, supported by Khenpo Sodargye Rinpoche's oral teachings. The goal of these learnings is to unlearn thoughts and attitudes that obscure the true nature of mind.

Such immersive, repeated, in-depth studies and applications allow practitioners to thoroughly internalize the Dharma, and to direct their Vajrayana practice.

Khenpo Sodargye Rinpoche's emphasis on systematic study and practice, which embodies the legacy and tradition of Larung Gar Five Sciences Buddhist Academy, may seem unfamiliar to some Western Buddhists. This is because Western Dharma students often are encouraged to develop meditation before, or instead of, studying texts.

To better understand the unbroken lineage tradition that Khenpo Sodargye Rinpoche upholds, it is important to first understand the difference between the two approaches to enlightenment embedded in Tibetan Buddhism. One is the approach of the *panditas* primarily based on study, and the other is the approach of the *yogis* primarily based on meditative practice. Many Buddhists often regard these two approaches as polarized and competing traditions—an "either-or" situation.

But Khenpo Sodargye Rinpoche's teachings bring these two approaches together by following lineage masters, notably Mipham Rinpoche and Khenpo's root guru, the great Jigme Phuntsok Rinpoche. This integration is rooted in Khenpo Sodargye Rinpoche's indivisible roles as a great Buddhist scholar and an achieved Dharma practitioner.

As Khenpo Sodargye Rinpoche often says, for most Buddhist practitioners it is essential to study the Dharma systematically instead of sporadically. Hearing, contemplation, and meditation on the Dharma are all vital, with meditation at the very core. Without meditation, study through hearing and contemplation is insufficient, like cooking a big meal but not eating it. Without hearing and contemplation, meditation can go dangerously astray, like a blind person walking along a cliff with little guidance. Once practitioners have gained intellectual understanding through hearing and contemplation, meditation develops into true realization, without any mistake.

For those wishing to receive pointing-out instructions as soon as possible, preferably on their first day as a Buddhist, the Larung Gar model may seem too slow. Yet, we all know the motto "More haste, less speed."

As Khenpo Sodargye Rinpoche reassures his Dharma students, starting slowly and continuing steadily is essential for most people's progress on the path to enlightenment.

Through systematic study and practice, many practitioners following the Larung Gar model steadily grow in the love and compassion of *bodhichitta*, while ego-clinging and negative emotions decline; their dark clouds of ego vanish, while recognition of the nature of mind emerges. Although realized Larung Gar practitioners rarely disclose their accomplishment, their awakening is often revealed through auspicious signs at the time of death.

As their appetite for Dharma practice grows, some Larung Gar practitioners start realizing that Khenpo Sodargye Rinpoche's teaching series that they first encountered is the start of something big, something transcendental, and something very substantial to their life and to their death.

Among these practitioners were a few members of the Wisdom and Compassion Translation Group. We have gratefully received Khenpo Sodargye Rinpoche's many teachings and have no way of repaying his kindness. Despite our extremely limited qualities as Dharma practitioners and translators, we decided to edit and translate the teaching series into this book.

We thought that because the teaching series has been so important in our study and practice, it would also benefit our extended Dharma circle of English-speaking families, friends, colleagues, and by extension, other Westerners. This English book covers fundamentals of Tibetan Buddhism that practitioners should know and internalize, whether following the Larung Gar model or not.

While translating the teaching series, we also edited the content by adding excerpts from Khenpo Sodargye Rinpoche's most recent oral teachings on related topics. As much as we aspired to retain his voice in the English version of the book, we must admit that his carefree manner, heartfelt warmth, and humor, which are miraculously contagious and inspiring during his oral teachings, were partially lost in transcription and translation. Only if you have been with Khenpo Sodargye Rinpoche in person or listened to his teachings will you fully understand what we mean here.

We are grateful to several of our Dharma companions, primarily our vajra sisters and brothers, who for years have been faithful disciples of Khenpo Sodargye Rinpoche. Without their generous help in transcribing and compiling Khenpo's teachings and providing feedback on our drafts, our translation and editing could not have proceeded fast enough. In its essence, this book project has been our collective guru yoga practice.

We offer special thanks to Ngawang Zangpo for his timely suggestions pertaining to translation and to Cecilia Luk for proofreading the manuscript tirelessly. We especially thank Steve Wilhelm for his great involvement in editing the first draft of the manuscript and his exemplary work ethic.

We are very grateful for the valuable help of Nikko Odiseos, Tasha Kimmet, Peter Schumacher, and other highly competent members of Shambhala Publications. It has been heartening for us to work with the Shambhala team!

Any errors in word choice, meaning, or understanding are entirely our own, and we ask forgiveness of the deities and protectors of the doctrines for all mistakes made out of lack of experience, unawareness, or otherwise.

May this book help you journey into the pinnacle of wisdom!

The Wisdom and Compassion Translation Group
May 30, 2022

PREFACE

IN 1987 my root guru the great Jigme Phuntsok Rinpoche[1] led a few hundred Larung Gar Five Sciences Buddhist Academy[2] disciples on a pilgrimage to Mount Wutai, a sacred site for the bodhisattva Manjushri, who embodies the knowledge and wisdom of all the buddhas. The pilgrimage lasted nearly one hundred days.

Once the great Jigme Phuntsok Rinpoche arrived at Mount Wutai, more and more pilgrims joined from across the country. They were deeply fascinated by his teachings on Tibetan Buddhism, as well as by his great compassion and wisdom.

Eventually some of them followed the great Jigme Phuntsok Rinpoche back to Larung Gar, where they started a new life journey in the fierce sunshine and thin air of the Tibetan Plateau and, most importantly, in the bliss of Dharma.

As their translator during the pilgrimage, I was appointed by my root guru to be their translator and teacher at Larung Gar.

"Your task," my root guru told me, "is to bring authentic Tibetan Buddhism to non-Tibetan Buddhists."

More than thirty years have passed since then, and I am still committing myself to the same task.

At the very beginning, I had to teach in the open air in the front yard of my makeshift cabin at Larung Gar. In winter the small group of us had to sit on the frozen ground—you can imagine how much we appreciated sunshine back then.

Over the years, more and more Dharma halls were erected at Larung Gar, and now I teach in a spacious hall where statues of Shakyamuni Buddha, Guru Rinpoche (Padmasambhava), and the great Jigme Phuntsok Rinpoche are venerated. Thanks to evolving information technology, now I can also reach more Dharma students living far away from Larung Gar.

Although the teaching venue has changed and the audience has grown larger, one thing remains unchanged: my teachings follow the long unbroken tradition of lineage masters, particularly including the great Jigme Phuntsok Rinpoche.

My root guru always emphasized the importance of establishing solid foundations of spiritual progress through systematic Buddhist studies and Dharma practice. As he often told us disciples, Buddhists without right views can hardly advance on the path to enlightenment, even if they may have received the highest teachings of the Great Perfection (Dzogchen).

I always try my very best to emulate my root guru in everything, including teachings. Whenever beginning Dharma friends ask about the sequence of studying and practicing Mahayana Buddhism, I suggest they start by establishing right fundamental views.

Over a dozen years ago, laypeople started following the Larung Gar curriculum and delving into systematic hearing, contemplation, and meditation. Responding to that interest, I delivered a series of oral teachings on several must-know subjects for beginning lay Mahayanists, some of whom also aspired to take the tantric path later. This entry-level teaching series serves as the prerequisite for their systematic study and practice of the Dharma. In a way, it prepares them for entry into the path to enlightenment. Its close resemblance in a worldly setting could be the prelaw or premed studies that prepare university students for entry into law school or medical school. This English book originates from that teaching series and has been edited to be reader-friendly for Western Buddhists.

Unlike monastics at Larung Gar who can thoroughly study foundational Buddhist texts to establish right views, most lay practitioners don't have the luxury of time and energy. So, my teaching series, as well as this book, aim to convey a big picture of the Mahayana path by highlighting the bullet points of the path.

This book is like the pencil sketches of a deity, like Manjushri, utilized to create a Tibetan Buddhist painting called a *thangka*. The pencil sketches don't show all the meticulous details, but they offer a clear outline so the final outcomes won't be wrong. This book is the "sketch" for the "thangka of the Mahayana Buddhist path."

As readers of this English-language book will be somehow different from the recipients of my original oral teachings, I have to customize my pedagogical approach and cater to the Western worldview. The key question was how to make this customization right.

Once a Tibetan Dharma teacher, who now teaches in North America, said to me, "When you teach Westerners, make sure you skip or fast-forward topics pertaining to rebirth and karma. They don't like them. They don't necessarily believe them. You'd better choose topics that they like, such as mindfulness meditation."

This may be his skillful means to attract Westerners, but I disagree with his ideas about "customization."

A Dharma teacher must teach Dharma students what they *should* know, whether they like it or not. Otherwise, for students who cherry-pick Dharma or worse yet twist it to suit what they already believe, Dharma is merely a pacifier that pampers or even grows their ego. This is the exact opposite of enlightenment, which entails the state of egolessness.

Foundational Buddhist views must remain the same for people from Asia and those from the West. If topics such as rebirth and karma are skipped, it is like the head or an arm of Manjushri is missing in a thangka—the painting is incomplete.

Of course, approaches used to introduce these topics to Asian people and Westerners can vary, and this is where the book is "customized." This customization is like the various ways thangka artists can sketch Manjushri: they can use pencil or charcoal; they can adopt thinner lines or heavier strokes; they can draw twenty or thirty petals for the lotus held by Manjushri. Nevertheless, the deity on the thangka remains intact, complete, and carries the legacy of the long tradition, which is also the guiding principle for this book.

While giving the teaching series to lay Mahayanists, I tried to present the Dharma in a direct and concise manner, offering quotes from sutras and shastras as scriptural evidence and support. I learned this teaching style primarily from my own guru, the great Jigme Phuntsok Rinpoche.

Even when my guru could not see well in his old age, he still taught in this way. He usually asked someone or me to record the root texts he was going to teach, and he would then listen to the audio and teach accordingly in front of a crowd. My root guru taught based solely on his memory, and he could perfectly quote Buddhist scriptures at will, without any error. He always said that the words of the Buddha and the eminent masters have inconceivable blessings and benefits. And so, dear readers of this book, even if all you remember after reading this book are a few quoted verses, this can already help you establish right views and dispel wrong views.

With the blessings of the lineage masters and the Three Jewels, may this book help you lay a solid foundation for the path to enlightenment.

May this book be the start of your systematic hearing, contemplation, and meditation on the Dharma.

With utmost gratitude, I dedicate this book to my peerless root guru the great Jigme Phuntsok Rinpoche, who is always present in my heart and mind. My root guru passed into *parinirvana* in 2004, but he has never departed from me.

Lama Chenno!

Sodargye
July 2020
Larung Gar, Sertar

TIBETAN BUDDHISM

1. THE FOUR DHARMA SEALS

The Heart of the Buddha's Teachings

THE MAN WHO would become the Buddha started life over 2,500 years ago as the prince Siddhartha Gautama. He enjoyed a privileged royal life in Kapilavastu, an ancient city on the Indian subcontinent. From the outside, everything seemed perfect in his princely life. Siddhartha had all anyone could dream of: a beautiful wife, caring parents, several splendid palaces, many fancy chariots, exotic food, elegant clothes, devoted servants, glorious fame, and a kingdom over which he was soon to reign. If it were today, Siddhartha would be featured as an icon of success on the covers of *Time*, *Forbes*, and *Vogue*.

Prince Siddhartha could have continued living this seemingly perfect life and succeeded his father as king. However, he was a man interested in truth, and this led him to earnestly investigate life outside the palace. Several eye-opening excursions beyond the palace walls took his life in a completely unexpected direction.

During these outings, at the eastern gate of the palace, Siddhartha saw an old man limping along; at the southern gate, he saw a sick person racked with excruciating pain; at the western gate, he saw a dead, lifeless body. Never in his life had he seen such things! After a life exposed only to pleasure and privilege, Siddhartha was deeply shocked by what he witnessed. Lastly, at the northern gate, Siddhartha came upon an ascetic practitioner who had renounced the world and devoted himself to seeking the end of suffering.

Feeling powerless and fearful of old age, sickness, and death, Siddhartha realized his privileged status would not protect him and his loved ones from these sufferings. In the hope of discovering a way to end this suffering, he relinquished his royal life and heirship and became an ascetic spiritual seeker.

Upon first hearing Siddhartha's story, we may wonder how things so seemingly mundane could impact him so profoundly that he sought to discover the source of suffering and how to eliminate it. Unlike ordinary beings who remain oblivious to decay and death, Siddhartha aspired to delve deep into the truth of impermanence upon witnessing these miseries. Inspired by the ascetic practitioner, he became convinced that there was a path to freedom from this suffering, although at the beginning he didn't know what that path might be.

During his spiritual quest Siddhartha sought many teachers. He first received meditation methods by which his mind could abide in the state of one-pointed serenity, in which awareness of the external world recedes. This gave him the impression that all his problems had disappeared. However, this experience didn't last. Once his meditation finished, he found his existential questions remained unanswered. Siddhartha decided to take up a different course of action. He conducted ascetic practices such as prolonged fasts, hoping that wearing down his body could help him find the truth. However, after six years of ascetic life, having starved himself to almost a walking skeleton, Siddhartha found himself enveloped by frustration. He realized that his ascetic experience brought no solution to the problems of suffering and that the path should be through the mind recognizing the true nature of everything. Siddhartha ended his asceticism and revived himself by accepting a small meal of milk porridge from a milkmaid.

Then, Siddhartha took a seat beneath a tree, which has since been called the Bodhi Tree, in Bodh Gaya, India, and vowed not to arise until he attained spiritual awakening. He entered a state of deep concentration, vanquished all obscurations, and recognized the ultimate truth of the universe after three days and nights, awakening to full realization at dawn.

From that time on, Siddhartha, the prince from the Shakya clan, was known as Shakyamuni Buddha, with Shakyamuni meaning "the sage of the Shakyas," and Buddha meaning "the awakened one." The Tibetan term for Buddha is *Sangye (sangs rgyas)*, in which *sang* means awakening from the sleep of ignorance and purifying the darkness of obscurations, and *gye* means opening consciousness to encompass the knowledge of the true nature of things and their multiplicity.

He rested in the bliss of the awakened state for forty-nine days before he took any action; then he began teaching. For the rest of his life Shakyamuni Buddha taught people the path of liberation and assisted them in ending their suffering through the three turnings of the wheel of Dharma.

Once, a disciple asked the Buddha, "After you are gone, if someone else comes along to give teachings and proclaims that to be the Dharma, how can we discern whether it is indeed the true Dharma?" The Buddha answered, "After I am gone, any teachings that incorporate the four Dharma seals are the true Dharma." The four Dharma seals are the four truths that encompass all of Buddhism and fundamentally differentiate it from other religions:

> All conditioned phenomena are impermanent.
> All tainted things are suffering.
> All phenomena are devoid of self.
> Nirvana is beyond extremes.

Here "seal" means a stamp or hallmark that denotes or confirms authenticity. Thus, the presence of the four Dharma seals in a teaching confirms its authenticity as true Dharma.

Buddhist teachings cannot deviate from the four Dharma seals. If a person practices Dharma that is consistent with the seals, they are a true Buddhist, in that they are on the true path to enlightenment. Otherwise, even if a person becomes a Buddhist after taking refuge in the Three Jewels by attending a refuge ceremony in a Dharma center or a monastery—a sort of equivalent of baptism in Catholicism—without embracing and integrating the seals, they are not yet a true Buddhist. Even for those who are not Buddhists, knowing and accepting the four Dharma seals can be of great benefit because the seals are not merely religious doctrines but the truth of all our inner and outer worlds.

FIRST SEAL: ALL CONDITIONED PHENOMENA ARE IMPERMANENT

The Buddha taught that nothing is permanent. The nature of every phenomenon, or every conditioned thing, is impermanence. This means everything changes. The word *phenomenon*, one of the many meanings of *dharma* in Buddhism, refers to all things that can be perceived. What does "conditioned phenomena" mean here? This means that all things, be they physical objects, mental factors, or their respective activities, don't exist independently; they arise from causes and conditions and are subject to cause and effect.

For example, this book you are holding is the result of a writer's thoughts, the work of an editor, a computer, paper, ink, glue, and printers coming together. This book doesn't exist independent of its parts. If we further examine each of the parts, we'll find they are also "conditioned." The paper, for instance, is the product of trees, loggers, truck drivers, paper mills, and more coming together. All these parts of parts also depend on causes and conditions. The trees depend on seeds produced by another tree, fertile ground filled with various nutrients, rain, sunlight, and so on. Therefore everything deemed "conditioned" arises through causes and conditions, everything is interdependent, and everything is subject to change.

Everything around us is a reminder of impermanence, yet we don't see that, or we simply ignore it. When I accompanied my root guru the great Jigme Phuntsok Rinpoche to New York City in 1993, we were able to stand at the topmost windows of the twin towers of the former World Trade Center, looking at the panoramic views of downtown Manhattan and the broader city. I visited New York again in 2017, after the September 11 attacks, and the twin towers had been replaced by two pools of water. I stood there, contemplating impermanence for a long while. The twin towers made of seemingly indestructible steel beams collapsed in no time; the law of impermanence is unfailing. In the National September 11 Memorial & Museum I saw photos of the 2,977 victims, many still very young, whose hopes and dreams for this life were erased.

Life is so transitory. We can be just one second away from dying. While many people believe the 9/11 victims encountered a rare catastrophe and that chances we will die in such an unexpected manner are small, this isn't true. They simply haven't embraced and internalized the truth of impermanence.

Alas! We often allow impermanence to slip out of our minds, consciously or unconsciously. Despite a devastating disaster such as 9/11 and endless other instances of impermanence, we still push impermanence to the back burner in our pursuit of long-lasting things and feelings. People continue to build new skyscrapers around the 9/11 site. Construction of the world's tallest buildings and longest bridges never stops. A prospective spouse spends three months' salary on an engagement ring because "a diamond is forever." A high school kid spends his pocket money on a bottle of happy pills hoping to attain a long-lasting high. We always tell ourselves, "I still have time," so we procrastinate, especially about our spiritual practice, telling ourselves, "I'll do it tomorrow." But are we sure there *is* a tomorrow?

Everything is subject to change, and nothing lasts forever. The Buddha taught about the truth of impermanence:

What is born will die,
What has been gathered will be dispersed,
What has been accumulated will be exhausted,
What has been high will be brought low.

Thus everything in this universe changes, including the entire Earth, all beings dwelling upon the Earth, and all the miracles of humans and nature. The Forbes world's billionaires list reshuffles every year as resourceful and relentless newcomers join the ranks while others go bankrupt. China's Old Summer Palace in northern Beijing, once the pinnacle of imperial design, is now reduced to ruins. Top government officials, who once enjoyed power and fame, are replaced or imprisoned. In one hundred years, nearly every person now alive will be dead, and the Earth will be populated with people not yet born.

Change is inevitable, and death is just part of life.

People may argue, "Wouldn't it be too pessimistic if one constantly reminds oneself of impermanence?" They believe that contemplating impermanence could put a person in a negative mindset. In fact, if we embrace impermanence and stop fantasizing that things are eternal, this may motivate us to live the best possible life. We won't get caught up in good or bad life changes and won't expect to control everything according to our hopes and fears. We will be less likely to blame others or drown in a whirlpool of remorse when things go wrong. Therefore, we are less likely to suffer.

Two Kinds of Impermanence

There are two kinds of impermanence: the coarse and the subtle. Coarse impermanence can be easily noticed and examined by an ordinary person: changes in the four seasons, sunrise and sunset, the moon waxing crescent to full, a nation falling from prosperity to poverty, an apple decaying, someone's health failing or improving, and the swing from emotional outburst to calm. Coarse impermanence is too obvious to go unnoticed.

Emotional change is an example of coarse impermanence. You may have felt hopeful yesterday but self-doubting today. Your new neighbor may appear friendly now but may stop saying hi to you six months from now. Your parents are delighted to know you'll fly back home for Thanksgiving but feel disappointed when your flight is canceled. Your kids who hit puberty constantly experience emotional roller coasters, which drives you nuts. As a result, you may become confused, preoccupied, and nostalgic. You may wish to always live in the good old days and remain happy all the time.

People who embrace impermanence perceive all those emotional changes through a difference lens. They understand that there is no such a thing as happily ever after. They don't even wish to be in the happily-ever-after state. It's like if a spring remains stretched all the time and hardly gets compressed, it will be permanently deformed. Likewise, if a person remains happy all the time, they will be like an outstretched spring. A healthy dose of unhappiness is part of our being, an indispensable component of our holistic living. Moreover, impermanence can also bring joy, albeit temporarily. After feeling blue, you may feel rosy; after a cold period, your neighbor may smile at you again at a potluck party; after a disappointing Thanksgiving, your parents may be thrilled to see you during the next holiday; after puberty, your kids may become more caring and warmhearted.

Death is another example of coarse impermanence. Death is thrust in our faces almost every day—in the news, in movies, on the Internet, and in our own lives. Young people sometimes say to me, "I am still young, so death is a long way off. It's pointless to discuss the end of my life now. It makes me very uncomfortable talking about dying and death." But, if they fully embrace impermanence, they will realize that however young they are, they are not exempt from death, and death is not necessarily "coming later" to young people. In our everyday life, far too many young people die prematurely on account of accidents, suicide, disease, and so on.

Many people accept that what is born will eventually die. They also accept that when and how to die can be uncertain. But for them death denotes "the eternal end," so they indulge recklessly in their worldly pursuits, hoping to stave off the inevitable. "Carpe diem," they tell themselves, "because life is impermanent, and we live only once." With this mindset, they may veer into a hedonistic lifestyle; they maximize the pleasures in life, sometimes even at the cost of virtues. "Who cares!" they tell themselves, "Birth is the start, and death is the end. Period!" Buddhists, on the other hand, believe birth is not a singular beginning nor is death a singular end. Actually, each is just one moment in the endless cycle called samsara. So, death isn't death—it's followed by the birth of yet another life (chapter 6 covers the topic of rebirth).

Knowing this, we start to understand impermanence and death at the deepest possible level, which allows us to appreciate their simple and profound truth and to merge ourselves with them fully. In so doing, we won't descend into misery and despair when thinking "death is unavoidable, and everything vanishes." Instead, we will be motivated to study and practice the Dharma with more diligence because we know it is the only path to liberation.

As humans we have the opportunity to make this life precious by practicing the Dharma and finding freedom from the cycle of suffering and rebirth. The Buddha taught us that unless we contemplate the preciousness of this human life and how easily it can be lost owing to impermanence, we will never be able to live fully and practice diligently.

Insight into the impermanent nature of human life can help us balance our priorities. When we begin to let go of our attachments, we will no longer put the most important thing in our life—our spiritual realization—on the back burner.

Subtle impermanence is the basis of coarse impermanence. While we can't perceive it with our bare eyes, all conditioned things change moment by moment. The Buddha taught that nothing stays the same, not even for a split moment. Therefore, impermanence isn't "later"; it's now. For example, though it's not visible, the physical body of any person is a continuum of causally related moments. The person reading this book at this very moment is not the same person as ten minutes ago; that person is gone. Likewise, the person who will take a coffee break in thirty minutes is not the same as the person who is reading right now. The person now reading is not the same person as even a second ago.

Buddhists adopt a specific system to divide each second into shorter moments. In the *Humane King Sutra*, the Buddha taught that one instant of thought lasts 90 *ksanas*,[1] and each ksana contains 900 sets of arising and ceasing moments of mental processing. When we discern anger or desire arising, the mind that observes our own mind is at the gross level—we notice the obvious change of our emotions. The instantaneous thought "I am angry" can be divided into 90 ksanas, each of which is further divided into 900 shorter moments.

Modern physics also seeks to identify the shortest measurable time interval. According to the International System of Units for time, for example, a second can be divided into centiseconds (1/100 second), nanoseconds (10^{-9} second), yoctoseconds (10^{-24} second), and Planck time (5.39×10^{-44} second)—the smallest physically meaningful interval of time.

Let's bring back the example of the instantaneous thought "I am angry." In theory, Buddhists can further divide this thought into even shorter moments than Planck time, until the moment is so small that it cannot be further divided—an indivisible moment. Within this indivisible moment, arising and ceasing happen at the same time, so that arising is ceasing and ceasing is arising. When we achieve this understanding of subtle impermanence, we'll realize that the conventional worldview that distinguishes the processes of becoming, abiding, and cessation is a complete illusion and misconception.

Some Buddhist scriptures explain that realizing subtle impermanence opens the gateway to realizing emptiness (Skt. *shunyata*; Tib. *tongpa nyi*), the absence of inherent existence in all phenomena. When we apprehend subtle impermanence, we'll easily understand the concept of the nonexistence of an indivisible moment for time and a partless particle for matter. We will discuss this in greater detail in the context of the third Dharma seal.

Practicing Impermanence

Practicing impermanence is the most important task for Buddhists, though we often find ways to avoid it. The Buddha once told a story that explains how ignorant we are about impermanence:

A man is running away from a wild elephant when he slips over an abandoned water well. Falling to his doom, he grasps some vines that arrest his fall. He hangs there, while below him is an evil dragon and around the well are four venomous snakes. Soon a little white mouse appears and starts gnawing away the vines to which he is clinging and then disappears. Then a little black mouse appears and does the same thing as the white mouse. Gradually fewer vines are left in the man's hand.

Meanwhile honey is dripping from a bee's nest above him, and five drops fall directly into the man's mouth. Wow, how sweet it tastes! He savors the honey so much that he completely forgets the dangerous situation he is in.

Our life situation is just like this man clinging to a clump of vines while dangling over a well. The white mouse is day, and the black mouse is night, representing the inexorable passage of time by which our life is gradually diminishing. Hanging in the well denoting life and death, we forget the immediacy of death because we are fixating on the honey, which represents the five worldly desires (fame, wealth, lust, food, and sleep). If we remain enmeshed in the trivial pleasures of our worldly desires, it may not end well after we die.

Despite this truth many of us struggle to fully embrace impermanence. We try to bargain with impermanence or remain in denial about it. As a result, we often focus our energy on the future that we assume exists, rather than concentrating on the present. For example, many elderly people, who will only live for another ten to twenty years at most, still make long-term plans as though they will live for another century. Many young people, thinking they are healthier and more energetic than the older generation, firmly believe they will live longer than their parents.

In the same way many Buddhist practitioners repeatedly procrastinate doing their practice, while they dive into worldly endeavors as swiftly as possible. Good Dharma practitioners, on the other hand, make Dharma practice their priority because they've deeply embraced the truth of impermanence. As Longchenpa (1308–1364), one of the most brilliant teachers of the Nyingma lineage, stated in *Finding Rest in the Nature of the Mind*:

> Death therefore is sure;
> Uncertain is its when and where and how.
> This life is ever-dwindling; no increment is possible.
> Many are death's circumstances;
> Those that make life possible are few.
> You have so little time to live!
> Rein in your projects for the future—
> Better far to strive in Dharma from this very instant![2]

Contemplating impermanence is of utmost importance. The Buddha taught in the *Nirvana Sutra*:

> Of all footprints, the elephant's tracks are the most reliable;
> Of all thoughts, the one of impermanence is the most sacred.

Why are the elephant's tracks more reliable? The elephant avoids precarious trails and only walks along a safe path. If we follow the elephant's footprints, we can keep away from dangers and arrive safely at our destination. Similarly, of all subjects of meditation for a practitioner, the idea of impermanence is the unsurpassed prelude that opens the way of all practices of the Dharma. At first, meditating on impermanence makes you take up the Dharma, then it motivates you to practice with great diligence, and in the end, it helps you attain realization. Therefore, the practice on impermanence is the most sacred.

The Buddha also said in other sutras,

> The merit of making offerings to one hundred enlightened beings such as Shariputra and Maudgalyayana is enormous, but it is still incomparable to the merit of meditating on impermanence for one instant.

A practitioner who takes impermanence seriously will make real progress, no matter which specific practice, basic or advanced, that person is undertaking. Without keeping impermanence in mind that person won't advance toward liberation, even if they receive empowerments and teachings on the highest Vajrayana Buddhist practices such as the Great Perfection (Dzogchen).

Once a devotee earnestly requested teachings from Drubthob Chöjung (1351–1408) but was constantly put off. The devotee insisted, and finally Drubthob Chöjung took the devotee's hands in his and said three times, "I will die, and you will die." Drubthob Chöjung then added, "That's all that my guru taught me, and that's all that I practice. Just meditate on that. I promise there is nothing greater than that." The devotee took the master's words seriously, practiced impermanence diligently, and eventually attained realization.

Because of this my own primary practice has always been impermanence. No matter what happens, I retain a sense of impermanence. For example, when I am enjoying a good weather day, I remind myself it is impermanent. When I am saddened by bad news, I remind myself it is impermanent. I practice impermanence often in my daily endeavors including walking, sitting, and sleeping.

Reflecting on impermanence motivates us to practice the Dharma. Thinking about the impermanence of human life—we'll all die, but when, where, and how we'll die are uncertain—generates particularly strong intention to practice. When we practice subtle impermanence, it helps build the basis for realizing emptiness.

As we more deeply realize impermanence, we become more positive and proactive rather than pessimistic as many people believe. We become more carefree and more compassionate, and we start to experience real progress in our practice.

SECOND SEAL: ALL TAINTED THINGS ARE SUFFERING

All conditioned phenomena, the leading actor in the first Dharma seal, are either tainted (Skt. *sasrava*; Tib. *zakche*) or untainted (Skt. *anasrava*; Tib. *zakme*). The word *tainted* means "impure," "defiled," "stained," "contaminated," or "flawed." Buddhist teachings in the *Mahavibhasa* state that "tainted" has the connotation of "trapping sentient beings." This means that sentient beings' taints trap them in samsara—the uncontrollable and endless rounds of existence—which entails suffering. A tainted phenomenon is either suffering itself such as mental illness, the condition for suffering such as a Louis Vuitton bag, or the root of suffering such as desire for the luxury bag. In contrast, untainted things are always pure, undefiled, uncontaminated, and free from suffering—a state attained by sublime beings according to Buddhism.

Contemplating the first and second Dharma seals concerning impermanence and suffering gives rise to the resolution to renounce the endless cycle of birth, aging, sickness, and death, so we become determined to put an end to samsara.

People often disagree with the idea of seeing all tainted phenomena as suffering, which, they argue, is too pessimistic and does not capture all of life experience. "There are also many happy things in life," they protest. "Life includes ice cream, a new iPad, Louis Armstrong's jazz, reuniting with old friends, falling in love, times on a beach or before a fireplace, becoming a CEO or an Olympic medalist, and so much more."

In fact, Buddhism does not deny the happiness that we sometimes experience. But happy experiences carry the nature of suffering. This is most obvious in the Pali term *dukkha* that corresponds to "suffering" in the Buddha's teachings. When the Buddha says, "all tainted things are dukkha," he doesn't only refer to the limited literal meaning of "suffering" as people today typically interpret it. Dukkha also has the connotation of "distress," "anxiety," "uneasiness," "dissatisfaction," or "unsatisfactoriness." Therefore, Buddhism considers the nature of all tainted things in this world, or everything we experience in samsara, to be suffering or dukkha. It either appears to be suffering in itself or is the very cause of future suffering. The happiness we now have—in owning a new iPad or winning an Olympic medal—actually causes suffering sooner or later. Such temporary happiness, which is suffering of change in its essence, is only a very few colorful dots scattered on the canvas of life, with suffering as its dominant background color. This is the true meaning of the second Dharma seal.

Three Fundamental Types of Suffering

Suffering was the Buddha's first teaching. "I teach suffering, its origin, cessation, and path; that's all I teach," declared the Buddha 2,500 years ago.

Suffering comes in many forms. Several obvious kinds of suffering correspond to what Prince Siddhartha witnessed during his excursions out of the palace: old age, sickness, and death. But suffering and its cause, according to the Buddha, goes much deeper than that.

In Buddhist teachings suffering doesn't just arise from physical pain but also from mental afflictions. As Aryadeva (second/third century) wrote in his *Four Hundred Stanzas on the Middle Way*:

> The high have mental suffering;
> For the common it comes from the body.
> Day by day, both kinds of suffering
> Overwhelm people in the world.[3]

Even when we are not suffering from physical distress like illness or hunger, we are nevertheless unsatisfied, frustrated, or anxious. To recognize all our sufferings, Buddhists are asked to contemplate the three fundamental types of suffering in our lives: suffering of change, suffering of suffering, and all-pervasive suffering of being conditioned.

Suffering of Change

The Buddha says, "The suffering of change is that which is pleasant when arising, pleasant when remaining, but painful when ceasing."

In his *Gateway to Knowledge*, Jamgön Mipham Gyatso, or Mipham Rinpoche (1846–1912), says,

> When changing, the previous pleasure itself becomes a cause
> of torments . . . no matter what the intensity of pleasure experienced, its previous moments gradually cease while its subsequent

moments gradually arise such that its continuity eventually ceases. Nothing is beyond that. Therefore, it is unreliable like a beautiful white autumn cloud.[4]

From the first Dharma seal, we know that all conditioned things are impermanent, including pleasant experience, and they can be as fleeting as a flash of lightning, a bubble, and a rainbow, or as changeable as running water. Therefore, everything changes and nothing stays the same in any consecutive moment. When causes and conditions are present, pleasure arises; when causes and conditions wear out, pleasure weakens; when causes and conditions vanish, pleasure ceases. As a result, suffering or unsatisfactoriness underlies any pleasure, and pleasure can easily change into suffering. Hence, pleasure is none other than suffering.

Happiness in our life doesn't last long. For example, the refreshing sensation that occurs when we eat ice cream on a hot summer day will gradually wear off; some long-married couples, once deeply in love, become disconnected and apathetic and eventually end in separation or divorce.

Sometimes, happiness vanishes very abruptly, and we plunge into suffering in the blink of an eye. For example, one moment a billionaire is sipping a glass of wine on his super-yacht, and the next moment his financial advisor calls, telling him he has lost all his wealth; or one moment some university buddies are having fun drinking, and the next moment two of them fall from a balcony and are badly injured.

Suffering of Suffering

The Buddha says: "What is the suffering of suffering? It is that which is painful when arising, painful when remaining, and pleasant when changing."

In *Gateway to Knowledge*, Mipham Rinpoche comments,

> [It] is the sufferings of the lower realms; birth, old age, sickness and death even within the higher realms; separation from what is dear; having to encounter what is undesirable; and not achieving what is desired even when pursuing it.[5]

This is the type of suffering with which we are all familiar: the pain of birth; the helplessness of getting old; the anxiety of being sick; the fear of death; the torments of separation from a loved one; the disappointment of failing a job interview; the shame of being laughed at in public; the anger of being framed for a crime; the frustration of denial. We feel pain when these situations arise and remain, and we feel pleasant when they change or disappear.

Even worse, many people will be subjected to yet another painful experience before the first one is over. As the saying goes, "When it rains it pours." In life some people have multiple heavy loads of suffering on their shoulders. For example, a man is hospitalized after being struck by a hit-and-run driver, then his mother dies from a heart attack; a single mom is laid off, then soon after diagnosed with breast cancer; a university student breaks up with his girlfriend and later fails his qualifying exam and has to leave the program.

All-Pervasive Suffering of Being Conditioned

The Buddha says, "The suffering of being conditioned is not apparent when it arises, remains, or ceases, but it is still the cause of suffering."

In *Gateway to Knowledge*, Mipham Rinpoche comments,

> The suffering of being conditioned is that once implicated in the aggregates that perpetuate defilements, no matter whether there is temporary pleasure, pain, or neutrality, all aspects of their instants form the material cause for perpetuating future aggregates. Consequently, it is the source of all future suffering.[6]

The phrase rendered as "all-pervasive suffering of being conditioned" is often translated as "composite suffering," in the sense that when causes and conditions come together, suffering arises. This type of suffering is harder to recognize than suffering of change or suffering of suffering, and it is considered the source of both.

At first glance, all-pervasive suffering of being conditioned often doesn't seem to be suffering because things can be going quite well at any moment. However, as Mipham Rinpoche says, everything we do is a composite of actions that can lead to suffering. We are, in fact, totally immersed in the causes of suffering, with our current actions planting the seeds of future suffering.

For example, a diner enjoying crispy fried chicken may be feeling pretty happy, humming, "Yummy, yummy, happy life comes from happy tummy," while consuming the bird. But while savoring the food, the diner is also con-

suming growth hormones and antibiotics added by chicken farmers, causing them future health problems. In addition, the high demand for chicken
supports factory farming, a notoriously cruel way to raise animals for food.
Even if a chicken is free-range and totally organic, the fact that it ends up on
a plate means that the diner's crispy, juicy, finger-licking enjoyment comes
at the cost of a being's life.

Embracing Suffering

When we are aware of the three types of suffering and develop a genuine
insight into the nature of suffering, true renunciation arises. We are eager
to end the suffering. Therefore, understanding suffering is the first requirement for the journey to enlightenment and freedom from suffering. Without understanding suffering, we won't be able to embrace it, and therefore
we will remain tormented by physical and emotional suffering. Without
understanding suffering the wish for freedom from suffering won't arise,
and we won't make Dharma practice our top priority.

We all want to be happy, and our longing for happiness is as old as life.
Thomas Jefferson enshrined the "pursuit of happiness" as a basic human
right in the United States Declaration of Independence in 1776. On March
20 of every year since 2013, the United Nations has celebrated the International Day of Happiness, recognizing the importance of happiness in the
lives of people around the world. More and more brands put "happiness" in
their taglines and slogans to sell products that may not even be good for us,
including sugary beverages, donuts, cigarettes, dating apps, and lottery tick-
ets. It seems the epidemic of happiness is spreading more than ever before.

Very often we believe that to achieve happiness we must avoid suffering.
We think that if we are richer, younger, smarter, slimmer, working harder,
loving deeper, laughing louder, living somewhere else, with a different partner, partying with more friends—you name it—we can dodge suffering, and
as a result we'll be happy or become happier. However, research findings in
neuroscience and psychology conclude that our pursuit of happiness, par-
adoxically, makes us feel unhappy at most times. Because we rarely know
what really makes us happy, we might not even know what happiness is, and
we are on a hedonic treadmill that can never bring us to the pursued goal.

If we embrace suffering instead of avoiding it, we'll remain strong and
even feel at ease in the face of adversity. We'll accept that suffering is inevitable, but it can also be a catalyst for our personal and spiritual growth and

freedom from suffering. For example, each year many pilgrims and tourists travel to the eastern Tibetan highland to visit Larung Gar, where many members of my Buddhist community (sangha) and I reside and practice the Dharma. But with the Larung Gar Five Sciences Buddhist Academy perched high in the mountains at 13,000 feet, visitors can encounter temperatures plummeting to −22° Fahrenheit in winter. If visitors accept Larung Gar's weather, they don't complain, even when the cold numbs their faces and hands, and their lips turn blue and their teeth chatter. "This is what is supposed to be," they say, and then they proactively deal with the suffering of cold weather by dressing warmly. However, if a visitor has no idea about the excruciating cold at Larung Gar, that person can be overwhelmed by a brisk winter breeze and suffer physically and emotionally. Likewise, if we understand and embrace the presence of suffering, this brings calm and relief.

Many great Buddhist practitioners are not afraid of suffering at all. Does this mean a Buddhist will have no painful feelings after starting to practice the Dharma? Of course not! Buddhists may still experience suffering, but unlike ordinary people they know how to deal with suffering more effectively. When suffering arises, Buddhists simply acknowledge and embrace it. For example, Shantideva (685–763) said in *The Way of the Bodhisattva*,

If there's a remedy when trouble strikes,
What reason is there for dejection?
And if there is no help for it,
What use is there in being glum?[7]

When a painful situation arises that we have the ability to improve, then why feel depressed or resentful? On the flip side, if we cannot change the situation, what good does it do to be miserable about it? For instance, if your laptop crashes while you are writing a thesis but technical support can fix the machine or your files are saved in off-site storage, why despair or become angry? If your laptop has completely died and there is no way to retrieve the thesis, nothing can be changed; therefore what is the use of becoming unhappy about it? Indeed, when suffering comes up, becoming unhappy will not only be of no use but will aggravate the situation further, causing even more suffering. Shantideva's verse is easy to understand in theory, but without steady contemplation and practice most of us find it difficult to apply in life.

To completely eradicate suffering, the Buddha prescribed removing its cause. If water is leaking into a boat, there is little use bailing the water out without also mending the hole. Likewise, if we can uproot the cause of suffering, we can prevent the recurrence of suffering forever.

According to Buddhism, we suffer because of our mistaken belief that at our core we have an independent, separate, and solid "I," a mistake that results in our grasping at this delusion of self.

In *The Words of My Perfect Teacher*, Patrul Rinpoche (1808–1887), one of the most illustrious spiritual teachers of the nineteenth century, wrote that Dharma practitioners should mobilize all their practice strength, skill, and power against the mistaken belief of "I." If we fully realize "I" doesn't inherently exist and that the nature of all phenomena is emptiness—the truth stated in the third Dharma seal—we will become entirely free from suffering.

THIRD SEAL: ALL PHENOMENA ARE DEVOID OF SELF

The third Dharma seal says all phenomena are empty and devoid of self (Skt. *atman*; Tib. *dak*). What is "self"? In this context, "self" means a permanent, singular, and independent identity. Being devoid of self, which we can call no-self (Skt. *anatman*; Tib. *dakme*), means the absence of a fixed identity. Buddhism divides "self" into two kinds: *self of the individual* and *self of phenomena*.

The Two Kinds of Self

Self of the Individual

Mipham Rinpoche defines "the individual" as: "That which we label as the agent of our actions or the experiencer of happiness and suffering, and which we assume to be the self, the individual, the agent and so on."[8]

Thus, "self" in *self of the individual* carries the connotations of "I" or "me" having a solid existence. More specifically, *self of the individual* is the incorrect consideration that there is an "I" that endures, in the sense that an "I" has a lasting continuity—"I was," "I am," and "I will be"—that there is an "I" that is a single entity with the name of "Elizabeth," "Francisco," or "Raphael," and that there is an "I" that is separate from or independent of the body, mind, feeling, external circumstances, and so on.

Our grasping for such an "I," or self-grasping, can be innate, meaning that we were born with it, and it can also be imputed, meaning that it is learned from wrong views and improper thinking. As early as infancy, we already cling to the notion that the self actually exists, and such a notion of "I am" is embedded deeply in our mind-stream. As time passes, we are systematically exposed to distorted views and improper thinking from classrooms, books, movies, television, newspapers, social media, and so on, and we learn to impute qualities to the self that are not inherently there—namely, perceiving something as part of the permanent, singular, and independent self.

As a result, we hold the mistaken belief that there is an "I." Many people are interested in boosting self-esteem, achieving self-actualization, and seeking self-identity. They often say, "I am not myself." "I just want to be myself!" "I am trying to find myself," and more, as if there were a separate "I," independent of anything. While this is particularly common in Western culture, it is more difficult to explain these expressions to native Tibetan speakers because their vocabulary lacks a corresponding word that carries the same connotation of "the self."

From boomers to millennials to the youngest zoomers, people are getting more and more centered around "me, me, me!" Nowadays, self-obsession has become the vital part of many people's everyday life, as shown from the selfie-obsessed culture pervading Facebook, Instagram, and TikTok. It is not surprising to see that our narcissism, a self-centered trait, has increased as quickly as obesity has since the 1980s, and has risen faster since the turn of this century. However, focusing too much on the notion of the self tends to make people more unhappy, anxious, and depressed.[9]

We don't have to become a narcissist to feel miserable. As long as we are still grasping at "the self of the individual"—even just a tiny pinch of it—mental afflictions, notably the "three poisons" of desire, aversion, and ignorance arise unavoidably, which sows the seeds of suffering and keeps the wheel of samsara rolling. The antidote is the realization of no-self of the individual, which is only part instead of the entire scope of emptiness, as I will discuss soon, but is enough to free us from samsara because such realization can destroy our mental afflictions.

Self of Phenomena

In *Ascertaining the Two Kinds of Selflessness*, Mipham Rinpoche defines "phenomena" as "All conditioned and unconditioned things other than 'I' or the self."[10]

It means that apart from the "I" or "self" to which a person clings, all things and events in the world are "phenomena," including the sun, the moon, the World Trade Center, diamond rings, ice cream, jazz, romantic lovers, fireplaces, dating apps, the lottery, becoming a CEO, winning Olympic medals, and so on. *Self of phenomena* refers to our mistaken belief that these things and events are real and truly exist, meaning each phenomenon is a distinct and permanent entity that exists independent of other things.

The truth is that all phenomena, in both samsara and nirvana, are just like the moon reflected in water or a dream: they appear while lacking inherent existence, so they are devoid of self and ultimately empty in nature. Not knowing this truth, we cling to the self of phenomena—mistaking phenomena as real, objectifying everything, and falling into the dualistic view of things. As a result, we are drawn to consumer materialism, buying more and owning more, because it affords us the pleasure and status that make us feel real; we are meticulous about the arrangement of an important event, such as a birthday, wedding, or graduation, to make it the "best day of my life"; we mentally label "me and others," "this or that," "good or bad," "like or dislike," and more, which reinforces our naïve assumptions of duality. In so doing, our life is shaped by these thoughts, and without doubt our grasping at "the self" of things and events brings desire, aversion, and ignorance.

The antidote to these mental afflictions is the realization of no-self of phenomena, culminating in the full realization of emptiness, freedom from samsara, and becoming a buddha—the state of nonduality. The realization of no-self of phenomena can be gradual before reaching the culmination. For example, at first an engaged couple is strongly attracted to the beauty, value, and symbolic meaning of a diamond ring, so their wish to get one arises, but they have to work hard to pay for this expensive piece of rock. Then, one day the couple remember their physics teacher taught that a diamond is composed of carbon atoms. "This thing called a diamond is merely a cluster of atoms," they think. "The diamond in itself is an illusion, a made-up concept! It doesn't inherently exist! Why bother spending three months' worth of salary on it?" Then, the couple meditate on this view, engender a form of certainty, and eventually realize the diamond lacks "the self" they were grasping on to, so they can let go of having a diamond, and escape the corresponding suffering.

However, their realization of the no-self of the diamond is partial and incomplete. Since they still hang on to an ultimate basis or origin of everything, which in the case of the diamond is the carbon atoms, they continue to embrace "concepts" and perceive the world dualistically: this is me, that is a thing independent of me, and I like or dislike it. So, they are still grasping. In Buddhism, such dualistic conceptualizations of "me," "thing," and "liking or disliking" are called cognitive obscurations. These obscurations prevent complete enlightenment.

It is not until the couple realize that there is actually no ultimate basis or origin of phenomena—that is, the carbon atoms, and the particles smaller than atoms, don't exist inherently, and even the concept of nonexistence doesn't exist inherently—that they can move even further in realizing the no-self of phenomena and get closer to becoming an omniscient buddha.

Of course, I oversimplified the realization of no-self in the diamond example, just for the sake of offering a basic explanation. To cut through our grasping at the self of phenomena, as well as the self of the individual, it is necessary to obtain conviction of no-self through logical reasoning. Although we cannot eradicate both forms of self-grasping entirely by logic, such investigation and analysis are the first step to transform the way we think. We then become certain within the mind that all things don't exist inherently in the way they seem to, and the way things appear is not the way they truly are. In the following sections, I therefore present logical arguments about the no-self of the individual and the no-self of phenomena.

No-Self of the Individual

Very often upon first hearing that we don't inherently exist, many of us will protest, "I have a body; I can think; I can move; I can feel. It doesn't make sense saying this 'I' doesn't exist!" This reaction is due to the fundamental ignorance that we believe "the self" inherently exists with its own identity, evolving under its own power.

But under the spotlight of incisive wisdom,[11] when we closely look at "the self" we find nothing inherently exists. The self we cling to so tightly is actually nowhere to be found.

In the *Questions of King Milinda*, the Buddhist yogi Nagasena presents the Buddhist doctrine of no-self to the king.

The debate starts with Nagasena saying that his own name is just a label because no permanent self can be found. King Milinda, who believed in a permanent, independent, and singular self, challenged Nagasena.

"If no permanent self can be found," he said, "who is Nagasena exactly? Is it the head?" King Milinda asked.

"Certainly not," replied Nagasena.

King Milinda continued, "Or is it then the ears, nose, mouth, neck, shoulder, hands, or feet?"

"Certainly not," said Nagasena.

The king asked, "Or is it then the liver, lungs, heart, intestines, or stomach?"

"Certainly not," answered Nagasena.

The king asked, "Or is it then the look?"

"Certainly not," replied Nagasena.

The king continued, "Or is it then the happy or sad feeling, the good or evil deeds, the body or the mind? Is it all of these combined? Or is it something outside of these that is Nagasena?"

"It is none of these," replied Nagasena.

The king asked, "Or is it the voice or the breath?"

And still Nagasena replied, "Certainly not."

King Milinda, who disagreed with Nagasena's views of no-self, posed a further question: "If no Nagasena can be discovered, then who is the person before the king?"

Nagasena defended his view with the well-known simile of the chariot. Specifically, Nagasena asked King Milinda to contemplate what a chariot is:

"Is it the axle, or the wheels, or the chassis, or reins, or yoke that is a chariot?" Nagasena asked. "Is it all of these combined, or is it something apart from them?"

"Certainly not," the king answered.

Nagasena asked, "Then, is it the sound that is a chariot?"

"Certainly not," the king replied.

Nagasena asked, "Then, what is a chariot?"

King Milinda realized that chariot, just like "Nagasena," is solely a label, a concept, a mere name we falsely impose on its constituent parts. A chariot is not an independent entity, is not a singular entity, and cannot exist independently without causes and conditions, as does the "I" or "me."

According to Nagasena's analysis, none of the "five aggregates" or their combination supports the concept of "I." These five aggregates are physical body or form, as well as the four mind-related aggregates—sensation, perception, mental formation, and consciousness—that make up our physical and mental existence. They are the basis upon which the "I" is projected. So, logical refutations on the self of the individual can be reduced to answering two basic questions: "Is our body the self?" and "Is our mind the self?"

Is Our Body the Self?

Let's examine the body. When you say "my body is the self," you refer to the body as the "I" that is permanent, singular, and independent.

Is the body permanent? Of course not, as said in the first Dharma seal. It changes all the time—from a fertilized ovum to a fetus, an infant, a grade-schooler, a teen, an adult, and a senior—and many people's bodies stop the process earlier. The body also changes from one instant to the next, in a subtle manner.

Is the body a singular entity? It is not. It has many body parts, as listed by King Milinda in the debate. It is by nature multiple and manifold.

Is the body independent? It is not. The body is the ripening result of the karma that one has accumulated from previous lives. It is fueled with food, sleep, water, air, and shelter to survive and thrive. Our bodily state also depends on our emotions—when in love we may notice a racing heartbeat and sweaty palms, and when jealous we may have stomach problems and insomnia.

If you think of your body as a single whole, then think again. When you divide the body into the head, trunk, and limbs, the concept of "body" is destroyed, and you are left with the concepts of these three major parts; when you further divide the parts into flesh, skin, blood, and bones, you destroy the concepts of the three major parts, and you are left with the concepts of flesh, skin, and so on. You may continue to analyze the conceptual parts and eventually find that none of the concepts can withstand the investigation. So, the body is not the self.

Is Our Mind the Self?

Next, let's examine the mind. Again, we tend to believe the mind is permanent, singular, and independent, but this incorrect consideration cannot withstand logical investigation either.

The mind is not permanent. Take a moment to examine your mind, and you will notice thoughts arising and ceasing endlessly. Research[12] has suggested that mind wandering—a form of distraction—makes up nearly half of our waking lives. Our mind can wander everywhere like the flow of a river—from negative emotions and thoughts like sadness or helplessness to positive emotions and thoughts like gratitude or forgiveness.

The mind is not singular. For example, Mahayana Buddhism breaks the mind (Skt. *chitta*; Tib. *sem*) into eight separate consciousnesses,[13] fifty-one mental states, and so on. In addition, mind can have many kinds of positive, negative, and neutral thoughts.

The mind is not independent. It depends on external objects including sights, sounds, smells, taste, and textures, as well as internal objects including thoughts, self-grasping, and memory.

After a close examination, you will also find that none of the concepts related to "mind" can withstand the analysis. So, the mind is not the self, either.

In a nutshell, the five aggregates, or simply put, the body and the mind, are the basis of our clinging to the self, but none of them is the "I." So, there is no such "I" that is permanent, singular, and independent. The so-called "self" cannot be found anywhere. It is just a projection of our deluded mind, which is conceptual, dualistic, and emotional and which obstructs us from realizing and manifesting the true nature of mind.

As I already mentioned, realizing no-self of the individual can free us from samsara, since it can uproot the three poisons of desire, aversion, and ignorance. It is like we are horrified when spotting a "snake" at dusk but feel relief when realizing it is just a coiled rope—the "snake" was a product of our deluded mind. Knowing and eventually realizing that the "I," like the "snake," is merely a groundless concept set up by our mind, we can escape the suffering of samsara because there doesn't exist an "I" who is actually suffering.

However, since we may still cling to the "existence" of the rope, the realization of no-self of the individual is only part of emptiness. Although we are freed from samsara, we cannot yet become a buddha. To attain complete enlightenment, we must also realize the no-self of phenomena—the entire scope of emptiness, that even the rope itself doesn't inherently exist.

No-Self of Phenomena

In *Ascertaining the Two Kinds of Selflessness*, Mipham Rinpoche says:

> Yet if we do examine them (phenomena) using logical reasoning, such as the argument of "neither one nor many," we come to understand that no entity, whether coarse or subtle, can be

said to be real. And that understanding of how things lack any basis or origin is what we call the realization of the "selflessness of phenomena."[14]

Through the logical reasoning of "neither one nor many," let's refute the inherent existence of the basis of phenomena, namely the partless particles as the ultimate basis of physical matter and the indivisible moments as the ultimate basis of mind.

Partless Particles

Most Buddhists, particularly *shravakas*,[15] have no difficulty accepting that everything, be it Nagasena or a chariot, is purely conceptual and devoid of self. However, they frequently believe that it is impossible for forms— material matter—to exist without a basis. They posit that forms exist as a collection of partless particles that cannot be broken down further. Unlike a chariot, they say, these smallest units of matter constituting a chariot truly exist. In other words, they believe partless particles truly exist as the basis of matter.

Mahayana Buddhists refute the existence of partless particles. For example, in his *Twenty Stanzas*, a Mahayana teaching on the Mind Only School (Chittamatra), Vasubandhu (c. fourth to fifth century) argued that objects are not built of partless, indivisible, and eternal particles. His reasoning is expressed in this famous verse:

> When six other particles are joined to it,
> The subtle particle will have six parts.
> If the six all simply converge together,
> Then even compounds will be infinitesimal.

Vasubandhu argued that since all physical objects have directional parts, the smallest particle must also have other parts associated with the six directions (south, north, east, west, above, and below), corresponding to the other particles surrounding it. That being the case, the central particle and the other particles surrounding it are not "directionless" after all. This implies that each particle is still divisible.

On another note, if each of the particles was without direction—if the eastern side of each particle was also its western side—then all other par-

THE FOUR DHARMA SEALS — 25

ticles would touch the same place. This would mean that there would be just one particle, no matter how many partless particles were put together. Therefore, it would be impossible to build the gross form of a physical object out of these partless particles, and Mount Meru—the sacred mountain at the center of the universe—would just be one partless particle. As such, the notion of partless particles is not viable at all.

If a single partless particle doesn't inherently exist, neither does the multiplicity of partless particles. As Sakya Pandita Kunga Gyaltsen (1182–1251) says in his *Treasury of Valid Reasoning*:

> Because things have the nature of neither one nor many,
> So objects and their properties don't exist inherently.

This means that the moon, the sun, the Himalayas, the iPad, fireplaces, old friends, romantic lovers, and so on, don't inherently exist, and neither do our eyes, ears, nose, tongue, and skin. From this, we may clearly infer that the nature of physical matter, or "form" as in the five aggregates, is indeed empty.

I hope Vasubandhu has cracked your previous views on the existence of things, even just a little bit. Besides the logical reasoning of the "neither one nor many" argument of the Mind Only School, we can also use the four great logical arguments[16] of the Middle Way (Madhyamika) to refute the true existence of any phenomenon and develop conviction in emptiness.

However, not everyone is ready to adopt this logical reasoning. Nowadays, people have come to celebrate science-oriented mindsets. They are willing to accept something only when science can prove it. But we should be aware that no matter how advanced modern science has become, it has at best moved one step closer to the direction of the true reality. Put differently, science may have a vague glimpse of the moon's image reflected on the surface of the water but not the moon in the sky—the true moon. Scientific understanding remains very, very far away from the truth of emptiness.

Scientists have deepened their understanding of the interrelationship between energy and matter, moving slightly closer to the Buddhist understanding of emptiness. Researchers first discovered ordinary matter is made of atoms. They then discovered that every atom is composed of a nucleus and electrons, and the nucleus is made up of protons and neutrons. Later scientists realized that quarks—fast-moving points of energy—are fundamental constituents of matter. Now quantum physicists' most advanced understanding is string theory, which proposes an underlying one-dimensional category of objects called "strings." However, scientists still believe in the inherent existence of matter and energy, which, in Buddhism, are empty in nature.

Indivisible Moments

Similarly, when we analyze the mind using logical reasoning, there is no solid, inherently existent mind to be found. As mentioned in the previous section related to subtle impermanence, we can also think about mind in terms of indivisible moments of consciousness. Because these mind moments don't inherently exist, the mind is also empty.

Let's imagine two scenarios when two indivisible moments would be adjacent to each other. The first scenario is when two such moments are connected tangibly. If they align together seamlessly in a sequential order, then each moment can be divided in two: one moment that is in touch with the neighboring indivisible moment, and the other that is not. As such, the so-called "indivisible" moment can still be further divided.

If two moments are connected both seamlessly and comprehensively—merged completely into one unit—then all the indivisible moments would just be one indivisible moment. Therefore, it would be impossible to constitute the continuity of consciousness.

As such, the notion of indivisible moments is not viable at all.

The second scenario is when two such moments are not connected seamlessly. Thus, there is always a void gap between two sequential indivisible moments. Each indivisible moment is preceded by a gap after the earlier moment, while there's another gap before the succeeding moment.

Now let's examine these two void gaps. If they are connected, then the indivisible moment supposed to be in their middle should also be a void gap. If they are not connected, then the two gaps belong to different entities. This means the start and end of the indivisible moment between these gaps can be further divided into two parts: one in touch with the preceding void gap, and the other in touch with the succeeding void gap. Regardless of whether the void gaps are connected or not, this means it's impossible for an indivisible moment to be inherently existent.

If indivisible moments do not inherently exist, how can our mind, consciousness, and emotions inherently exist? The mind itself is empty. Ultimately it doesn't exist, and on the phenomenal level the mind is like a mirage.

This lack of inherent existence has significant meaning in our human lives. When we experience emotional ups and downs, although it all seems very real and solid, these emotional appearances, like a rainbow or an illusion, arise solely from causes and conditions, according to the rules of interdependence. When we look closely at these emotional states, there is nothing inherently there.

Based on the above analysis I hope you've started to accept the third Dharma seal, that all phenomena are empty and devoid of self.

We must always keep in mind that emptiness is the central tenet of Buddhism and what makes it unique among religions. Emptiness doesn't mean things don't exist at all. Emptiness is not "nothingness" or a "vacuum"; many beginning Buddhists misunderstand its meaning in this manner.

In fact, emptiness is beyond all four extremes: existence, nonexistence, both existence and nonexistence, and neither existence nor nonexistence. Ordinary beings initially tend to believe everything truly exists, and upon first hearing the teachings of emptiness, they may go to the other extreme believing everything is nothingness. In this chapter, I have mainly addressed the first erroneous extreme of "existence."

To deepen your understanding of emptiness, it is very important to distinguish between the two truths: ultimate truth and relative truth (chapter 5 covers the topic of the two truths). "All phenomena are empty" means "all phenomena are empty of inherent existence and transcend any dualistic extreme" at the ultimate level. The dualistic phenomena that we perceive in our deluded mind and that make up our lives—ourselves, other beings, concepts, material objects, thoughts, emotions—are not nothingness; they do appear at the relative or conventional level, like dreams and illusions.

Upon reading here, I hope you've at least gained some intellectual understanding of no-self of the individual and no-self of phenomena. To fully realize no-self, we must transcend our ordinary mental processes through meditation practice.

According to lineage masters, our realization of no-self or emptiness has several stages. Let's use the analogy we heard earlier involving a snake—which we realized is actually a rope—to explain the stages. A person's initial fear of the snake may not have completely disappeared upon learning it was a rope. It is only after he examines the rope himself and is completely assured of the nonexistence of a snake that his fear is entirely overcome. Moreover, if this person carefully scrutinizes the rope, he'll realize that the rope lacks inherent existence because it is a collection of just so many strands of wool. Further scrutiny will make him realize that the strand of wool also lacks inherent existence because it is simply a collection of atoms. Furthermore, he'll also realize that atoms are not real either because they are also in a state of emptiness. Eventually, this person will realize that even this emptiness itself is empty.

The process of fully realizing no-self or emptiness follows similar stages. At the very beginning we mistake what is not self as self, so we suffer. Later, through studying and practicing the Dharma, we start to learn that everything is without inherent existence. However, since we haven't yet delved deeply enough into practice, we haven't fully realized no-self. It is through steadfast practice, and blessings from our Buddhist teacher or guru, that we can fully realize no-self.

A Dzogchen master may help their Vajrayana disciples to realize emptiness through skillful tantric methods including presenting a crystal ball, using the analogy of space or the ocean, or showing special images of peaceful and wrathful deities. As a result, those disciples, who are adept at settling the mind, find it easy to develop certainty in emptiness.

Nevertheless, beginners should start by studying the texts of the Middle Way (the list is covered in chapter 5) to establish a solid understanding of emptiness before going further to the Vajrayana practice. One issue I want to address especially is that although nothing truly exists at the ultimate level, it does appear and function at the relative level, as mentioned earlier. Thus, before we attain full realization, we are still subject to phenomena including the law of karma.

In addition to cultivating guru devotion (see chapters 7 and 9), accumulating merit and purifying obscurations are very important in our Dharma practice. As the Buddha said, "Innate absolute wisdom can only come as the mark of having accumulated merit and purified obscurations, and through the blessings of a realized teacher. Knowing that, those who rely on other means are fools." Eventually when realization arises, we see things—good or bad— the same as illusions or mirages. We become fully aware that what appears to exist is merely imputed by the mind. We become free from the entanglements of hope and fear. We achieve nirvana.

FOURTH SEAL: NIRVANA IS BEYOND EXTREMES

By practicing the first three Dharma seals we can achieve nirvana: a state of total peace and great bliss without clinging to self, without any defilements and obscurations, without any suffering, and without further cyclic rebirth.

Our mind awakens from delusion, recognizes the true nature of everything, is beyond duality, and is driven to benefit sentient beings effortlessly and spontaneously. This is what the fourth seal is about—nirvana, the final goal we strive to attain when we fully realize emptiness and reach a state that is beyond extremes. This seal is not practiced by practitioners but is the end result of practicing the first three Dharma seals.

The state of nirvana is achievable by every one of us. Some may attain it swiftly—if a person of great capacity studies and trains in certain Vajrayana teachings, the possibility of enlightenment within one lifetime is within reach. Others may spend many more lifetimes purifying obscurations and accumulating merits to eventually reach the enlightened state.

Nevertheless, all of us can become enlightened.

Every living being has Buddha nature, which is just temporarily veiled by our obscurations, and therefore the potential for achieving perfect buddhahood. We must firmly believe in this innate potential.

Nirvana is nothing more than awakening to the true nature of our mind.

2. FAITH IN BUDDHISM

Not Just a Mere Belief

SHORTLY AFTER my monastic ordination in the 1980s, I accompanied my root guru the great Jigme Phuntsok Rinpoche on his teaching tours to the West. In the years that followed, I tried to find time to deliver Dharma teachings abroad. The trips gave me the opportunity to closely observe and engage with Buddhists in the West.

From my perspective, the many Westerners I encountered during my trips were straightforward and driven by logic and reason; they were interested in philosophy and in an earnest quest for truth. These traits are aligned with the rational wisdom acclaimed in Tibetan Buddhism.

If these same Western practitioners also allow themselves to be driven by heart—to cultivate the emotional wisdom arising from their profound faith in the Three Jewels and the guru—their practice will become transcendent.

Faith is an important concept in Buddhism that does not necessarily carry the same meaning as the term used in the West. The word for faith is *shraddha* in Sanskrit or *depa* in Tibetan. Both carry the meaning of "confidence" or "trust," whereas the term *faith* in the West often has a theistic connotation.

I have encountered Westerners who said to me, "I came to Buddhism to get away from faith." Perhaps because of their previous backgrounds in theistic religions, they didn't interpret the word *faith* in a way that resonates with its true meaning in Buddhism. From their descriptions, I sense that sometimes the word *faith* could bring up fear. In fact, in Buddhism faith is an antidote to fear.

True faith in Buddhism is developed by verifying and validating the teachings through our own experience and insight, not through mere belief. Throughout a Dharma student's practice, faith plays a significant

31

role. Without true faith, studying Dharma is no different than worldly academic research, which at best provides some Buddhist knowledge but hardly brings any fundamental change to one's mind.

FAITH WITH WISDOM

The Buddha taught in the Four Reliances[1] that anyone studying the Dharma should "rely on the message of the teacher, not on his personality." This means Dharma students should rely on the Dharma itself, not those expounding it, although this does not mean students should avoid teachers.

We should not rely on Dharma teachers according to their fame or social status, because if they don't have true wisdom and realization, our belief in them will blind us—at the sight of a misdeed, we may not discern it and choose to believe in the teacher instead. This will put us at risk.

Buddhism advocates wisdom and faith based on rationality. The Buddha said in the *Nirvana Sutra*:

> If a person possesses faith, but not insight,
> Then his ignorance will be increased.
> If a person possesses insightful wisdom, but not faith,
> Then his distorted views will be increased.

Faith, if not accompanied by wisdom, will increase a person's ignorance; thus that person may do something unwholesome or unwise. Wisdom, if not accompanied by faith, will boost a person's wrong views, such as constantly seeking faults in others. We need both faith and wisdom.

Many religions are theistic, which means they embrace the belief in the existence of a god or gods, especially believing in one God as the divine creator of the universe. Buddhism is different. It is neither totally theistic nor totally atheistic but instead has its own unique viewpoint: the Buddha was the revealer of the truth, instead of a creator of the truth or a creator of the universe; the Dharma is the truth of all phenomena taught by the Buddha; and the sangha is the community that seeks the truth by following the Buddha's path.

Some religions rely on divine truth proclaimed by an infallible authority, therefore their dogmas cannot be tested by an ordinary person. In comparison, the Buddha asked followers to examine his teachings rather than to unquestioningly accept his words as true. If after this examination followers thought the Buddhist teachings made sense, they could accept them; if not, they could discard them. The Buddha urged his followers to refrain from blind faith, saying:

> O bhikkus and wise men, just as a goldsmith would test his gold
> by burning, cutting, and rubbing it (on a piece of touchstone),
> so you must examine my words then accept them, but not merely
> out of reverence for me.[2]

Buddhism also recognizes different degrees of faith. The highest degree of faith is based on wisdom. The *Flower Ornament Sutra* (*Avatamsaka Sutra*) says: "Wisdom is of the utmost importance in the Dharma."

You may feel a bit confused. At first, I say faith is important and now wisdom is important—isn't that a conflict? Well, it is not. People first entering the gateway of Buddhism need faith to bring them in; when they study the profound Dharma, they need wisdom. Nagarjuna said in his *The Treatise on the Great Virtue of Wisdom*:

> For the great ocean of the Buddha-dharma,
> With faith one can enter into it,
> With wisdom one can cross it over.

The Dharma is as vast as the ocean, encompassing profound qualities and merits. One enters that ocean in the canoe of faith and crosses that ocean with the paddles of wisdom.

FOUR KINDS OF FAITH

Possessing faith, according to Mipham Rinpoche, is to have a vivid and eager mind for, and confidence in, that which is authentic and true. It is faith that opens the gateway to taking refuge in the Three Jewels. We experience faith on many levels, and here I will introduce four kinds of faith.

Vivid Faith

Vivid faith, as defined in Patrul Rinpoche's *The Words of My Perfect Teacher*, is the faith that is inspired in us by thinking of the immense compassion of the buddhas and great teachers.

We might experience vivid faith when seeing representations of the Buddha's body, speech, and mind, namely the images of the Buddha, scriptures, and stupas, or after encountering a great teacher or an eminent master in person or whose inspiring life story or great qualities we just heard described. Touched by their vast compassion, we feel lighthearted, uplifted, or deeply moved.

When closely examining vivid faith, we realize it is primarily an intense emotional state. This state, which can include excitement, awe, ecstasy, and gratitude, wavers and doesn't last long. Many people can't help but shed tears when they see the Buddha's statue, hear sutras chanted, or prostrate themselves in front of a stupa for the first time. These people may weep emotionally when encountering a great Buddhist teacher, saying, "Dear teacher, you look so compassionate. The more I look at you, the more I want to cry!"

I have met Dharma students who cried very easily at the beginning. But perhaps this exhausted their reservoir of tears, because later they shed not even a single tear of faith. I often tease my disciples, "Maybe it's better to 'cry smartly,' so there is always some stock of tears left for your future use."

Vivid faith generates great merit, as related in a story in the *Miscellaneous Treasures Sutra*:

A girl was riding a chariot on her way to a garden when she happened to meet the Buddha, who was heading to the city. She immediately gave way to the Buddha, and owing to his majestic appearance, she was filled with joy and appreciation. This vivid faith brought her rebirth in the god realm.

When Dakini Muntso Rinpoche[3] was heading to the Larung Gar Nun's Dharma Hall for the consecration of the site, I saw many laypersons cry upon seeing her, shedding tears of joy and faith. A non-Buddhist might think the laypersons were silly, asking, "Why did they cry like that?" The answer is that their tears signaled the awakening of their dormant virtues.

Vivid faith is important for a Buddhist. If you remain emotionless like a rock when seeing an image of the Buddha or meeting a teacher, or even worse if you give a scornful or disdainful look, the blessings from buddhas, bodhisattvas, and teachers cannot enter your mind.

We don't need to question people experiencing vivid faith, asking, "Why are they so emotional? Why are they crying? Why are they so ecstatic?" When someone jumps with joy upon seeing their teachers, we should not think they are abnormal. Their joy simply reflects their vivid faith.

FAITH IN BUDDHISM — 35

Eager Faith

Eager faith arises when we are eager (1) to be free of the sufferings in the three lower realms of hell beings, animals, and hungry ghosts; (2) to enjoy the happiness of the three higher realms of humans, demigods, and gods; and (3) to eventually attain ultimate liberation when we hear what these realms are like. Eager faith also arises when we long to engage in positive actions because we understand the benefits they bring, and to avoid negative actions because we acknowledge the harm they cause.

Compared to the temporary excitement or ecstasy of vivid faith, eager faith arises when we start to understand the Buddha's teachings. This means eager faith is more reliable and stable.

For example, we may not at first understand the need for engaging in positive actions. But as we become more aware of the benefits of positive actions through studying Buddhist teachings, we're less likely to stumble. For this reason eager faith enables us to progress steadily on the path to liberation, and to eventually free ourselves from all suffering. The *Discourse on Meeting of the Father and the Son* (*Pitaputrasamagama Sutra*) says:

> Hearing the Buddha's teachings in Dharma assemblies,
> Thus generating pure faith and ultimate understandings,
> And then diligently practicing the Dharma that leads to bodhi,
> One will be free from the samsaric ocean of birth and death.

Eager faith is far more powerful than vivid faith, but both kinds of faith, together with the other two kinds yet to be introduced, are important along the path to liberation. Faith itself is like an admission ticket to liberation, without which one cannot enter the "Dharma Theater" to watch the miraculous show of the Three Jewels.

Confident Faith

Confident faith is faith in the Three Jewels from the depth of our hearts once we understand the Three Jewels' extraordinary qualities and the power of their blessings. With this faith, we deeply trust in the Three Jewels and become very certain that they are the only unfailing refuge, or protection. By taking refuge we commit ourselves to the Buddhist path and seek protection from the suffering in samsara. Thus, whatever circumstances we are in—happy, sad, painful, ill, living, or dead—the Three Jewels are always with us.

Confident faith is to the bone, not just skin deep. Confident faith brings total trust in the Three Jewels, so a practitioner says, "In this life and in many lives to come, whether happy or in pain, I trust you in everything. You are my only refuge." This confident faith is like that of an orphan who places total trust in the person who wholeheartedly helps them. A story on confident faith is recorded in the *Dhammapada:*

Once upon a time, there was a country where *tirthikas*[4] lived. People there suffered tremendous hardship because no rain had fallen in three years. The king called upon all the Brahmins of the nation and requested them to find answers from the celestial god: Why had this severe drought arisen?

After some observation, the Brahmins proposed a big sacrifice to the gods. The king was asked to prepare as many as twenty chariots of firewood, cheese, honey, ointment, oil, flowers, incense, banners, gold, silver, and sacrificial utensils. In addition, the king had to select seven people to send to the celestial realm by cremation, so they could ask for the cause of the drought.

After the prayer ceremony the crowd watched the seven people climb to the top of the woodpile, which was soon set on fire. When the flame reached them, they started to cry for help, but to no avail. They cried in great desperation, "We'll take refuge in whomever can relieve our suffering from the burning fire!"

Hearing them the Buddha appeared and said,

> You may take refuge in a mountain or a tree god
> And draw images of those refuge objects,
> And then pray in front of them for protection.
> But this is not the most auspicious and supreme refuge,
> Because it cannot liberate you from sufferings.
> Taking refuge in the Three Jewels is the most auspicious and
>   supreme,
> Because it can free you from all sufferings.

Then the flames extinguished and the seven people were saved. Upon witnessing the whole event, all the Brahmins generated confident faith— they fervently and totally trusted the Three Jewels. They all decided to take ordination from the Buddha, and later they attained arhatship, a state of enlightenment. The king, the ministers, and the citizens also took refuge in the Buddha and started to practice the Dharma. Very soon, it started to rain, and the crisis of drought was finally over.

The verses the Buddha said to the Brahmins have been quoted in many Buddhist scriptures.[5] When in danger, a worldly person may try to take refuge in a person, a spirit, or a mountain. However, this is not the ultimate refuge that brings the ultimate liberation. In this world, the Three Jewels are the only unfailing refuge that can guide us and free us from the ocean of samsara. The *Sutra on the Mahayana Principle of Six Paramitas* says:

> Only the Buddha Bhagavant,[6]
> A great noble teacher with the sunlike wisdom,
> Can exterminate our doubts,
> So he is the only genuine refuge.

How many people in the world really understand the meaning of taking refuge in the Three Jewels? There are some Buddhists who received stamped-and-signed refuge certificates from a temple or a master in a refuge ceremony a dozen years ago, yet they haven't generated total trust in the Buddha, rendering their refuge (and accompanying certificates) superficial. As true Buddhists, we should aim to free our minds from doubts and pray to the Three Jewels with full trust and genuine confidence.

Confident faith is not blind faith based only on someone praising the extraordinary qualities of the Buddha. Most ordinary Dharma students start to generate confident faith through systematic hearing and contemplation. For example, through studying the "Pramanasiddhi" chapter of *The Commentary on Valid Cognition (Pramaṇavarttika)*, we become convinced that the Buddha is a valid source of knowledge for those seeking spiritual freedom. Through studying the *Noble Sutra of Recalling the Three Jewels*, we no longer doubt the inconceivable qualities of the Three Jewels.

Confident faith is more solid than the first two kinds of faith and cannot be shaken by temporary circumstances and events. Yet there remains a chance, however miniscule, for confident faith to regress. Therefore, we should all strive for irreversible faith.

Irreversible Faith

Irreversible faith is the deepest level of faith, remaining unshakable under all circumstances no matter how difficult, even at the cost of our own lives.

When we truly realize the ultimate truth of all phenomena, we'll give rise to irreversible faith and take the ultimate refuge in the ultimate Three Jewels, which is none other than the very nature of our own mind. When irreversible faith arises, it'll become integral to us—in our heart, mind, blood, and bone marrow.

As Patrul Rinpoche says in *The Words of My Perfect Teacher*:

> As you develop a faith quite beyond the commonplace, by its power the blessings of the teacher and of the Three Jewels will enter you. Then true realization will arise, and you will see the natural state as it really is. When that happens, you will feel an even more extraordinary and irreversible faith and confidence in your teacher and in the Three Jewels. In this way faith and the realization of the natural state support each other.[7]

During this degenerate age,[8] irreversible faith cannot surface without serious study, thorough contemplation, and diligent meditation practice. Practitioners with irreversible faith, who acquire knowledge and direct experience, won't waver for one microsecond even if the whole world denounces Buddhism.

I remember a conversation with Khenpo Norbu, a monk who came to Larung Gar at roughly the same time as I did. We reflected on our faith, agreeing that although neither of us dared suggest we'd attained realization, our faith in the Dharma and the Buddha was indeed hard to regress. As we both age we feel more and more that the only refuge is the Three Jewels, and that everything else—wealth, fame, status, relationships—is unreliable, transient, dreamlike, and meaningless.

I sincerely hope every Buddhist takes authentic refuge in the Three Jewels. This may start from vivid faith, gradually evolving into eager faith and then confident faith, and finally become irreversible faith. As our faith deepens, we can start to significantly contribute to Buddhist activities such as propagating the Dharma and benefiting sentient beings. Here is a story that reflects this:

Kanishka, the king of the Kushan Empire, was an aggressive, hot-tempered, and rigid person who liked to hunt. Once in a forest he spotted a little white rabbit, so he went after it with his bow and arrow. Suddenly, the rabbit disappeared, and a boy appeared making a meter-high stupa.

The king asked, "Why are you making this?"

The boy answered, "Before his *parinirvana*, Shakyamuni Buddha foretold that five hundred years later, a king named Kanishka would erect a stupa on this spot and contribute greatly to Buddhism. I am here to give you a hint with this mud stupa." After saying that, the boy disappeared.

Hearing this King Kanishka instantly generated faith and a sense of joy, thinking, "How extraordinary was Shakyamuni Buddha! He knew I would be here! Since the Buddha has prophesied, I should convert to Buddhism." After his conversion to Buddhism, gradually he became an openhearted, benevolent, and faithful ruler.

He not only believed in Buddhism but also encouraged its teachings. He built a Dharma hall in his palace, and invited different learned masters to give teachings on a daily basis. Through his study, King Kanishka's faith was getting stronger. As he progressed further on the path, his trust in the Buddha and the Dharma ripened.

Soon King Kanishka noticed that each master had his own interpretation about the same section of the sutra. Befuddled, the king didn't know which one he should follow, so he asked Arya Parshva, a renowned Buddhist monk, why so many variations existed. Arya Parshva answered: "It has been five hundred years since Shakyamuni Buddha's parinirvana. Various Buddhist schools disagree with each other on the interpretation of the Buddha's teachings. It is time to organize the Fourth Buddhist Council, which will mark an important turning point for Buddhism."

Knowing this could bring great benefits to sentient beings, the king adopted Arya Parshva's suggestion and gathered five hundred monks in Kashmir, headed by Vasumitra, to systematize the *abhidharma* texts. The main fruit of this council was the vast commentary known as the *Great Exegesis* (*Mahavibhasa*). This council also signaled the development and transmission of Mahayana Buddhism to China.

This story shows that vivid faith arose when King Kanishka first heard the Buddha's prophecy. After he systematically studied and contemplated the Buddha's teachings, he generated the mind of renunciation and devoted himself to propagating the Dharma, a sign of confident faith.

The faith of many Dharma students follows a similar progression. Inspired by their first encounter with a great teacher or the Three Jewels, they are guided to Buddhism by their karmic connection even though they don't know much about the Dharma. Later they develop confident faith through systematic study and contemplation. As they advance further on the path to liberation, they strive to eventually attain irreversible faith.

THE IMPORTANCE OF FAITH

Without Faith

If faith is absent, the compassion and blessings of the Three Jewels cannot reach you. It says in the *Great Jewel Heap Sutra* (*Maharatnakuṭa Sutra*):

> In those who lack faith
> Nothing positive will grow,
> Just as from a burnt seed
> No green shoot will ever sprout.[9]

Without faith, it is hardly possible to receive blessings from lineage masters or from the buddhas, bodhisattvas, and *dharmapalas* (Dharma protectors), let alone gain enlightenment.

Not only Buddhist practice requires faith. Faith-related intentions are crucial factors in worldly achievements, such as curing diseases and winning an Olympic medal, and without faith success is almost unattainable.

Without faith, even meeting the Buddha in person and being accepted as his disciple would bring no benefit. Nobody compares to the Buddha in this world, but because his disciples Sunakshatra[10] and Devadatta[11] lacked faith, they couldn't tame their minds and failed to attain realization even after years of hearing the Buddha's teachings.

Someone once said to me, "There are people who have been staying at Larung Gar for so many years and heard so many teachings given by their gurus, yet why do they still conduct such misdeeds and hold such wrong views?" The answer lies in their degree of faith. As the Buddha said in the *Sutra of the Manifestations of the Tathagata* (*Tathagata-utpatti-sambhava-nirdesa Sutra*), like a blind person who cannot see sunshine, a person who is overwhelmed by his own contaminated thoughts can hardly be aware of the inconceivable blessings of the lineage gurus and the Three Jewels; neither can they generate devotion and faith in the Three Jewels.

Therefore, a person who lacks faith and holds wrong views can hardly achieve any realization, no matter how many years that person walks the Dharma path. Here is a story in the *Ekottaragama Sutra*:

One day the Buddha was giving teachings to the sangha at Kalandaka Venuvana (Bamboo Grove Monastery).[12] A senior bhikshu blatantly disregarded stares from sangha members while pointing his feet toward the Dharma seat where the Buddha sat—inappropriate etiquette signaling disrespect—and then fell asleep during the teaching. Meanwhile an eight-year-old novice monk sat beside the Buddha, keeping his back straight in the proper manner and attentively listening to the teachings with great appreciation and respect.

Seeing this, the Buddha decided to offer a special teaching, saying to the sangha, "The title of 'venerable master' is not necessarily appropriate for monastics who long ago received ordination. If the minds of these venerables lack wisdom, mindless behavior will surface. But if someone really knows the truth of the Dharma and his mind isn't tainted by afflictions, even if that person is a novice monk, he is eligible for the title of venerable master."

Then the Buddha asked, "Do you notice the senior bhikshu sleeping with his feet pointing toward the front?"

"Yes, we do," the sangha answered.

Next the Buddha asked, "Do you notice the eight-year-old *samanera*?"[13]

"Yes, we do," the sangha answered.

The Buddha continued, "They differ greatly in their levels of faith in and respect for the Three Jewels. The maturations of their karma also differ significantly. The senior bhikshu was a naga[14] in five hundred previous lives. After this life, he will be reborn as a naga again as a result of his lack of faith in the Three Jewels. The novice monk listened to the Dharma teaching with great veneration, so within seven days he will attain realization."

No matter how long Dharma students have been studying Buddhism, if they're without faith, they're simply lip-service Buddhists. Whatever teachings such students hear, just like Sunakshatra and Devadatta, they always think, "I know it already," and their minds fail to integrate with the Dharma. This is truly pitiful!

There are many faithless people around us whose minds can hardly be tamed. The Buddha also said in the *Ekottaragama Sutra*, "Mentioning the practice of generosity to a person who is frugal and teaching the Dharma to a person who lacks faith are both very difficult."

It is difficult to help a person with no faith even if we really want to.

With Faith

The *Flower Ornament Sutra* says:

> Faith can grow the tree of bodhi,
> Faith can increase the supreme wisdom,
> Faith can reveal all the buddhas.

This verse explains that whenever with sincere faith we visualize, pray to, or prostrate to the Buddha, the Buddha is there.

Many shastras[15] share the same viewpoint, for instance, telling us that when we visualize Shakyamuni Buddha or Amitabha[16] in the space in front of us and pray one-pointedly, the Buddha is there bestowing blessings. When we call our teacher from afar, whether the teacher is alive or not, their inconceivable blessings can reach us.

The Buddha's blessings are everywhere—in rooms, on trains, in planes, in libraries, at farmers' markets. The Buddha's body, qualities, and activities are ubiquitous. The *Mahayana Sutra of Tathagata's Inconceivable Secrets* says:

> Just like empty space that is vast,
> The Buddha's body is vast;
> Because the Buddha's body is vast and boundless,
> The Buddha's luminosity is vast likewise;
> Because the Buddha's luminosity is vast,
> The wisdom of the Buddha's speech is vast likewise;
> Because the wisdom of the Buddha's speech is vast,
> The wisdom of the Buddha's mind is vast likewise.

Similarly, the body, speech, mind, precious qualities, and activities of our gurus are everywhere. If we remember and pray to our guru often, we'll without doubt receive their blessings.

Whichever deity or buddha it is, their compassion toward living beings is the same. As long as we pray all the time, the Buddha's compassion and blessings are always there for us. Patrul Rinpoche quoted a verse from a sutra in *The Words of My Perfect Teacher*:

For all who think of him with faith
The Buddha is there in front of them
And will give empowerments and blessings.[17]

When we pray with faith and devotion, the Buddha's blessings emerge effortlessly, as the moon's reflection appears in clear water. Whether the blessings of the Three Jewels reach us or not depends entirely on our faith and devotion. The *Mula-sarvastivada Vinaya Sutra* says:

Even when the ocean tides stop rising and falling,
The Buddha will never stop liberating sentient beings.

Someone may wonder: "How come a buddha of a particular era can continue liberating beings even after his era has ended?" The answer is that when the era of his teaching has ended, it is only over in terms of time; the blessings of the buddha and his teachings continue even after the era is complete. Whomever of the thousand buddhas of the good kalpa[18] we pray to, be it Vipassi or Kassapa Buddha of the past or Maitreya Buddha of the future, their compassion and blessings will always reach us swiftly.

There are many corresponding stories in Buddhist history. For example, when the founder of Tibetan Buddhism Guru Rinpoche (Padmasambhava) was about to leave Tibet for the country of *rakshasas*,[19] a place full of demonic beings, Tibetans supplicated him to stay and continue bestowing empowerments and blessings on the Land of Snows. Guru Rinpoche told them:

For all men and women with faith in me, I, Padmasambhava,
Have never departed—I sleep beside their door.
For me there is no such thing as death;
Before each person with faith, there is a Padmasambhava.

Even now, many years later, whenever we pray to Guru Rinpoche by chanting his mantra—OM AH HUM VAJRA GURU PADMA SIDDHI HUM— his blessings are there for us although we do not see him. It is like a blind person who receives help from another and knows he is being helped, even though he cannot see the helper.

It took Asanga[20] twelve years of practice to finally have a vision of Maitreya. At the sight of Maitreya, Asanga cried, "How unkind you are! I have been praying to you for such a long time, yet you didn't show me your face until now!"

"It is not that I have not shown myself," Maitreya answered, "You and I have never been separated. But your own negative actions and obscurations were too intense for you to be able to see me."

When praying to the buddhas and bodhisattvas, we should firmly believe they are right in front of us. With confident faith, we'll receive unfailing blessings from them, whatever situation we get into. Faith is crucial because a person with little faith may see the buddhas and bodhisattvas as no different than ghosts or spirits. In this case, if a person sees no immediate effect from praying, his thin faith in the Three Jewels dissipates easily. Hence, the person won't receive the blessings.

Most Tibetans know a story of an old woman who was helped toward buddhahood by her faith in a dog's tooth. The woman believed the dog's tooth was a relic of Shakyamuni Buddha, so she placed the tooth on her shrine table and day after day she prayed before it very fervently. Owing to her strong faith and devotion, there appeared a canopy of rainbow light around the old woman and other signs of accomplishment when she died.

The dog's tooth in itself did not contain any blessings. However, the old woman's faith was so strong that after she mistook the dog's tooth for a real tooth of the Buddha, she had no doubt that this tooth would most certainly give her full blessings. Through her confident faith and devotion, the dog's tooth was permeated with the Buddha's blessings, until finally it was in no way different from a real tooth of the Buddha. The message is that when we have strong faith, the Buddha's blessings can be present in anything, anywhere, and at any time.

A similar incident happened to a practitioner from Dhomang Monastery,[21] my home monastery in Garze Tibetan Autonomous Prefecture. In the late 1990s, I found a small bronze statue of Guru Rinpoche in a local store in Barkam, a county in the eastern Tibetan region, and gave it to the practitioner as a gift. The statue cost five Chinese yuan, then equivalent to seventy cents USD, and its quality was not very good.

After receiving the statue, this practitioner always kept it with him, and never put it away. Recently he showed me the statue, and I offered to replace it with a better-quality one. But he immediately declined, saying, "I have great faith in this statue. In the past years, it helped me dispel many unfavorable conditions. Last year when I was going through Indian customs, I was so afraid it would get confiscated when the customs officer went through my luggage. Luckily, everything was fine."

I replied jokingly, "Of course this statue of Guru Rinpoche wouldn't be confiscated. Since it can dispel your adversity, it surely can dispel its own adversity."

This practitioner vividly demonstrated the importance of faith. Without faith he wouldn't have carried with him a poor-quality statue for more than a dozen years. With faith, he has received many extraordinary blessings from Guru Rinpoche throughout his practice. Each of us should try to develop such an untainted faith!

According to the abhidharma, faith is a virtuous mental state. Once it arises, its effect on the practitioner is inconceivable. As Patrul Rinpoche said in *The Words of My Perfect Teacher*,

> If you have immense faith and devotion, the compassion and
> blessings you receive from your teacher and the Three Jewels
> will be equally immense.
> If your faith and devotion are just moderate, the compassion and
> blessings that reach you will also be moderate.
> If you have only a little faith and devotion, only a little
> compassion and blessings will reach you.
> If you have no faith and devotion at all, you will get absolutely
> nothing.[22]

It is not just Buddhism that stresses the importance of faith. Other disciplines such as psychology, medicine, and philosophy also value faith. For example, Pietro Pomponazzi, a leading philosopher of sixteenth-century Renaissance Italy, said: "If the bones of any skeleton were put in place of a saint's bones, the sick would nonetheless experience beneficial effects if they believed they were verifiable relics."[23] In *The Power of Your Subconscious Mind*, author Joseph Murphy explains the effect of faith in medicine. If a healthy patient receives a misdiagnosis saying he is severely ill, that patient may soon die from fear. The diagnosis error arouses despair in the patient and exhausts their hope and faith. Whereas a severely ill patient who holds faith, hope, and courage toward life may survive longer. Many similar studies parallel the Buddha's teachings on faith.

FAITH AND ULTIMATE TRUTH

Faith can invoke compassion in a practitioner and the blessings of the Three Jewels. Actual realization of the ultimate truth of emptiness or the accomplishment of the Great Perfection rely on faith alone.

In his *Introduction to the Middle Way* (*Madhyamakavatara*), Chandrakirti (c. 600–c. 650) says those with great faith in the profound teachings of emptiness will become great vessels of the Dharma. The Buddha once told Shariputra: "Ultimate truth is only realized through faith."

With our extraordinary faith, and by the supreme blessings of the teacher and the Three Jewels, true realization of ultimate truth will naturally arise in us. When realization arises, our faith in the teacher and in the Three Jewels becomes irreversible. Thus, realization of the ultimate truth and faith are complementary and concurrent. Faith enables us to realize the natural state of all phenomena, as written in the *Mahayana-Uttaratantra Shastra* (*Buddha Nature*): "This ultimate truth of the spontaneously born is to be understood through faith alone. The orb of the sun may shine but it cannot be seen by the blind!"[24]

This verse explains that ultimate truth can only be understood and realized through faith, and not by any other means. Ultimate truth refers to emptiness, the central teaching of Buddhism. Though hard to assimilate, an ordinary person with fervent faith can realize emptiness through diligent study, contemplation, and meditation, and this realization then further makes faith irreversible.

HOW TO DEVELOP FAITH

It is very important to develop faith through frequent practice. People who have strong faith but are less learned scholastically can still attain high levels of realization and benefit sentient beings. A story in the *Legends of the Himalayan Mahasiddhas*, a Chinese book about enlightened masters from all walks of life, shows the power of faith:

Once somewhere in northern Tibet a senior died. His family couldn't find monks to perform *phowa*, a practice to help transfer the consciousness of the deceased to the Pure Land, a blissful buddha-field of Amitabha. Then it happened that a beggar-looking yogi passed by the tent. With no other option at hand, the family invited the yogi for phowa.

The yogi said, "I am illiterate, so I am not able to chant the sadhana of phowa. But I do know how to chant the mantra KARMAPA CHENNO.[25] It can also transfer the deceased's consciousness."

The yogi started chanting, holding complete faith in the Karmapa in his mind. After every one hundred repetitions of the mantra, he tapped the body of the deceased with his mala beads. Soon miraculous signs of successful phowa practice emerged: a small drop of blood oozing out directly from the center of the deceased's vertex (skull midline), and a canopy of rainbow light appearing around him.

Later the yogi saw the Karmapa in person. The Karmapa told him, "Recently in northern Tibet, we collaborated to transfer the consciousness of a deceased senior. It was not an easy task." Saying this the Karmapa tapped a person beside him with his mala beads, in exactly the same way the yogi had tapped the deceased senior. The yogi gave the Karmapa a knowing smile and had even stronger faith in him from then on.

Allow me to repeat one more time: it is only through our devotion and faith that we receive the blessings of the teacher and the Three Jewels and that we attain true realization of the ultimate truth. Here is a story about Jowo Atisha (982–1054), the great Indian Buddhist master who reintroduced Buddhism in Tibet:

One day one of Atisha's disciples loudly knocked on his door, calling out his name, "I am sick. Jowo, give me your blessings!"

After the disciple knocked three times Atisha opened the door, seemingly discontented.

"Lax disciple, show me your devotion," he said, "It is not through hard knocks at my door that blessings reach you."

There is another story about Atisha and his disciple:

Once a disciple bent down before Atisha and asked, "Master, may you grant me some blessings?"

To his surprise Atisha didn't place a hand on his head to bestow a blessing. Instead Atisha bent even lower, and asked back, "May you grant me some devotion?"

I myself often encounter people with no faith in Buddhism who ask me to bestow blessings on them. They say, "Come on! Place your hand on my head! Tap me, tap me!" When I indeed "tap" them, they don't bother to bend down even a little bit, as if their spines were steel poles. With this kind of attitude, they cannot receive any blessing, not even from the Buddha himself. Unwavering faith and devotion are indispensable for a Dharma practitioner. A Buddhist can develop faith through studying the Dharma and praying to the lineage teachers.

Studying the Dharma

Sometimes you might complain, "What's wrong? I have been praying every day but get no result at all!"

Maybe you should run a full "scan" on yourself. While your body is prostrating and your speech is praying, is there firm faith in your mind? If the answer is no, it makes sense that you cannot receive the inconceivable compassion and blessings of the teacher and the Three Jewels.

Faith can grow through studying the Dharma, thus hearing the Buddha's teachings and contemplating them are essential. The *Flower Ornament Sutra* says:

> If one often has trust in the supreme Dharma,
> He won't get weary of hearing the Dharma;
> Not weary of hearing the Dharma,
> His faith in the Dharma is inconceivable.

The *Treatise on the Great Perfection of Wisdom* contains a story about Hastaka, a layperson who took rebirth in the heaven of the Pure Abodes (*suddhavasa*). During a conversation with the Buddha, Hastaka said there were three reasons for his rebirth in a higher realm: "First, I never wearied of seeing the buddhas and making offerings to them; second, I never wearied of hearing the Dharma; and third, I never tired of making offerings to the sangha."

Like Hastaka, we should continue listening to and contemplating the Dharma. The better we understand the Dharma, the more faith we'll generate and this, in turn, motivates us to keep studying the Dharma.

Unless we've already achieved irreversible faith, if we put the Dharma aside and only focus on mundane issues, our faith, however strong at the beginning, will surely fade. Without faith as well as motivation for the Dharma, one is unlikely to embark on the Dharma path.

Many people hold strong eternalist or nihilist views that prevent them from entering the Dharma path. Sometimes these people aspire to a life of meaning, but end up being constantly distracted with mundane pursuits like wealth, fame, or making a living. In so doing, they miss out on what's really important.

There are as many different kinds of wrong views as there are mental states of living beings. Dignaga (c. 480–c. 540), an Indian Buddhist scholar and one of the founders of Buddhist logic, said:

> Because the number of wrong views is limitless,
> It is hard to negate them one by one.

Those with wrong views have no opportunity to practice the Dharma because their minds are influenced by their mistaken beliefs. As Dignaga said, we don't have time, energy, and interest to refute each of the wrong views. Continuous study of authentic Dharma is imperative to make sure our minds aren't tainted by such views. When we develop right views through studying the Dharma, our faith steadily grows, which reinforces our motivation to engage the Dharma.

Praying to the Lineage Teachers and Practicing Guru Yoga

Learned masters of past and present stress the importance of praying to lineage masters during Dharma practice. They themselves did this, with many Dzogchen teachers showing inconceivable faith in their gurus.

For example, my root guru the great Jigme Phuntsok Rinpoche would shed heavy tears whenever he mentioned his root guru Thubten Chöpel Rinpoche (aka Thupga Rinpoche, 1886–1956). My root guru continued this even into his seventies, as he approached his own parinirvana. "All my wisdom comes from my lineage masters," he always said. Thus, whenever he remembered their kindness, he felt so grateful that he couldn't stop crying.

This is just like a person whose life is saved by a philanthropist's donation during urgent need and who then never forgets the donor's kindness. The *Dhammapada* says:

> Faith helps one cross the river (of suffering);
> Its merits are hard to be grabbed away;
> Faith inhibits others from stealing (his treasure of life).
> This is the bliss of a *shramana* (who practices) in the wilderness.

Our gurus' blessings and teachings empower us to eradicate suffering in the ocean of samsara, so we should feel grateful to our gurus and pray to them often.

What has touched me most in the biographies of Buddhist masters is their devotion to and faith in their gurus. These masters didn't care about their own status, fame, and living conditions, yet they felt deep gratitude whenever they remembered the lineage gurus who transmitted the Buddha's wisdom to them. For example, in his autobiography *Brilliant Moon*, Dilgo Khyentse Rinpoche (1910–1991) wrote that even in his seventies he was still moved to tears when remembering his root guru. Did Dilgo Khyentse Rinpoche cry easily? Of course not! In his youth, he hardly cried over mundane things such as relationships and family issues, and he persevered through the rigors of thirteen years of solitary retreat. He cried from gratitude to his guru, who transmitted to him spiritual treasure whose value far exceeded any worldly wealth.

I hope that for the rest of this life you see your root guru as a buddha or a bodhisattva, such as Shakyamuni Buddha, Avalokiteshvara,[26] or Manjushri,[27] and always pray to the guru with this conviction. If your guru has a specific guru yoga prayer, you should practice it every day. We should pray to our guru when we wake up, and again before we go to bed.

Many Tibetan Buddhist teachers say guru yoga is the most essential practice of all. They say that no matter what Dharma practice we are doing, we cannot attain true realization without the guidance of guru yoga and the guru's blessings. Karma Chakme (1613–1678), one of the most highly realized masters of Tibet, said that if every morning and night we chant the mantra LAMA CHENNO (which means "calling the guru from afar" or "calling the perfect teacher") and remember our guru throughout the day, this in itself is the practice of guru yoga.

I would suggest that those people who often have little time for lengthy meditation practices undertake the simple yet essential guru yoga practice. I always practice guru yoga after I wake up and before bedtime, never skipping even one day.

THE CRITERION OF SOLID FAITH

Each of us should try our very best to develop faith in the teacher and the Three Jewels, until that faith becomes indestructible and irreversible. This means faith becomes so integral to us that we would never give it up, even at the risk of our lives.

As I said previously, I dare not claim I've attained any realization. But after more than thirty years of Dharma study and practice I dare to defend, in front of anyone, statements such as "The blessing power of the Dharma is inconceivable," and "The wisdom of the Buddha is beyond the logical mind." I cannot be 100 percent certain of many things in this life, but I am completely confident that my faith in Buddhism is now indestructible. Had I been an ordained monk during the Cultural Revolution of the 1960s and 1970s (I was still a young boy), I don't know whether my faith would have been strong enough that I would not have lied about it to avoid the torture experienced by many Buddhists. Now the Dharma has internalized and mingled with my mind, and my faith is bone-deep and unchangeable.

Many Buddhist teachings say a Dharma practitioner should grow solid faith, while temporary vivid faith or a sense of joy is not enough. But nowadays upon first encountering a teacher, Dharma students often say, "Dear teacher, you are really no different from the Buddha. I have great faith in you." The next day, these students feel discontented with the teacher, thinking the teacher is incompetent. They may even slander the teacher and try to find a new one. This is definitely not solid faith.

Those with solid faith firmly believe the Buddha's teachings as incomparable and vast as the ocean, far exceeding anyone's worldly wisdom. They also understand the Buddha's compassion to be deeper than any worldly kindness, as reflected by the Buddha's willingness to suffer the worst torments in the hell realm for millions of kalpas just to benefit one being.

The Buddha said in the *Sutra of the Irreversible Dharma Wheel* (*Avaivartikacakra Sutra*):

> Having faith in the noble Shakyamuni Buddha
> Who offers the Dharma to sentient beings,
> I should also emulate such activities.
> Thus is called solid faith.

This verse suggests that one with solid faith in the Buddha is as dedicated to protecting the Dharma as they are to protecting their own precious life. Such a person wants to utilize the Dharma to benefit sentient beings.

I believe the Dharma is the best antidote to mental afflictions including greed, anger, and ignorance. Therefore, in this life and many lives to come, we should steadily follow the footsteps of Shakyamuni Buddha and grow bone-deep faith from the bottom of our hearts.

Real solid faith is irreversible. Even if hundreds of thousands of people oppose us and say no to our actions on the path to liberation, we won't be intimidated and change our beliefs. Without solid faith no matter how hard you try, how good you appear to be, you cannot pass the "qualifying exam" to become an authentic Buddhist.

3. BODHICHITTA

Becoming a Buddha for Others

B ODHICHITTA is the quintessence of the Buddhist Mahayana path and the state of mind of a bodhisattva, an individual who seeks full awakening to benefit others. The word *bodhichitta* refers to the "awakening mind"—*bodhi* meaning "awakening" or "enlightenment" and *citta* meaning "mind" or "heart"—that aspires to attain full enlightenment in order to free all beings from suffering and lead them to ultimate liberation.

Bodhichitta is the root of the whole path. In the *Sutra of the Great Assembly* (*Mahasamnipata Sutra*), Bodhisattva Ratnapani asked, "What is the foundation of all Dharmas?" "Bodhichitta," Bodhisattva Akashagarbha replied. "All Dharmas are grounded in bodhichitta and are advanced by bodhichitta."

Therefore, arousing bodhichitta is indispensable for Mahayanists. To have bodhichitta is enough by itself, but to lack it is sure to render everything else in vain.

THE BENEFITS OF BODHICHITTA

Qualified teachers of Mahayana Buddhism always put bodhichitta at the core of their teachings. Many eminent masters have advocated the benefits of bodhichitta. For example, Shantideva said in *The Way of the Bodhisattva:*

> For many aeons deeply pondering,
> The mighty Sages saw its benefits,
> Whereby unnumbered multitudes
> Are brought with ease to supreme joy.[1]

According to Shantideva, for three countless eons and more, the perfect buddhas had been searching for the best way to bring immediate benefit and ultimate bliss to sentient beings. In every case, they found it is bodhichitta that brings the most benefit to beings—it enables us to halt the suffering of samsara for ourselves and others, and to attain ultimate enlightenment.

The end of the samsaric cycle of birth and death nears when authentic bodhichitta arises in our mind. Even if bodhichitta flickers on for just a split second in our mind, the benefits it brings are substantial. As Nagarjuna said in his *Commentary on Bodhichitta*:

> A person who for an instant
> Meditates on bodhichitta,
> The heap of merit accumulated from this,
> Not even the buddhas can measure.

On the flip side, without bodhichitta we can't attain complete and perfect enlightenment, and therefore we can't guide sentient beings to ultimate liberation. As Patrul Rinpoche said:

> Without generating renunciation and arousing bodhichitta, you won't plant a single seed of liberation in your mind, even if you are in a nine-year retreat focusing on the practice of the Great Perfection

As indicated in the great Jigme Phuntsok Rinpoche's vajra song called *The Song of Victory*, a Mahayanist should start from building virtuous characteristics, followed by the three principal aspects of the path, namely, arousing renunciation, then generating bodhichitta, and lastly attaining non-dual wisdom.[2] Such a path to enlightenment has been addressed extensively in other Buddhist works, including the renowned *The Three Principal Aspects of the Path* by Lama Tsongkhapa (1357–1419).

Without bodhichitta, even hearing and practicing the most profound teachings won't help practitioners attain the ultimate enlightenment. While the extraordinary Vajrayana practices offer a swift path to enlightenment, if there is a lack of bodhichitta, essentially, these practices may not differ significantly from ordinary mental exercises. It is only within the context of bodhichitta that tantric practitioners can attain buddhahood in one lifetime.

A story of the great Indian Buddhist master Atisha illustrates why bodhichitta is essential for enlightenment:

Atisha was a great Indian pandita[3] in the eleventh century. He was initially a prince of what is now eastern Bangladesh, and was expected to inherit the throne. Tara, a female Buddha, one day vividly appeared to him in a dream. She told Atisha, "For five hundred consecutive lives you have been a pandita. It is your mission to help free sentient beings from the ocean of samsaric suffering. You must not fall by the wayside."

Upon waking from his dream, Atisha remembered his past-life aspirations, so he left royal life and ordained as a monk. Guided by his guru Rahula, Atisha became well versed in the Buddhist scriptures and memorized all the texts.

One day while reading, a question arose in Atisha's mind.

"Which path to enlightenment is fastest?" he thought. "According to the bodhisattva path of Mahayana Buddhism, a Mahayanist must benefit others for countless kalpas before becoming a buddha. Is it even possible for me to attain enlightenment?"

Atisha sought an answer from Rahula, who responded, "You care too much about your own enlightenment. The only path to ultimate liberation is to cultivate bodhichitta. You must forgo egoistic concerns and develop altruism, because self-centeredness is the very cause of suffering!"

Shortly afterward Atisha went on pilgrimage to the vajra seat at Bodh Gaya, a small town in the northern Indian state of Bihar where the Buddha reached enlightenment, where he overheard a conversation between two celestial maidens. The first asked, "What is the fastest way to attain enlightenment?" The second responded, "The cultivation of the egoless and altruistic bodhichitta." Atisha was slightly inspired.

On the next day of his pilgrimage, while circumambulating the Mahabodhi Stupa and the Bodhi Tree, he noticed a beggar and a leper talking about the Dharma. The leper asked, "What is the fastest way to attain enlightenment?" The beggar answered, "The cultivation of the egoless and altruistic bodhichitta."

Hearing this, Atisha thought, "Whoever I meet, be it a higher- or lower-positioned person, or a pretty or ugly person, all tell me bodhichitta leads to the fastest enlightenment. This is consistent with my teacher's answer. It seems I am the only person not aware of this!" Atisha started to belittle himself for his ignorance.

On the third day, when walking inside the stupa's temple, Atisha noticed a little bird had landed on the knee of the Avalokiteshvara statue. The bird asked Avalokiteshvara, "What is the fastest way to attain enlightenment?" The statue's answer was the same, "The cultivation of the egoless and altruistic bodhichitta."

At that very moment, Atisha fully understood the importance of bodhichitta.

To generate and strengthen his bodhichitta Atisha later traveled to Indonesia, where for twelve years he received teachings from Suvarnadvipa (b. tenth century), his most important teacher. During this period, Atisha only focused on the practice of bodhichitta. Eventually authentic bodhichitta arose in him, and Atisha attained enlightenment.

WHAT IS BODHICHITTA?

Maitreya, the bodhisattva who will be the next buddha after Shakyamuni Buddha, gave the famous definition of bodhichitta in his *Ornament of Clear Realization*:

> Arousing bodhichitta is: for the sake of others,
> Longing to attain complete enlightenment.

Two aspects of bodhichitta are embedded in this definition: the impartial compassion for all, and the wisdom of complete enlightenment.

The Impartial Compassion for All

The first aspect of bodhichitta means one aspires to compassionately free all sentient beings from the sufferings of samsaric existence. Often referred to as "Great Compassion," it is impartially directed toward all sentient beings, for instance, without discriminating between friends and foes, or animals and humans.

Why *all* sentient beings? As recorded in the *Brahmajala Sutra*, the Buddha said,

> All males have been my father,
> All females have been my mother;
> I was born from them, through life after life;
> So, all beings within the six realms have been my parents.

In *The Words of My Perfect Teacher*, Patrul Rinpoche offered the same argument: "There is not a single being in samsara who has never been our father or mother, since beginningless time."[4]

We ignorant beings don't remember these relationships because many of these parent-child relationships happened countless eons ago. In addition, we have lost memory of past lives when going through the process of death, intermediate state, and rebirth.

When these innumerous beings were our parents, their only thought was to raise us with the greatest possible kindness and love, and to protect us from any harm. They always gave us the very best of everything, and when faced with danger they were willing to die for us. We are enormously indebted to them. We should repay their kindness in any way possible.

Some people who have been neglected or abused by their parents find it hard to respond positively to the idea that others have been their parents. In this case, it's not easy to repay kindness that has not been felt. While I understand their difficulty, they might think of the question this way: "At birth I was a helpless infant and my parents provided food and clothing, so I didn't die of hunger or cold. This is a great kindness I should repay." If you still have difficulty feeling gratitude for your parents, you may substitute a cherished grandparent, sibling, friend, uncle, or aunt, whom you are convinced loves you and cares for you. From this beginning, imagine that every sentient being has loved and cared for you in the same way, until you are convinced.

Like everybody, these beings want to be happy and to avoid suffering. But they don't know how to give up the root of suffering—fundamental ignorance—so no matter how hard they try, they are tormented by the miseries of the six realms (the three higher realms and the three lower realms) of existence. Realizing this, we should practice compassion and loving-kindness equally toward all sentient beings.

The Wisdom of Complete Enlightenment

The second aspect of bodhichitta focuses on the transcendent wisdom of perfect enlightenment. To bring perfect buddhahood to all beings including ourselves, we aspire to attain the wisdom of fully realizing emptiness.

Allow me to reiterate: whatever positive things we do, including attaining enlightenment, we should avoid doing it for the pursuit of our own happiness or fame; instead, we must be motivated by the wish to free all beings—our parents of this life and past lives—from their habitual patterns, karmic debts, and sufferings of samsara, and to lead them to buddhahood.

Then how do we attain enlightenment? The Buddha gave his answer in the *Medium Prajnaparamita*:

> To obtain the Buddha's perfect unsurpassable enlightenment, one must practice the *prajnaparamita*. Even one who wishes to obtain the fruit of an arhat, shravaka, or *prateyekabuddha*[5] must still practice the prajnaparamita.

Prajnaparamita, the "Perfection of Transcendent Wisdom," refers to the wisdom of emptiness. As you've known from the first chapter of this book, emptiness means that things do not inherently exist as they appear to; instead, they are like illusions and dreams. Put another way, there is not a truly existent "self" or "phenomenon." The realization of emptiness is crucial for the attainment of liberation and perfect enlightenment, and Mahayana Buddhism provides a particularly effective means for realizing emptiness.

Given the definition of bodhichitta, it should be inscribed in our hearts and minds that the heart essence of bodhichitta is the union of compassion and wisdom. As a result of not fully understanding bodhichitta, many people, including some Buddhists, reduce bodhichitta to nothing more than compassionate loving-kindness. Often, they simply equate bodhichitta with charitable endeavors, altruistic actions, and selfless and loving concern for others. They fail to notice the crucial aspect of the wisdom of emptiness.

In a nutshell, bodhichitta is about having great compassion toward all sentient beings and the wisdom to complete enlightenment—to become a buddha for all. All of us should be crystal clear about this: the ultimate goal of a Mahayana practitioner is not to attain buddhahood for oneself, but for all sentient beings. It is because buddhahood empowers bodhisattvas to perfectly benefit others, that the aspiration to attain full enlightenment is needed.

RELATIVE AND ABSOLUTE BODHICHITTA

According to its nature, bodhichitta can be categorized into "relative bodhichitta" and "absolute bodhichitta," the former of which includes the distinction between "aspirational bodhichitta" and "practical bodhichitta."

Aspirational bodhichitta, practical bodhichitta, and absolute bodhichitta are all equally important to a Mahayana practitioner. It is not appropriate to think that one specific type of bodhichitta outweighs the others. In the case of most beginners, it is better to start by practicing aspirational bodhichitta and gradually advance to practical bodhichitta and absolute bodhichitta.

Relative Bodhichitta

Relative bodhichitta is consciously cultivated and is accessible to everyone. It refers to the wish to attain full enlightenment for all sentient beings impartially, and the actions needed to achieve that goal.

Relative bodhichitta includes the component of an altruistic mind. There are different levels of altruism. A mother's compassion for her child is a sort of altruism, but it cannot be considered an example of relative bodhichitta because it is partial.

Relative bodhichitta has two aspects: "aspirational bodhichitta" and "practical bodhichitta." Aspirational bodhichitta is a compassionate wish: "From this time onward I'll always aspire to attain full enlightenment so that I can dedicate myself to the benefit of all sentient beings. That's going to be my aim. That's going to be my purpose."

Practical bodhichitta means enacting the wish. We actually engage it, putting the wish into action through the six transcendent perfections (*paramitas*) of generosity, discipline, patience, diligence, meditative concentration, and wisdom.

In *The Way of the Bodhisattva*, Shantideva used the analogy of a journey to distinguish the two subdivisions of relative bodhichitta:

> Bodhichitta, the awakened mind,
> Is known in brief to have two aspects:
> First, aspiring bodhichitta in intention;
> Then active bodhichitta, practical engagement.
> As corresponding to the wish to go
> And then to setting out,
> The wise should understand respectively
> The difference that divides these two.[6]

Thus, aspirational bodhichitta is like setting a goal to go somewhere, perhaps Lhasa, Tokyo, or Paris. Practical bodhichitta is like embarking on the journey, on foot or by air, to reach the destination. To better explain this, let's continue with the story of Atisha.

After gaining full realization of bodhichitta, Atisha returned to India and resided at Vikramashila Monastery, a leading Buddhist monastic university. During this same period, Buddhism in Tibet suffered a severe setback due to repression by King Langdarma.

A later Tibetan king named Lhalama Yeshey-Ö strongly wished to invite Atisha to Tibet to revitalize Buddhism. After Atisha received the invitation, he prayed to Tara for guidance. In a vision he met Tara again, who told him his journey to Tibet would benefit Tibetans enormously.

"But if you remain in India you will live to be ninety-two years old," she said, "While if you go to Tibet your life span will be shortened to seventy-two years."

Atisha really wanted to help Tibetans, and felt it was worth sacrificing twenty years of his life to do so. Therefore, without hesitation he went to Tibet to propagate the Dharma.

Atisha regarded bodhichitta as the essence of all the Dharma practices, so he focused on teaching bodhichitta to Tibetans. When being asked how to reduce any practice to its essence, Atisha answered:

> "By training in bodhichitta with love and compassion for all living creatures throughout space.
>
> By making strenuous efforts in the two accumulations for the benefit of all those beings.
>
> By dedicating all sources of future good thus created to the perfect enlightenment of each and every being.
>
> And finally by recognizing that all these things are empty by nature, like dreams or magical illusions."[7]

Absolute Bodhichitta

Absolute bodhichitta is the direct insight into the ultimate nature of reality—emptiness. It is the nature of mind recognized by realized sublime beings, which is difficult for ordinary individuals to comprehend. Unlike generating relative bodhichitta, of which beginning Buddhists follow a ritual to take the vow, absolute bodhichitta comes about through meditation instead of rituals.

According to the viewpoint of great Tibetan Buddhist masters such as Longchenpa, Jigme Lingpa (1730–1798), and Tsongkhapa, the person who truly arouses absolute bodhichitta, that is, who realizes emptiness, is a bodhisattva having attained at least the first stage of the path (*bhumi*[8]).

The *Sutra of Arousing the Great Bodhichitta* says this about absolute bodhichitta:

> Bodhisattva Kashyapa asked the Buddha, "How can we arouse bodhichitta?"
>
> The Buddha responded, "All phenomena are like the empty space without innate nature, and they are primordially luminous and completely pure. That is called enlightenment. Giving birth to the realization of being in accord with that, the precious realization that has not arisen before, is called arousing bodhichitta."

In the above context, bodhichitta is synonymous with completely awakened mind or buddha-nature. It is the union of emptiness and luminosity. This non-dual state of realization is beyond any dual verbal explanation. Therefore, while an ordinary beginner may start to have intellectual understanding of the meaning of absolute bodhichitta, it is still beyond their reach to realize absolute bodhichitta. Therefore, beginners should start from developing relative bodhichitta.

AROUSING BODHICHITTA

Bodhichitta first must be established in one's mind through aspirational bodhichitta. As said, it's best that beginning Buddhists start by practicing aspirational bodhichitta and gradually work up to practical bodhichitta and absolute bodhichitta. Without setting intention through aspirational bodhichitta, simply acting compassionately or doing seemingly virtuous acts is not sufficient to be bodhichitta practice.

Practical bodhichitta must be guided by aspirational bodhichitta. Let's use Shantideva's analogy of a journey here. Suppose you aspire to reach Lhasa, so you act accordingly: you pack your backpack, grab your wallet, and head toward your destination. During the long journey, you must keep your mind focused on the destination—your initial aspiration—otherwise, you will stop or go astray.

Aspirational Bodhichitta

The Dharma can be like a supermarket offering fulfillment of all kinds of goals. The reason why "customers" end with different results is that they have varied goals or aspirations.

As Mahayana Buddhists, our goal is to lead all sentient beings to buddhahood. To fulfill this, we must constantly examine the motivations behind our actions, whenever we are walking, standing, sitting, lying down, running errands, hearing Dharma talks, or meditating. We should always ask ourselves, "Why am I doing what I'm doing?"

Sometimes we may realize we have no particular goal behind an action, or we are simply copying others' actions. Also, we may be motivated by a drive for self-achievement, such as, "I myself want to have a good rebirth," or "I want to get fame or wealth."

Of course, these are totally normal goals for us ordinary people when we first embark on the path of Mahayana Buddhism. Gradually we must develop the higher aspirations of bodhichitta.

When I reflect on my "aspirations"—albeit transient ones—from when I was a novice monk more than thirty years ago, I still feel a bit embarrassed. At that time, the chant leader at my home monastery had a melodious voice, and many of us in the sangha admired this monk. Attracted by this admiration, for some time the aspiration of becoming a chant leader hovered over me. Also, at the monastery there was a lama whose monk's robe was the most elegant, so I aspired to appear as elegant as him with a robe like his.

The aspirations of many beginning Buddhists may be similar to mine during my early monastic life. Don't feel bad about that. Such aspirations are normal when you are new to the path. The key is this: now that you have encountered the profound teachings of Mahayana Buddhism, you should gradually revamp your aspirations and start to generate an altruistic mind.

Eventually, the aspiration of bodhichitta should permeate your ordinary daily life and your Dharma life. You should always aspire to help others through your expertise, wisdom, and wealth. This is a must for a Mahayana practitioner.

Aspiration Guides Actions

My root guru the great Jigme Phuntsok Rinpoche once said:

Any virtuous deed not guided by bodhichitta, be it prostrating, chanting mantras, or bowing, is not able to surpass the deed guided by bodhichitta. Without bodhichitta, even if one has finished millions of mantra recitations, accomplished ngöndro (preliminary practices) dozens of times, or attained a higher level of meditative equipoise, the merit one accumulated from these deeds is insignificant. Such actions may just result in worldly merit, which doesn't lead to ultimate liberation.

However magnificent virtuous deeds may appear, without bodhichitta they don't bring substantial merit onto our Mahayana path to enlightenment. As Jigme Lingpa wrote in his *Treasury of Precious Qualities*:

What makes an action good or bad?
Not how it looks, nor whether it is big or small,
But the good or evil motivation behind it.

Some people appear to do good deeds on a large scale, for example, studying the Dharma for years, making substantial offerings to the sangha, or building grand Dharma halls. However, sometimes the motivations behind these endeavors are not entirely pure, contaminated by worldly intentions of rivalry, competitiveness, gaining fame and status, or flaunting wealth.

For example, the primary goal for some Tibetan lamas studying the Dharma is to receive the title of *khenpo* or *geshe*, while for some householders attending Buddhist teachings is to become Dharma instructors or to achieve worldly benefits such as family harmony, prosperity, healing, or eloquence. People like this are not yet authentic students and practitioners of Mahayana Buddhism no matter how much they've studied the Dharma because Mahayana Buddhists have only one ultimate goal in mind: to benefit all sentient beings and to lead them to enlightenment.

Seeking fame or building one's personal image is not an appropriate goal for a Mahayana Buddhist. To be sure, some great masters naturally and involuntarily gain fame when their Dharma activities grow; this fame is not their goal but a natural consequence or by-product of the aspirations and actions of their bodhichitta.

Moreover, if it is not guided by bodhichitta, engaging in any practice, no matter how profound it is, will sidetrack or even backfire. One day Atisha appeared sad, and his disciple Dromtönpa asked him why. Atisha said, "I have a disciple who had been practicing Hevajra. Today, he entered the shravaka path of cessation."

This may seem surprising, because the deity practice of Hevajra in Vajrayana Buddhism is considered an extraordinary and high practice that can lead to the state of buddhahood, not a shravaka practice per se that at most leads to the state of arhatship. However, as Atisha further commented, rather than *what* one practices, it is one's motivation, or *how* one practices, that is most important. Therefore, if a practitioner has an ill-intended aspiration, the deity practice may throw them into a lower realm; if they have an egocentric aspiration of renunciation, the deity practice may bring them to the shravaka path of cessation; if they have the aspiration of bodhichitta, the deity practice may project them to the level of buddhahood.

The point is that aspiration determines the outcome, and if aspiration is pure, outcomes will be pure. According to Patrul Rinpoche, this is like a tree. If a tree has a poisonous root, its branches, flowers, and fruit will all be poisonous; if a tree has a medicinal root, its branches, flowers, and fruit will all bring miraculous healing.

It is worth mentioning that however small virtuous bodhichitta deeds may seem, the merits of the actions won't be exhausted until buddhahood is attained. Therefore, at the very beginning of any action we must examine our aspiration and adjust our motivation to ensure that the action is guided by bodhichitta. As Shantideva said in *The Way of Bodhisattva*,

> When you feel the wish to move about,
> Or even to express yourself in speech,
> First examine what is in your mind,
> For steadfast ones should act correctly.[9]

Whatever Dharma activity we engage in, Mahayanists should hold bodhichitta in mind. This includes listening to Dharma teachings, visualizing a deity, chanting the hundred-syllable Vajrasattva mantra, prostrating as part of preliminary practices, or circumambulating any sacred site or object.

Arousing bodhichitta before starting an action is referred to as "good in the beginning" or the "preparation" in the three supreme methods. These three are the ultimate methods of cultivating virtue and training the mind, which will be explained in greater detail in chapter 4.

The Practices of Aspirational Bodhichitta

All our daily activities should be guided by the aspiration of benefiting sentient beings. Those of superior faculties always keep bodhichitta in their minds in all endeavors, regardless of time and place. The *Flower Ornament Sutra* describes in great detail how to arouse bodhichitta in everyday life.

As beginning Buddhists, if you can't do so throughout the day, at least you should try to arouse bodhichitta in the morning, wishing that your daily activities benefit others, and then concluding your day by keeping others in your mind. This is a practice of bodhichitta.

I don't suggest beginning Buddhists go after "magical" signs including clairvoyance, visions of *bindu* (the essence-drop), direct realization, or the experience of luminosity. Arousing aspirational bodhichitta is beginners' primary mission and task, and they should ensure all their virtuous actions become a source of good on their bodhisattva path.

Some Buddhists may retain non-Buddhist residuals from their previous experience or have been shravaka practitioners of the Hinayana (Common Vehicle), so the idea of attaining enlightenment for all beings, instead of for oneself only, is unfamiliar to them. Thus, it is difficult for them to generate bodhichitta. They may even experience negative emotions such as fear, anxiety, and bewilderment upon hearing the vast aspirations and actions of Mahayana bodhisattvas. However, they need not worry because these emotions can be transformed through practice. As long as these people constantly cultivate the idea of helping and enlightening others, their negative reactions will gradually diminish.

Of course, it is easy to talk about bodhichitta or simply recite the bodhichitta prayer; everyone can pay lip service, but, as Patrul Rinpoche pointed out:

> The most important thing about bodhichitta is not arousing it,
> but rather that it has actually arisen.[10]

Developing genuine, uncontrived bodhichitta in our minds depends on diligent practice. I will briefly introduce two renowned methods for arousing bodhichitta, including *tonglen* practice and the four boundless qualities. You will receive detailed teachings on the methods when you study texts like *Seven Points of Mind Training, The Way of Bodhisattva, The Words of My Perfect Teacher,* and *Finding Rest in the Nature of Mind.*

Tonglen

Tonglen practice, also known as "taking and sending," is taking in the suffering and pain of others and sending out your happiness, peace, or whatever is beneficial to others. The heart of this bodhichitta meditation is to exchange oneself and others, as Langri Thangpa (1054–1123) says:

> Offer gain and victory to others.
> Take loss and defeat for yourself.

The practice was brought to Tibet by Atisha, who learned it from his guru Suvarnadvipa. For many years, this mind-training teaching from Atisha was kept secret and transmitted only to close disciples, which gives you an idea of how precious the practice is. Tonglen became more well known after Geshe Chekawa Yeshe Dorje (1102–1179) summarized the practice in his *Seven Points of Mind Training*, and it has since been practiced by all the major lineages of Tibetan Buddhism.

Sometimes, my Dharma students would earnestly request me to offer them a "pith instruction." Tonglen is the genuine pith instruction! This practice is extremely important, as Shantideva says:

> If I do not interchange
> My happiness for other's pain,
> Enlightenment will never be attained,
> And even in samsara, joy will fly from me.[11]

Tonglen invokes our compassion, awakens our bodhichitta, and enables enlightenment. We may do tonglen as a formal sitting meditation practice, as well as a simple exchange for a real-life situation such as witnessing someone's angry outburst. In our daily life, we should constantly remind ourselves of the abovementioned verse from Langri Thangpa or the verse from Shantideva's *The Way of Bodhisattva*:

> To free myself from harm
> And others from their sufferings,
> Let me give myself to others,
> Loving them as I now love myself.[12]

You may find it quite embarrassing and feel helpless when you first begin the tonglen practice, as you realize how stubborn your old patterns of self-ishness are. It seems like a mission impossible to do a genuine tonglen with a friend, let alone a stranger, or even an enemy!

But, if you hang on to the practice, gradually at your own pace, you will find you care less and less about yourself and more and more about others; your selfishness yields to selflessness; you become more open and compassionate; and you start to glimpse emptiness.

The Four Boundless Qualities

Buddhists, especially those following the Nyingma lineage, can also train the mind in the four boundless qualities, as per the guidance of enlightened masters including Longchenpa, Mipham Rinpoche, and Khenpo Ngawang Pelzang (1879–1941).

In his *Finding Rest in the Nature of Mind*, Longchenpa explains that aspirational bodhichitta is based on the four boundless qualities, the practice of which is considered essential for Mahayanists. Lineage masters always suggest steady and enduring contemplation and meditation on the four boundless states. Good practice on the four boundless qualities can facilitate the arising of genuine bodhichitta, whereas bad practice renders your bodhichitta insincere—you just talk the talk when saying "I vow to liberate all sentient beings."

This traditional Tibetan Buddhist prayer summarizes the essence of the four boundless qualities—love, compassion, joy, and equanimity, respectively:

> May all beings have happiness and the cause of happiness.
> May they be free of suffering and the cause of suffering.
> May they never be disassociated from the supreme happiness that
>   is without suffering.
> May they remain in the boundless equanimity, free from both
>   attachment to close ones and rejection of others.

They are called "boundless" qualities because sentient beings—the object of our focus in the meditation practice—are boundless, the form the qualities take in our mind is boundless, and the result from the practice is boundless.

According to the pith instruction of Longchenpa, beginners should start the practice with equanimity by considering everyone as equal, by recognizing everyone as your parent, and by acknowledging that everyone seeks happiness. With equanimity as their base, the other three boundless qualities banish pride, desire, hatred, jealousy, and other blockers of bodhichitta.

Quite like what happens through the tonglen practice, with effective practice on the four boundless qualities, our grasping eases, ignorance atrophies, the self-other distinction blurs, loving compassion grows, and we also gain access to the wisdom of emptiness. Gradually and surely, our bodhichitta arises.

Practical Bodhichitta

As mentioned earlier, aspirational bodhichitta is like the wish to go somewhere, and practical bodhichitta is like making the journey. The responsiveness to the wish is through the practice of the six transcendent perfections (paramitas). Whichever paramita you are engaging in, make sure it is motivated and guided by the wish to enlighten all sentient beings.

The first paramita, generosity, refers to giving material, Dharma, or protection from fear to others without expecting to be paid back. The second, discipline, consists of avoiding negative actions, undertaking positive actions, and bringing benefit to others. Patience is the third paramita and means gentle forbearance when being disturbed or even harmed by others, endurance when encountering hardships for the Dharma, and acceptance when receiving profound teachings. The fourth, diligence, is being courageous and perseverant, never separating from virtues, and never feeling satisfied with your practice until you attain buddhahood. Meditative concentration, the fifth paramita, gives up distraction and rests in a state where there is no grasping for anything.

These first five activities are skillful means to channel your aspirational bodhichitta into real actions, and they are infused with wisdom, the sixth paramita. The wisdom paramita refers to the non-dual wisdom of emptiness. It is wisdom that makes the first five activities "transcendent perfections."

We don't just train our practical bodhichitta once in a while or during scheduled time slots. Everything we do in the twenty-four hours of a day can be practical bodhichitta, as long as we remember the aspirations of bodhichitta. There shouldn't be a clear-cut division between our "Dharmic life" and "ordinary life." Every moment of our "ordinary life" can be the bodhisattva path.

In addition, beginning Mahayanists should start practical bodhichitta with small steps, despite the vast aspiration of bringing all sentient beings to buddhahood. It's better if beginners start the practice with caring for one person or one family, giving smaller donations, doing shorter meditation sessions, and so on. Eventually, as we become more experienced and capable after practice—lots of practice—we can *do* more and *do* something bigger and better.

BODHICHITTA FOR BEGINNERS—FURTHER THOUGHTS

Dreamers and Doers

Some people think those who practice aspirational bodhichitta are dreamers or wishers. "They just talk the talk," such people say, "Isn't it better to walk the talk, to actually do something, to be a doer?" This question is not uncommon nowadays. Most people seem to prefer doers to dreamers. For example, in political campaigns candidates repeatedly claim they are doers to attract votes.

In the spiritual world, sometimes it is wiser to be a dreamer at first. You may have read touching stories in which compassionate beings put bodhichitta into action, including Prince Great Courage giving his body to a starving tigress, Nagarjuna giving his head to the son of King Surabhibhadra, and Princess Mandabhadri feeding a tigress with her own body. Such people have at least reached the first stage of the bodhisattva's path and realized emptiness, so they can take such actions with vast and pure intentions.

In comparison, ordinary beings are incapable of such exceptionally great giving of body or life. Instead, beginners may use their minds to visualize offering their bodies to beings in need. Beginners should practice developing strong aspiration, wishing, "One day I will physically and practically perform bodhichitta in action, just like highly realized bodhisattvas."

That said, beginning Buddhists shouldn't undervalue the power of aspiration. Shantideva said, "A simple thought to help others exceeds in worth the worship of the buddhas."

Here is a story from the *Sutra of the Wise and the Fool* about the power of aspiration:

During the Buddha's time there lived a poor beggar woman named Nanta. She relied on begging for goods or spare change to survive. She used to watch kings, princes, and other people making offerings to the Buddha and his disciples.

One day she heard about people going to make a light offering to the Buddha.

Seeing people devoutly purchasing exquisite, perfumed oils and candles, she also wished to make an offering. She thought, "Because in the past I didn't cultivate any merit, in this life I am poor and miserable. Now that I've met such a great field of merit, I should take this opportunity to make an offering to the Buddha."

Nanta went out begging, but by the end of the day all she had received was one small coin. She took the coin to an oil vendor but found it was only enough to buy the smallest amount of oil, not sufficient to make a lamp. Out of sympathy, the vendor gave her the oil she wanted, so Nanta could finally offer an oil lamp to the Buddha.

As darkness descended upon the city, people gathered and lit their lamps for the Buddha. Nanta was amid the crowd, respectfully lighting her oil lamp. When her very ordinary oil lamp started to glow among all the other lamps, Nanta made a wish:

"I have nothing to offer but this tiny lamp, but through this offering, may the light of this lamp pervade through the ten directions, guiding all sentient beings out of the miserable ocean of cyclic birth and death, dispelling the darkness of their ignorance, and leading them to enlightenment."

After making the aspiration, Nanta prostrated in front of the lamp, and left.

By the next day, all the oil lamps had gone out after burning all night, except Nanta's lamp, which was still shining brightly and full of oil with a wick like new. When the Buddha's disciple Maudgalyayana came to collect all the lamps, he tried to blow it out, but Nanta's lamp kept on burning. He tried to snuff it out with his fingers, but it stayed alight. He tried to smother it with his robe, but still, it burned on.

Maudgalyayana was astonished. "Whose lamp is this that is still burning?" he wondered.

The Buddha had been watching all along. He said: "Maudgalyayana, the person who offered this lamp made a great Mahayana aspiration of bodhichitta to enlighten all sentient beings. It cannot be extinguished by a shravaka like you, no matter how much supernatural power you possess. Even if you exhaust all the water in the four great oceans, you will still not be able to extinguish this lamp."

When the Buddha said this Nanta approached him, and the Buddha prophesized that in the future this beggar woman would become a perfect Buddha, called "Light of the Lamp."

Therefore, although this bodhichitta aspiration was made by the poor beggar woman Nanta, its power was substantial!

Perhaps you find Nanta's story hard to resonate with because it happened nearly 2,500 years ago. I'll share another story of aspiration that is still unfolding today. This inspiring story is about Dharma Master Cheng Yen, with whom I am not personally acquainted but whose great kindness I've read about in articles.

Dharma Master Cheng Yen seems at first sight to be a very ordinary Taiwanese Buddhist nun. She is thin, gentle, and very humble. However, she has developed an extremely vast aspiration of bodhichitta, which has generated her great capacity to help others.

In 1966 Dharma Master Cheng Yen founded the Buddhist Compassion Relief Tzu Chi Foundation, which started as a group of thirty housewives who saved fifty cents in Taiwanese currency—about two cents USD–from their daily grocery money to help families in need. After more than forty years, Tzu Chi has grown to ten million members worldwide, providing Buddhist support in terms of medical aid, disaster relief, environmental protection, and much more.

When asked how Tzu Chi became one of the world's largest humanitarian organizations, Master Cheng Yen's answer was simple: "Because we have vast aspirations—the bigger the aspiration, the more powerful the actions."

The power of aspiration is inconceivable, as said in the *Flower Ornament Sutra*:

> To attain the wisdom lamp of luminosity and purity of all the
> buddhas,
> One shall generate vast aspirations, and swiftly arouse bodhichitta.

After reading this far, I hope you have realized that arousing aspirational bodhichitta is a crucial part of your spiritual training. With the inconceivable power of our vast bodhichitta aspiration, we will definitely benefit sentient beings when causes and conditions ripen.

There are many disciples who started to follow the great Jigme Phuntsok Rinpoche when he was still alive. While some of these disciples were relatively unknown back to thirty years ago, they aroused intense aspirations to bring all sentient beings to enlightenment. Because of this aspiration, later they were able to guide numerous beings on the path to liberation.

To benefit sentient beings, we don't have to possess exceptional intelligence or wealth. As long as we firmly embrace bodhichitta in our minds, we will develop the capacity to bring all sentient beings to ultimate happiness and enlightenment.

Bodhichitta and Ego-Clinging

Mahayana Buddhists often ask themselves this: "Have I started to arouse bodhichitta?"

To answer this question, we should carefully examine whether we have altruistic intention because bodhichitta arises only when altruistic mind is present. Admittedly, it is hard for an ordinary person to eradicate all egoistic thoughts. Yet, if we try our very best to lessen our ego-clinging—the greatest obstacle to bodhichitta—we'll gradually increase altruism.

The key to this, as many eminent masters have asserted, is that the altruistic mind is weaker when the egoistic mind is stronger. This is easy to understand since egoism is the opposite of altruism. Thus, altruistic motivation is the antidote to ego-clinging.

In conventional life, it seems legitimate to pursue one's happiness, so it can be hard to let go of egoistic concerns. However, as Shantideva said in *The Way of Bodhisattva*:

> All the joy the world contains
> Has come through wishing happiness for others.
> All the misery the world contains
> Has come through wanting pleasure for oneself.[13]

Thus, starting today, we should aspire to cultivate strong altruistic mind. Then we should gradually develop this altruism into bodhichitta—the longing to obtain unsurpassable buddhahood for the sake of others.

Practicing the Dharma is a gradual process. We should aim high yet move steadily and surely. If we set our expectations too high in the beginning, hoping to quickly generate bodhichitta and then to liberate all sentient beings, we are likely to become disappointed, frustrated, and discouraged. We may even give up entirely.

In my own life, I feel delighted whenever I've done something helpful to others, no matter how trivial it is. As we engage in altruistic endeavors, others may misunderstand us or even mock us. Shantideva suggested this response:

> This body I have now resigned
> To serve the pleasure of all living beings.
> Let them ever kill, despise, and beat it,
> Using it according to their wish.
> And though they treat it like a toy,
> Or make of it the butt of every mockery,
> My body has been given up to them.
> Why should I make so much of it?[14]

It is very helpful to keep this suggestion in mind. If our egoistic concerns are too strong, we can easily perceive others as hostile and ill-intentioned, and our bodhichitta will never mature. Recognizing that it's nearly impossible for ordinary people to completely eradicate ego-clinging, some may wonder if they can ever arouse bodhichitta. Bodhichitta, especially aspirational bodhichitta, can start to arise despite the presence of ego-clinging. Relatively speaking, aspirational bodhichitta is quite an easy practice for beginning Buddhists.

Bodhichitta is the antidote to ego-clinging, but completely eradicating ego-clinging is not a prerequisite for arousing aspirational bodhichitta. Since bodhichitta and ego-clinging stand at opposite ends of a continuum, when bodhichitta becomes stronger, ego-clinging becomes weaker accordingly. It's like in a tug-of-war with bodhichitta and ego-clinging pulling at the opposite ends of a rope—bodhichitta can start to pull while ego-clinging is also pulling at the same time; it is not the case that bodhichitta can only start to pull when ego-clinging surrenders with hands off the rope.

Sometimes, beginners feel their aspirations are not authentic, although they are trying hard, and they feel they are just faking it. "I cannot stop thinking about Me! Me! Me! I mostly think about my own enlightenment." They are so frustrated: "Then my aspiration is just like a bad check I write when there is not enough money in my bodhichitta account to pay for it."

Please rest assured that it's not wrong for a beginner to "fake" it. In fact, it is quite normal for a beginner to experience this feeling. Just make sure you continue making effort and practicing it, and eventually you will become less likely to feel that your bodhichitta is just paying lip service. A great Kadampa master described the right relationship between egoistic concern and bodhichitta with this story:

Many people are sunk deep in a mud pit, and among them is one person who wants to rescue everyone. Since he himself is also trapped, this person is not capable of helping others. So first, he does everything he can to get himself out of the mud pit, then he rescues others from danger. In this case, his self-rescue is not for his own safety, but for the safety of all the others.

When we first practice arousing bodhichitta, it is impossible to proceed without thinking, "My own attainment of enlightenment is more important." But the sprinkle of egoistic aspiration doesn't prevent us from generating authentic bodhichitta. To be capable of bringing all sentient beings to buddhahood, "I" must attain buddhahood as soon as possible.

As we advance on the path, through diligent study and meditation on emptiness, we realize the no-self of the individual and phenomena, which uproots our attachment and grasping. By then, we can generate the perfect bodhichitta free of any ego-clinging. Before that, bodhichitta and ego-clinging cohabitate within us.

In this chapter, aspirational bodhichitta is covered in greater detail than practical bodhichitta since most readers are beginning Mahayanists or want to revisit the foundations of practice. This chapter has served its purpose if you understand two important takeaways: bodhichitta is indispensable to enlightenment, and, particularly for beginners, aspiration is the primary mission and task.

Concluding this chapter, let me share with you a story about Khenpo Kunga Wangchuk (1921–2008) whose bodhichitta has touched and inspired many people.

Khenpo Kunga Wangchuk, a disciple of a great Tibetan lama, was imprisoned from the age of thirty-nine to sixty-one during the political turmoil of the Cultural Revolution—twenty-two years of punishment for being a Dharma teacher. He underwent excruciating torture in prison and was left blind in one eye.

In 1981, Khenpo, already an old man, was released from prison and received letters from Dzongsar Jamyang Khyentse Rinpoche—his root guru's reincarnation—inviting him to India to reestablish the Dzongsar Shedra. Despite his poor health, Khenpo soon embarked on an arduous and secret seven-month journey, mostly on foot, starting from his village in eastern Tibet.

When he finally arrived in India, people got to know more about his prison experience through inquiries. Deeply touched and impressed, someone asked Khenpo Kunga Wangchuk, "Did you fear when you were undergoing the torments in prison?"

He answered, "Yes. I did have fears. My biggest fear was that I would lose compassion for those who tortured me. Thanks to my guru's blessing, I didn't break my bodhichitta vows."

To remind himself to generate no hatred, to carry on his compassion for every being, and to retain his bodhichitta intact, Khenpo Kunga Wangchuk composed the prayer below and secretly recited it every day during his twenty-two years in prison.

THE ASPIRATION PRAYER TO TRANSFORM ADVERSITY INTO THE PATH

I take refuge in the guru and the Three Jewels.
With love, compassion and bodhichitta, I make the aspiration for
all the deluded mother-like beings whose mind, owing to not
knowing its primordial nature, fabricates the illusions of samsara.

May my body, provisions, speech, mind, and merits accumulated
through the past, present, and future be the cause of
innumerable beings' freedom from samsara and their attainment
of perfect enlightenment.

Some people generate faith because of me,
Some people become greedy because of me,
And some people get angry because of me.
Whatever mind arises in them, whatever connection they build
with me,
May all these beings who have an affinity with me attain
buddhahood,
Thus, our connection is endowed with a profound meaning.

Though I committed no evil,
Somebody is furious with me, seeing me as the killer who
murdered his father,

And attacks me directly or indirectly.
May I satisfy him with the Dharma one day.

Feeding and clothing me as if I were a pig or a dog,
Assaulting, insulting, slandering and framing me,
May all these frightening actions be the cause of buddhahood.

Because I did harm to others in the past,
I receive the karmic fruit—being harmed by others—in the
    present.
May this be the cause of virtues, so I will harm no one in the
    future.

The body is the cause of all harms in samsara;
Knowing that my own body has made me suffer,
May my suffering be the ally on the path to enlightenment.

With my kindness and pure power of increasing devotion,
May my loving family including my parents and siblings,
And everyone who has an affinity with me,
Be reborn in the western Pure Land of Amitabha.

May all male and female donors who, without reservation,
Offer me food, medicine, gold, silver, and other goods,
Perfect their generosity and please the buddhas.

May all attendants who provide me sitting and bedding
    equipment,
Provisions for living, affection and care when I was sick,
As well as respect and veneration,
Perfect their discipline and attain the perfect appearance.

May all beings who had been my parents in many lives,
Yet whom I, without any compassion and appreciation, have
    enslaved, ridden, and loaded,
And whose flesh, blood, and milk I nourish myself with,
Perfect their patience and swiftly attain buddhahood.

All in all, may all beings who have connection with me
Never be reborn in the lower realms;
May they always be reborn, life after life, in a period when a
buddha has appeared;
May they listen to the Dharma, arouse bodhichitta and attain
buddhahood.

Once I become like a bodhisattva including Manjushri,
Samantabhadra, or Avalokiteshvara,
Following the bodhisattva's aspiration,
May I be the protector of sentient beings as infinite as empty
space.

With the compassion of the guru and the Three Jewels, and
through the unfailing power of karma, may all my fervent
wishes come true.

4. THE THREE SUPREME METHODS

How to Seal Merits

IN THIS FAST-PACED digital age that fiercely promotes efficiency, almost everyone opts for something that yields the highest return with the least effort. We want to lose ten pounds in one week while sitting down, become a fantastic parent by adopting five easy and quick tips, or master alpine skiing after two private coaching sessions.

Modern Buddhists, of course, are not immune to this efficiency mindset. We wish to get the most trouble-free, effortless, yet effective pith instruction for our Dharma practice. Luckily there exists such an essential instruction in Mahayana Buddhism—the three supreme methods. This instruction is not an invention of the twenty-first century. It was taught by Shakyamuni Buddha 2,500 years ago and has since been passed on to Mahayanists, generation after generation.

Specifically, the instruction of the three supreme methods includes the motivation of bodhichitta (good in the beginning), practice with mind free from conceptualization (good in the middle), and dedication of merit (good in the end).

To both novice and veteran Mahayanists being good in the beginning, middle, and end must be applied to any kind of practice because it constitutes the difference between the practice just bringing temporary joy and peace, and that leading to ultimate and full enlightenment.

Many of the greatest Tibetan Buddhist masters of past and present have emphasized the importance of the three supreme methods. For example, Patrul Rinpoche said in *The Words of My Perfect Teacher*,

> Before beginning, arouse the bodhichitta as a skillful means, to make sure the action becomes a source of good for the future.

79

While carrying out the action, avoid getting involved in any conceptualization, so that the merit cannot be destroyed by circumstances.

At the end, seal the action properly by dedicating the merit, which will ensure it continually grows ever greater.[1]

Longchenpa said: "Begin with the thought of bodhichitta, do the main practice without concepts, conclude by dedicating the merit. These, together and complete, are the three vital supports for progressing on the path of liberation."[2] My root guru, the great Jigme Phuntsok Rinpoche, frequently stressed the importance of the three supreme methods, while giving Dharma teachings at Larung Gar and elsewhere.

As followers of these great spiritual teachers, we should try to comprehend the methods' essence and follow them impeccably, thus all our actions will become sources of good for our enlightenment and for the enlightenment of others.

Here I briefly summarize teachings on the three supreme methods that I received from my teachers.

THE MOTIVATION OF BODHICHITTA
(GOOD IN THE BEGINNING)

You've learned from the previous chapter that the quintessence of Mahayana Buddhist practices is the cultivation of bodhichitta, the motivation to awaken for the sake of all sentient beings.

On our path to the ultimate enlightenment, bodhichitta is imperative when we perform all good deeds, whether big or small. Without being motivated by bodhichitta, even Buddhists who have practiced for years won't advance much on the path, and their practice will lack substance and meaning.

Modern psychology breaks motivation into three major aspects. The first is activation—proactively initiating a behavior. The second is persistence—the continued effort toward a goal despite obstacles. The third is intensity—pursuing a goal with concentration and vigor. Motivation is a combination of these three elements, working at different levels.

In the same vein, the motivation of bodhichitta also consists of these three aspects. First, a practitioner initiates practice with eagerness and confidence; second, the practitioner persists with invincible determination;

and last, the practitioner vigorously and intensely concentrates on practice, from beginning until end.

Everything we do is preceded by motivation. So, we Buddhists should always turn our mind inward and check our motivation when we start a practice. When carefully examining our mind, we'll notice three kinds of motivation that drive our actions: unwholesome, neutral, and wholesome.

It is only when our motivation is pure and wholesome that we can proceed to the action for a meaningful effect. Otherwise, we should stop and reconsider.

Unwholesome Motivation

Whatever Dharma we practice, the primary requirement is that we are not driven by the unwholesome motivations pertaining to desire, aversion, selfishness, and other destructive emotions. If we are, we cannot succeed in our practice.

This requirement also applies to worldly actions. Any mundane actions we take should not be conditioned by excessive self-interest or selfishness. Such motivations will undermine our goals.

I've noticed the West promotes the ideology of individualism. Westerners value the idea that each person is unique and self-reliant and that their primary motivation should be to care for themselves.

Being self-interested might appear reasonable from an individual perspective. However, from a social and national perspective, it is not optimal. For example, while voting for president, a person with selfish motives might vote for a candidate who demonstrates no leadership competency yet whose policy may bring the most benefits to the voter's own family. Such a president would not greatly benefit the country.

Moreover, actions with ill intention can be detrimental to society, as we have all seen how a person or an organization with malice can bring harm to others. It has happened that some people pray and make offerings to the Three Jewels, wishing to cause harm to their opponents. For instance, they prostrate to a statue of the Buddha in a temple, requesting, "Dear Buddha, may you please make my enemy very sick?" Such a person is not a true Buddhist, and this malice is definitely not appropriate.

Some Buddhist practitioners are never driven by the intention of deliberately harming anyone, yet they may practice Dharma with a self-serving intention to gain fame, health, wealth, and the like. I've encountered

Buddhists who meditate so they can make better business decisions with a clearer mind, Buddhists who attend a retreat to dodge social responsibility, and Buddhists who participate in philanthropy and later boast of their superiority over others. While this kind of motivation may seem acceptable to people at large, it is a serious flaw to use Dharma for fulfilling one's own worldly desire, so it is still considered an unwholesome motivation in Buddhism.

Besides fulfilling hopes of worldly success, some other Buddhists practice Dharma to relieve fear of disease, evil spirits, bankruptcy, and similar worldly conditions. The practice may protect practitioners from these fears, but it won't benefit them in ending the suffering of samsara and attaining buddhahood. We should therefore also avoid this kind of unwholesome motivation.

Neutral Motivation

Some people's motivations are neither good nor bad but neutral, so these people are simply indifferent to their actions, unconcerned about anything. Easily affected by people around them, they are blind followers. They are disinterested in what they do, and primarily do things because other people are doing them.

Social psychologists refer to this phenomenon as the herd mentality. Some Buddhists participate in Dharma activities by imitating others mindlessly, without any intention of upholding the Dharma or developing compassion toward sentient beings.

Their actions may appear wholesome, but with neutral motivation they are little different from aimless eating or walking. While people's neutrally motivated actions may not harm individuals or society, those people's practice will hardly come to meaningful fruition, that is, it won't become the direct cause to the ultimate liberation. Even from a worldly perspective, the herd mentality is undesirable. Therefore, a Buddhist practitioner should avoid practicing with neutral motivation.

Wholesome Motivation

There are three levels of wholesome motivation: those of lesser beings, of middling beings, and of great beings.

The Motivation of Lesser Beings

What is the lesser being's motivation? It is the motivation only pertinent to one's hope and fear in the future life or lives. An example would be if one makes a wish such as, "I want to be reborn in the god realm in my future life," "I wish to reincarnate to a place of great happiness," or "I want to avoid being reborn in the lower realms." These wishes are just for oneself and for nobody else. This motivation, albeit wholesome, is egocentric.

As mentioned above, from a Buddhist viewpoint any actions taken with the motive to advance one's own fame, wealth, credit, or gratification are considered unwholesome. However, actions taken with the motive to attain a favorable rebirth are considered wholesome.

Why is it then, when both motivations are seemingly about oneself, that one is considered unwholesome and the other wholesome? The key is in the frame of reference.

The first is unwholesome because the intentions are focused on one's current lifetime, with no consideration for the next life or lives. The second is not just about this life, but about the next life or lives. In Buddhism, the ultimate motivation of spiritual practice can never be focused on the present life; only motivations concerning long-lasting and perpetual benefit are considered wholesome. As the great Sakya master Sachen Kunga Nyingpo (1092–1158) said, "If you are attached to this life, you are not a true spiritual practitioner."

Lesser beings practice Dharma to avoid rebirth in the three lower realms, and to gain rebirth in the three higher realms. However, even if they successfully attain a higher rebirth out of this motivation, they are still trapped in samsara. Their actions, while virtuous, will hardly bring them closer to full enlightenment.

The Motivation of Middling Beings

What is the middling being's motivation? It is a wish only for one's own liberation from suffering in samsara. Such Buddhists are called shravaka or pratyekabuddha practitioners. While they can realize the no-self of the individual,[3] this is not yet the ultimate liberation. The story of Shariputra offers a good example here.

Shariputra was one of the two chief male disciples of the Buddha and the one foremost in wisdom. According to Buddhist classics, including the *Lotus Sutra*, Shariputra practiced Mahayana Buddhism in his previous lives, but later lost his faith and turned to shravaka Buddhism. There is the detailed story about Shariputra's change of motivation in the *Treatise on the Great Virtue of Wisdom*.

Shariputra, who had practiced the bodhisattva path for sixteen kalpas, wanted to cross over the river of generosity.

One day a beggar came to him and asked for his eye. Shariputra said to him, "My eye will be of no use to you; why do you want it? But if you asked me for my body or my goods, I would give them to you immediately."

The beggar answered: "I do not need your body or your goods; I only want your eye. If you really practice generosity, you will give me your eye."

Then Shariputra tore out one of his eyes and gave it to him.

The beggar took it and, in front of Shariputra, he sniffed it, spat upon it with disgust, threw it on the ground and stamped on it with his feet.

Shariputra said to himself, "People as vicious as this are hard to save. My eye was of no use to him at all, but he demanded it violently and, when he got it, he threw it away and stamped on it. What can be more vicious? Such people cannot be saved. It is better to tame oneself; one will free oneself sooner from samsara."

Having had this thought, Shariputra left the bodhisattva path and returned to shravaka Buddhism.

This is what is called "not reaching the other shore".

But if one travels one's path directly without turning back (*avinivartana*) and reaches buddhahood, that is called "reaching the other shore."[4]

Shariputra later returned to the Mahayana path and will eventually attain buddhahood, as stated in the third chapter of the *Lotus Sutra*.

Therefore, people may practice the Dharma for their own liberation, but this liberation does not lead to buddhahood if the practitioners don't care about the liberation of others.

Of course, shravaka and pratyekabuddha practitioners do develop compassion toward sentient beings. However, they are unwilling to generate bodhichitta to help all sentient beings and end their sufferings in samsara selflessly and unconditionally. Instead, they prioritize their own liberations to resolve their own cyclic existences. As Kunga Nyingpo said, "If you are attached to your own self-interest, you have no bodhichitta.

The Motivation of Great Beings

What is the motivation of beings of great capacity? It is bodhichitta. This is the most supreme and noble motivation.

Whichever virtuous action a Mahayana Buddhist takes—saving life, teaching Dharma, chanting mantras, circumambulating stupas—they should think, "May this action be of benefit to all beings." Having such an aspirational thought seems a simple mental activity, yet it denotes the most meaningful and effective motivation of a Mahayanist.

With bodhichitta in mind, we are sure to gain all merits. In the *Sutra of the King Lion*, the Buddha said,

> For all beings' liberation, we now arouse bodhichitta;
> It magnetizes all kinds of goodness,
> It brings happiness and joy, both temporary and ultimate.

To liberate limitless sentient beings in this borderless universe we should arouse supreme bodhichitta, as it helps us perfect all positive actions and merits. With bodhichitta, we can effortlessly obtain both temporary and ultimate happiness.

THE MAIN PRACTICE (GOOD IN THE MIDDLE)

Wisdom of Emptiness

While carrying out actions we should avoid being caught in conceptualization. This is the second supreme method. Strictly speaking, practice without conceptualization is a state of non-duality, referring to an enlightened being's state of realization of emptiness.

According to Buddhist teachings, such a state is realizing the truth that, ultimately, all phenomena are like empty space, beyond all four extremes and free from any concepts and elaborations, and, relatively, every phenomenon is like a magical illusion, a dream, or the reflection of the moon on water.

When examining the nature of appearances with wisdom, we realize that dreamlike or illusory appearances don't inherently exist; they are free from the three concepts of a subject, an object, and an action.

What does it mean to be "free from the three concepts?" As an example, let's consider making a donation. When we practice generosity, we normally conceptualize a donor, a recipient, and a gift. However, when we examine the nature of these three things, we realize they have no inherent existence, and they appear in the manner of illusions or dreams.

Donor, recipient, and gift are all empty of inherent existence. The three are constructed concepts and labels in our minds, with no inherent nature of their own. Realizing this frees us from the three concepts, so that we are no longer bound by the dualistic mind—the root cause of our sufferings.

To deeply understand emptiness, one should study texts such as Chandrakirti's *Introduction to the Middle Way* and Longchenpa's *Finding Rest in the Nature of the Mind*. I'll cover this in greater detail in chapter 5.

Regarding the main practice, the great treasure revealer (*terton*) Dechen Lingpa (1829–1870) said: "When you merge the accumulation of conceptual merit with the accumulation of nonconceptual wisdom into one, this skillful practice is called 'the main practice without conceptualization.'"

What happens if we fail to free our mind from concepts? The Buddha said in the *Sutra of Upholding Virtuous Merits*,

> Even if one has been upholding his vows for a long time,
> Even if one has been practicing patience for a long time,
> Without the wisdom of suchness in his mind, he is a
> non-Buddhist.

Therefore, even when practitioners have firmly upheld precepts and practiced patience over a thousand great kalpas, without the wisdom pertaining to the empty nature of all things, there is no fundamental difference between them and non-Buddhists. Or, as Kunga Nyingpo said, "If there is grasping, you do not have the View." Here the "View" refers to the true reality of emptiness.

Practitioners of other religions also practice compassion and patience and uphold their own precepts, so behaviorally they are not different from Buddhists. That said, there is a key point in which Buddhism differs from other religions. Take actions of compassion, for example, Buddhists accompany the compassionate actions with the wisdom of emptiness. Understanding this distinction is extremely important for Buddhists.

Advice to Beginners

Beginners find it hard to start the main practice without conceptualization, since ordinary, unenlightened beings haven't realized emptiness. Therefore, many masters suggested that once a practitioner concentrates their mind, this is considered an acceptable alternative to the practice without conceptualization. For example, when you listen to a Dharma teaching, you sit still, maintain silence, and wholeheartedly concentrate.

But if your mind strays to something else while listening to the teaching, or if your mind is filled with rambling thoughts, you are no longer engaged in this alternative practice to the main practice free of conceptualization. In the *Sutra of Great Clairvoyance*, the Buddha said:

> The unmovable stability of your body, speech, and mind,
> Is called the precept of being free from the three concepts.

Thus, when engaged in positive actions such as listening to teachings, we should keep our bodies as still as the Himalayas. During teachings, we should not distractedly look around or lie down for even a single moment. We should remain silent, not indulging in irrelevant and meaningless chatter. If the situation permits, we should stay silent as best as we can. Our mind should remain unwavering and undistracted, but this doesn't mean we must meditate in a state of calm abiding where the mind rests one-pointedly. Instead, we may simply focus on the ongoing positive actions and keep our mind concentrated.

Similarly, when we engage in the compassionate Buddhist practice of returning animals about to be slaughtered to the wild, how do we refrain from distractive thinking? We might think, "May these suffering beings attain good fortune and merit now and the ultimate buddhahood in the future. Many more beings still need to be liberated, and I will try my very best to help them. If there is no chance to save them in this life, I vow to save them in my next life."

Another way of interpreting practice without conceptualization is the practice of reducing attachment to anything in our lives and reminding of ourselves that all phenomena are simply dreamlike or illusory.

What does this mean? For example, while we may experience insecurity and unhappiness in our daily lives, we should know all these emotions are transitory and don't exist inherently. The Buddha taught us not to cling to anything lacking inherent existence. Not clinging means we are not attached to the phenomenon or to the emotion. If we can gradually reduce our attachment little by little, happiness will arise naturally.

In our mundane daily lives, many of us encounter negative emotions and unquiet minds. If we can apply Buddhist wisdom in our life—viewing our life as a dream, living with compassion, and understanding emptiness—we will always be happy.

DEDICATION (GOOD IN THE END)

The best motivation is bodhichitta. The main practice requires the wisdom of emptiness. The dedication of merit combines both the motivation of bodhichitta and the wisdom of emptiness.

According to Mahayana Buddhism, at the end of any virtuous action we should dedicate all the merits, including that accumulated through arousing bodhichitta at the beginning and practicing concentration in the middle, to all sentient beings. In that dedication we wish for beings to be free of suffering and its causes and to eventually attain perfect buddhahood. Meanwhile, we should apply the wisdom of emptiness, realizing that we who dedicate, the act of dedication, and all sentient beings to whom we dedicate the merits are all devoid of inherent existence. This concludes a perfect practice of dedication.

The Why of Dedication

Past eminent masters said merit could be destroyed through four circumstances, if one failed to dedicate the merit for the sake of others' enlightenment. The four are:

1. *Anger*. When anger arises in our mind, even just for a split second, all the undedicated merits we accumulated through positive actions over a thousand great kalpas will be destroyed completely.
2. *Bragging*. If we announce to everyone our positive actions— how many mantras we have chanted, or where we have donated money—this showing off will gradually destroy our merit. Nowadays I notice that many people like to broadcast their philanthropic acts, listing them and letting everyone know. If you've dedicated the merit, then telling others is fine. If not, any merit might be easily destroyed.
3. *Regret*. A person might donate to a good cause starting with very pure intention. However, later the person might regret these deeds, considering the donations impulsive decisions. Such

regret may exhaust the merit of the person's positive actions.

4. *Unwholesome dedication.* If a person dedicates the merit of positive actions toward their opponents getting sick or even dying, this kind of dedication is not virtuous at all.

Ordinary people often generate wrong views, anger, and regret, which can easily destroy their merit. To prevent such destruction one of the most skillful practices is to dedicate the merit promptly and correctly after positive actions.

Any time we complete a virtuous action, we must conclude with a dedication. Such dedication prevents destruction of the merit by negative emotions and unfavorable circumstances, while enabling the merit to keep growing. This is like depositing money in a bank, where it generates interest. The longer we maintain our deposit, the more interest we'll receive.

Once I met a person who told me, "I am very rich now. The interest alone from my bank account can feed me easily." Similarly, if we dedicate the merit of our actions properly, then the "merit interest" we gain will be unlimited, and this root of virtue will keep growing.

The What of Dedication

What exactly is the merit that we dedicate? According to the abhidharma, the ultimate merit—liberation—cannot be dedicated to sentient beings because it is ever-present and unchangeable. But the other types of merit, which we obtain through virtuous actions of body, speech, and mind in the past, present, and future, can be dedicated. The *Flower Ornament Sutra* says: "All the merits sentient beings gained in the past, present, and future are dedicated for beings to attain the fruition of the primordial buddha Samantabhadra; may all of them gain perfect auspiciousness."

The merits of the three times described in this sutra rely on four virtuous conditions:

1. The merit should be dedicated to all sentient beings, instead of to only a few individuals;
2. The dedication is not for temporary happiness, but for the perfect buddhahood of all beings;
3. The merit should be dedicated in a skillful way, accompanied by compassion and wisdom; and
4. The merit should be accumulated through virtuous actions.

Merit that meets these four virtuous conditions is the best merit. If dedicated to all sentient beings, the merit becomes the root for attaining buddhahood. The *Sutra of Dedication* says: "May all these merits of virtue become the root of enlightenment for all beings."

The How of Dedication

Some Buddhists claim to have studied Dharma for ten years or even twenty years, yet they still dedicate in this way: "Oh Buddha Amitabha, please bless me to be reborn in the Pure Land. May all my family be healthy, safe, and happy. May I have good fortune." Their minds are always surrounded by these self-serving motivations, and their dedications lack essential meaning. Then, how should one dedicate as a Mahayanist?

We may dedicate merits in various ways. For example, we may recite chapter ten of *The Way of the Bodhisattvas*, or the following verses from *The King of Aspiration Prayer: Samantabhadra's Aspiration to Good Actions*:

> Just as the bodhisattva Manjushri attained omniscience,
> And Samantabhadra too,
> All these merits now I dedicate
> To train and follow in their footsteps.
> As all the victorious buddhas of past, present, and future
> Praise dedication as supreme,
> So now I dedicate all these roots of virtue
> For all beings to perfect good actions.

At Larung Gar, we normally dedicate merits with the following verse:

> Through this merit, may all beings attain the omniscient state of
>   enlightenment,
> And conquer the enemy of faults and delusion,
> May they all be liberated from this ocean of samsara
> And from its pounding waves of birth, old age, sickness, and death!

My root guru the great Jigme Phuntsok Rinpoche said that whichever verses or prayers we use, dedication always contains two components: to wish for the liberation of all sentient beings, and to wish that the Dharma thrives in the world.

Sentient beings can indeed receive the benefit from our dedications of merit, as reflected in many Buddhist stories. For example, the hungry ghosts in Vaishali were reborn in the Heaven of the Thirty-Three[5] thanks to dedication of merit by Shakyamuni Buddha.

Sometimes, the merit accumulated from one individual's virtuous action is sufficient to benefit others. In other cases, dedicating the merit of one individual is not enough to liberate beings, so it requires the sangha to jointly dedicate merit. A story in the *Ullambana Sutra* is a good example:

After his mother passed away, Maudgalyayana searched for her with his clairvoyance and found that she was reborn as a hungry ghost, suffering from hunger and thirst.

Maudgalyayana tried to feed her, but the food immediately turned into flame before she could even take a bite. Then he went to ask the Buddha for a solution.

The Buddha told him: "Your mother had very heavy karmic debts in her previous lives, so there is nothing you can do alone. It would be best to make an offering to the sangha, and ask the sangha to do a dedication prayer for her, which then will liberate her."

Maudgalyayana followed the Buddha's advice, and his mother left the realm of hungry ghosts and was reborn in the heavens as a god.

Since then, seeking the help of a sangha to liberate deceased parents has become a popular practice. For example, Chinese Buddhists use a ritual called the *ullambana puja*, which is held every year on the fifteenth day of the seventh month of the lunar calendar. This puja aims to liberate all the parents of our past lives.

When we dedicate the merit, we should abandon selfish thoughts. Nevertheless, there are some legitimate occasions when we can dedicate to a specific being. For example, if we often meet a deceased person in our dreams, we can ask a sangha to chant prayers and dedicate the merit to that person, which will surely benefit them. If it is impossible to find a sangha for this, we can always recite the *Diamond Sutra* by ourselves, and dedicate the merit to the deceased.

My root guru the great Jigme Phuntsok Rinpoche once taught, "While doing virtuous deeds, if we don't use the three supreme methods, we are not qualified practitioners of Mahayana Buddhism." A Mahayanist should refrain from undertaking any action without virtuous motivation at the beginning, concentration in the middle, and dedication of merit at the end. Also, a Mahayanist shouldn't dedicate merit in the unwholesome way earlier described, or in a self-concerned way only for worldly gain like food, clothes, or happiness.

The *Flower Ornament Sutra* says: "If one has bodhichitta in his mind, he will gain strength that frees him from all obstacles, and be accompanied by all favorable circumstances."

As long as we genuinely care about all sentient beings with bodhichitta in our minds, we will naturally attain precious qualities, powers, and spiritual accomplishments. Without bodhichitta, no matter how ascetic or noble we appear, or how solemn the Dharma assembly we organize, it will not be very beneficial to ourselves or other beings. Therefore, what we appear to be, or what we appear to do is not important; the most important is having the right motivation, and most preferably, the motivation of bodhichitta.

Buddhists should first establish a wholesome motivation. Practitioners of Mahayana or Vajrayana Buddhism must apply the three supreme methods as the only way to perfect their merit.

Thus, I do hope we all keep the three supreme methods in our minds whenever we carry out positive actions. If we do, even if our actions look insignificant, the merit is vast.

The three supreme methods are three skillful means. Therefore, even if we can't spend a lot of time and effort on our practice, through these skillful means we can still easily attain great merit and benefits.

I will end this chapter with a story that has touched me deeply.

During the Cultural Revolution Gachuk Rinpoche, a renowned lama from Qinghai Province of China, was the victim of struggle sessions[6] almost every day.

The public humiliation and torture included forcing him to admit various "crimes" before crowds of people, who would then verbally and physically abuse him. Normally after Gachuk Rinpoche's "confessions," several men would beat him badly.

Every time he was beaten, Gachuk Rinpoche would take the opportunity to practice patience using the three supreme methods.

When he was about to be beaten, he would make an aspiration: "I'll start to practice patience. Now it's time for me to generate bodhichitta for the sake of benefiting all sentient beings."

When he was being beaten, Gachuk Rinpoche concentrated his mind, making sure no anger or hatred arose. His mind was free from the three concepts.

After being beaten, he would dedicate the merit of practicing patience to all beings, especially to those who just beat him. When time allowed, he would recite *The King of Aspiration Prayers: Samantabhadra's Aspiration to Good Actions*.

Of course, he would recite this in his mind without moving his lips, because otherwise he would be beaten again. If he was short of time, or people were still beating him on the way back to his prison cell after the struggle session, he would recite a shorter dedication prayer. When he arrived at his cell, his dedication prayer would be finished. He would be happy since the practice was complete.

When the Cultural Revolution was over, those who had harmed Gachuk Rinpoche came to him for confession.

Rinpoche said peacefully, "You have no need to confess to me. Without you, I wouldn't have had the opportunity to practice patience. I don't hate you, not even a little bit. On the contrary, I do believe you have your own precious qualities. Please, you don't need to confess and ask for my forgiveness."

5. The Two Truths

What Is the Dharma Based On?

THE BUDDHA'S teachings of the Dharma are based on the two truths: relative truth and ultimate truth.[1] All phenomena subsist in the manner of these two truths. Without understanding the distinction between the two truths, a Dharma practitioner won't understand, let alone realize, the nature of reality revealed in the profound teachings of the Buddha, as Nagarjuna states in *The Root Stanzas of the Middle Way*:[2]

> Whoever fails to understand
> How the two truths are distinguished
> Also fails to understand
> The profound suchness taught by the enlightened ones.[3]

When I started my monastic training at Larung Gar in the mid-1980s, the curriculum required that my fellow Dharma peers and I master the doctrine of the two truths through intensive studies of the Middle Way (Madhyamaka) teachings. Based on lineage masters' instructions and my personal experience, I truly believe that without assimilating the doctrine of the two truths, neither Sutrayana[4] nor Vajrayana Buddhists will succeed in their practice.

Often, I encounter Buddhists who have not systematically studied the Dharma and tell me the two truths are rather simple.

"I know it well," they say, "Nothing exists in ultimate truth, while all exists as dreams and illusions in relative truth." This may be easy to say and to think, but it is much harder to assimilate and realize.

Many Buddhists seem to accept the notion of ultimate truth, yet they believe all things and beings that appear in each moment still undoubtedly

95

exist. "Everything in my life—family, friends, pets, NBA players, cars, pent-houses, broken hearts, and eureka moments—still truly exist," they say. "It is only when I fully realize the ultimate truth of emptiness that I will experience a spiritual makeover and upgrade my realization to a higher level. By then, I will finally possess a completely new wisdom and the three *kayas*,[5] and enter a fresh new world governed by ultimate truth."

This belief is shared by many Sutrayana practitioners, who practice what is known as the Causal Vehicle. In fact, when you fully understand the profound meaning of the two truths, you'll know that the true nature of all phenomena at that very moment, including this book and your mind, is ultimate truth.

WHAT ARE THE TWO TRUTHS?

The Definition of the Two Truths

What exactly are relative truth and ultimate truth? Indian and Tibetan masters offer various definitions. One explanation is from Shantideva, who states in *The Way of the Bodhisattva*:

> Relative and ultimate,
> There the two truths are declared to be.
> The ultimate is not the object of the mind.
> The mind is said to be the relative.[6]

Therefore, ultimate truth is beyond words and thoughts, and is only the sphere of non-dual, nonconceptual reality, whereas relative truth is the object of ordinary mind, which is dualistic and conceptual. As mentioned in chapter 1, all phenomena lack inherent existence and are empty in nature, they nevertheless appear in the manner of illusions, dreams, or mirages. Their appearance is relative truth; their nature, or the way they actually are, constitutes ultimate truth.

Another explanation comes from Chandrakirti, a renowned Buddhist scholar of the Middle Way School. In *Introduction to the Middle Way*, Chandrakirti said:

> All objects may be seen in truth or in delusion;
> They thus possess a twin identity.

The Buddha said the ultimate is what is seen correctly;
The wrongly seen is all-concealing truth.[7]

Since all objects and events can be seen truly or deceptively, they have a twin identity, or two aspects. That which is perceived correctly by the authentic primordial wisdom of the sublime beings is ultimate truth, and that which is perceived falsely by the deluded mind of ordinary beings is relative truth.

When conceptual mind analyzes the ultimate mode of phenomena, it has a distinction between object and subject: the object is *dharmadhatu*—the union of appearance and emptiness[8]—the subject is non-dual wisdom, and the action is wisdom cognizing dharmadhatu.

Yet please understand that ultimate truth is not an object per se apprehended by the conceptual mind. The wording "object" is used in a metaphorical sense in the definition. Essentially, from the perspective of the buddhas, there exists no dualistic structure of subject and object. That is, there is neither the object to be apprehended nor the subject apprehending the object, so no action of cognizing either.

The distinction of the two truths is made for the purpose of helping ordinary people understand the ultimate reality of everything. From the perspective of the buddhas who have fully realized reality, there is no such a thing as "two truths." As such, the distinction of the two truths is not ontological—concerning the nature of reality—but primarily epistemic: a subjective division depending on the observers. In other words, the distinction of the two truths itself is what the ordinary mind conceives and the language expresses—the object of words and thought; so "two truths" is actually relative truth.

Two Models of the Two Truths

The two truths can be understood in two distinct ways, or in two models. To better understand the two models, we must understand what Shakyamuni Buddha taught through the three turnings of the Dharma wheel—the three major series of teachings.

In the first turning the Buddha taught the four noble truths, which primarily pertain to relative truth. In the second turning the Buddha taught the perfection of transcendent wisdom (prajnaparamita), which focuses more on the ultimate truth of emptiness. In the third turning the Buddha taught the luminous clarity of buddha-nature, which is on ultimate truth, as well as the teachings concerning relative truth, such as how to establish the bodhisattva path and stages and how things appear, the latter of which can be referred to as the tenets of the Mind Only School.

According to the second turning of the Dharma wheel, relative truth is the appearance of things in their multiplicity, while ultimate truth is the true nature of the things—emptiness. In this model, the two truths are appearance and emptiness. It is worth reiterating that emptiness is not complete nothingness. It doesn't mean that nothing exists at all. What it does mean is that things do not exist the way our ignorant mind supposes they do. The correct understanding is that the two truths are united in such a way that whatever appears is empty and whatever is empty necessarily appears. Thus, the two truths are inseparable and indivisible.

According to the third turning, relative truth is when there is discordance between appearance and reality, whereas ultimate truth is when there is concordance. In brief, relative truth is inauthentic experience, while ultimate truth is authentic experience. More specifically, in this authentic/inauthentic model of two truths, relative truth consists of inauthentic phenomena that appear to be real to the erroneous minds of ordinary beings, while ultimate truth is reality that unmistakably appears to the non-erroneous mind of awakened beings, or the buddhas. Here is an analogy to help you better understand this conceptual distinction. Imagine there is a white conch shell. If someone's eye is compromised by the visual distortion of color, that person's mistaken perception of yellowness in this white conch shell is false. Whereas if a person's eye is healthy, their unmistaken perception of whiteness in the same conch shell is real. Of course, here the "white conch shell" is just a metaphorical example, which represents all phenomena as they really are—the ultimate truth that transcends all conceptual elaborations, rather than a specific object per se. Therefore, when reality is perceived without distortion by the buddhas, this authentic experience is the ultimate truth.

THE SEQUENCE OF REALIZING THE TWO TRUTHS

How can we realize the two truths? Can we directly jump to studying the perfection of transcendent wisdom⁹ or Buddhist scriptures on the doctrine of emptiness?

The answer is that we should first study Buddhist teachings on relative truth, and only then move to teachings on ultimate truth. Nagarjuna said in *The Root Stanzas of the Middle Way*:

> Without recourse to the conventional,
> The ultimate cannot be shown.
> Without the realization of the ultimate,
> There is no gaining of nirvana.[10]

Therefore, this sequential order is very important, because one can hardly reach for the sky with only a single step.

Relative Truth First

King Gurupala of Suvarnadvipa once sent the monk Devamade to see Atisha. Devamade's goal was to persuade Atisha to write a text of instruction on the two truths.

In the *Introduction to the Two Truths* that Atisha composed in response to Devamade's request, he wrote:

> Without the ladder of valid relative truth,
> One wishes to gradually ascend to
> The top of the palace of the true nature—
> The wise say it is untenable.[11]

To reach the top of a palace, one must start from the bottom by taking the elevator, climbing the stairs, or using a ladder. There is no other way.

Likewise, to reach the rooftop of ultimate truth,[12] one must rely on the "ladder" of relative truth. This includes teachings on Buddhist logic and epistemology, ethics, the ten virtues, the six compassionate acts of a bodhisattva, and others.

The understanding and realization of relative truth leads to the understanding and realization of ultimate truth. Unless we know and accept this fully, we will have trouble on the path.

Some beginners enter the Dharma path and come to Larung Gar for their Dharma studies. However, they disdain the basics of Buddhist teachings on relative truth, and don't want to allot time and effort on the must-have foundations. They ask me, "Can I enroll in Vajrayana courses so I can start my Vajrayana training right away?" Alas!

At Larung Gar we do study and practice the Great Perfection, the pinnacle of the Nyingma School, which contains the quintessence of Mahayana and Vajrayana teachings and the final and ultimate teachings of all the buddhas. I do give high teachings, such as Longchenpa's *Treasury of Dharmadhatu* in which the very essence of the Great Perfection and the most profound teaching of emptiness—self-liberation—is covered, but the reality here is the same as everywhere: without the foundations of basic Buddhist philosophy, especially the teachings on relative truth, it's very hard to comprehend this profound Vajrayana teaching.

There are teachers, in the East and in the West, who like to give the highest Vajrayana teachings to Buddhists who haven't yet established a proper foundation. But this way only very few Dharma students can benefit from the teachings in the long term because they have not built the necessary foundation to properly understand them.

Because of this, I urge most Dharma students to follow a sequence: start with teachings on relative truth, and after the foundation is properly established, move up to teachings on the ultimate truth of emptiness. In the same way, start by establishing a solid foundation in Mahayana, then move up to the profound Vajrayana teachings.

Sequential Order and Enlightenment

We need to be very clear about the link between the sequential order and enlightenment. Ultimately, nothing inherently exists in ultimate truth, so even the concept of virtue or vice is a mere mental fabrication; at the same time everything appears like a dream or an illusion in relative truth, so the law of karma still functions on us ordinary beings.

Therefore, before the attainment of full realization, we must stick to cultivating the virtue of ethical behavior. Ethical behavior functions as the raft that takes us to the other shore. We cannot abandon this raft before reaching the destination, because we know what will happen if we abandon our raft in the middle of the river.

This sequence was created in response to most people's mental dispositions, but there are exceptions. For instance, those with sharp faculties can be exposed to the profound teachings of the Middle Way at the very early stage. As an example, such practitioners can easily understand and internalize the instructions regarding ultimate truth in the prologue to Nagarjuna's *Root Stanzas of the Middle Way*: "not ceasing, not arising, not annihilated nor yet permanent, not coming, not departing, not different, not the same.[13]

However, for most ordinary Dharma practitioners, following the sequence steadily is essential.

Refuting the Extremes

Through negating the four extremes—the deluded views that trap us in samsara—most Dharma practitioners can gradually comprehend the doctrines of the Middle Way School, and stop falling into the wrong views of eternalism and nihilism. There are four great logical arguments of the Middle Way that can be used to refute deluded views, but I'll skip them here as the lengthy explanations may confuse beginning Buddhists.

Such refutation should start from the extreme of existence, then the extreme of nonexistence, followed by the extreme of both existence and nonexistence, and lastly the extreme of neither existence nor nonexistence. By following this sequence, one can eventually understand emptiness.

Nagarjuna said in *The Root Stanzas of the Middle Way*:

> To say that things exist means grasping at their permanence;
> To say they don't exist implies the notion of annihilation.
> Thus the wise should not remain in "this exists"
> Or "this does not exist."[14]

Nagarjuna described the Middle Way as a "middle path" between the extremes of existence and nonexistence. Is the "middle path" something that inherently exists? The answer is a definite no.

Even from the viewpoint of relative truth, the "middle path" is a conception that doesn't inherently exist either. It is not a midpoint on the same continuum as the two extremes. While the "middle path" refutes the extreme view, it does not lapse into any position.

Chandrakirti, in his commentary on Nagarjuna's *The Root Stanzas of the Middle Way*, quoted the *King of Samadhi Sutra*:

> "It exists" and "it does not exist" are both extremes;
> "Pure" and "impure" are both extremes.
> The wise man, avoiding both extremes,
> Likewise does not take a stand in the middle.[15]

These viewpoints aren't simply a play on words, nor do they randomly pop out of a conceptual mind. Following in-depth examination and analysis, these viewpoints may bring one to assimilating the ultimate truth of emptiness: "Oh, this is it!"

This realization is beyond thought and words, like a person sampling sugar can taste the sweetness but is unable to transfer the sensation to others only by words. Similarly, when we realize the emptiness of all things, we cannot articulate our experience. Direct realization of emptiness is devoid of any concept, analysis, or inference, as is the case with the emptiness of all phenomena, and even emptiness itself.

UNDERSTANDING RELATIVE TRUTH

Now that you understand the importance of following the sequential order of teachings of relative truth and ultimate truth, here is more food for thought.

Our Deluded Minds

Except for a very few realized beings, most people, even those who literally know this life is an illusion or a dream, remain attached to conventional reality. In theory we may know very well that nothing exists inherently, yet in our lives we remain trapped inside the dream of conventional reality on account of our deep-rooted habitual tendencies.

For example, many people like to watch movies or TV shows, and some binge on miniseries until they finish all the episodes. Do the stories and characters really exist? Of course not! Nevertheless, the viewers are totally immersed in, and often deeply moved by, what they've watched.

We know everything that our six sensory receptors see, hear, smell, taste, touch, or perceive does not exist inherently, yet we still mistakenly believe these objects of perception are real.

Here are classic analogies in Tibetan Buddhism: a cataract patient sees hair falling all the time; a squinting person sees two moons in the sky; a cross-eyed person has double vision. The things they see are all defective and don't intrinsically exist, but they often cannot help but grasp the views.

Because our minds are deluded, when causes and conditions arise it is hard for us as ordinary beings to avoid getting attached to our experience. It is just like an anamorphic Rubik's cube illusion, in which we are attached to the idea that we are seeing a three-dimensional Rubik's cube, while in reality it is just a two-dimensional image.

Scientists have conducted extensive studies on our sensory perceptions, but significantly fewer on the nature of the mind. I learned an English idiom from one of my Western disciples: the elephant in the room. This expression means there is a difficult situation or an obvious problem that people notice but do not want to talk about. I would like to apply this idiom to research on the mind.

In some scientists' opinion, "mind" or "consciousness" lacks the rigor of a scientific concept since it cannot be measured yet. As a result, there are limited scientific breakthroughs on the nature of the mind. Many scientists acknowledge that mind is a huge mystery, and the science of consciousness feels stuck. For scientists who want to avoid this muck of consciousness studies, "mind" is like an elephant in the room that needs to be addressed but typically is omitted.

Buddhism, on the other hand, has something clear to say about this "elephant." In the Buddhist view everything we see, hear, and think is conditioned by karmic imprints latent within our mind or in the continuum of our consciousness. Therefore, our mind is a karmic mind. For example, we human beings perceive a variety of objects in our daily lives, and our conceptual minds designate these objects as good versus bad, pleasant versus bitter, pretty versus ugly. Are these qualities we perceive through our sensory faculties and designate with our minds inherently real? Are they in accord with reality?

The answer is no. Such perception of reality as it exists is mistaken because we fail to see things as they really are. The relative truth of what you perceive is composed of the distorted, dualistic, and inauthentic modes of appearance. Our deluded mind often thinks what appears is what it is. We make such mistakes in our daily mundane life as well as our spiritual life.

It is worth mentioning that what appears varies among beings from different realms. Human beings and animals perceive objects differently—an object perceived as white by a human appears gray to a dog or yellow to a yak. Some animals are completely color-blind, so the conception of color doesn't even register in their mind.

While scientists ascribe these differences primarily to the physical structures of brains and neurons, Buddhists believe that mind and consciousness play a central role, and therefore the karmic mind must be taken into consideration. For example, when an object is placed in front of us, what exactly makes us "see" it? Is it our brain, or our consciousness? According to scientists, we see the cube because areas of our brain process visual sensations from our eyes through the optic nerve. But Buddhists also consider the role of eye consciousness and mental consciousness. Without inviting consciousness to the equation, we won't be able to explain why we can discern, analyze, and evaluate an object.

While scientists limit their comparisons to humans versus animals, Buddhists consider perceptions among all the beings in the six realms, backed up by the concept of karmic mind. In his *Beacon of Certainty*, Mipham Rinpoche described how beings differ in what they perceive. For example, when looking at a glass of water, a human sees it as water; a hungry ghost sees it as blood or pus; a samsaric god sees it as blissful nectar; a hell being sees it as molten lava. When obscurations accumulated by negative actions have been purified, a hungry ghost will start to see water as water, or a human will see water as blissful nectar.

Please keep in mind that even within the same realm, differences exist. For instance, individuals display different value systems within the human realm, and one person's values can change at different ages. As French philosopher Jean-Jacques Rousseau wrote in his *Émile, or On Education*: "At ten his mind was set upon cakes; at twenty it is set upon his mistress; at thirty it will be set upon pleasure; at forty on ambition; at fifty on avarice; when will he seek after wisdom only?" As we age, we change our values. Rousseau's stages of life seem to be an accurate description of many people.

That Which Entirely Obscures Reality

In the illusory relative world, sentient beings are all in a "dream." In Tibetan, relative truth is *kundzob denpa*. While *denpa* is sometimes translated as "truth," it actually means "reality" in this context, *kun* has the connotation of "all" or "entirely" and *dzob* means "obscuring"; taken together, *kundzob* means "that which entirely obscures."

Therefore, relative truth is "that which entirely obscures reality." As Chandrakirti said, "The wrongly seen is the relative truth."

We all live within a dream in which we take the impermanent as permanent, suffering as pleasure, no-self as self, and the impure as pure. These four upside-down views are the results of our karmas and ignorance. Through Dharma study and practice, we'll finally understand, "Oh, so it is just a dream!"

While many people are aware of the "dream," they remain manipulated by their powerful karmas. Let's consider digital entertainment such as YouTube or TikTok videos. Someone may know he or she shouldn't waste time on such distractions, but yields to the obsessive inner voice saying, "No way, I have to watch it!"

We know the dream is illusory, yet the temptations seem so real, and we become helplessly trapped. What should we do? We may think we should get over relative truth and reach a very pure place belonging to ultimate truth. But it is not like this.

Kundzob does mean "all-obscuring," but it is not like a curtain that "obscures" the ultimate truth behind it for everyone. So, it is not the case that you remove or pull back the curtain of relative truth—and voilà—here comes the wonderland of ultimate truth. When we feel helplessly trapped, the problem is not the dream but our mistaken belief that the phenomenon is not a dream, that it is real; so we are attached to what appears to us. Thus, what we should do is to stop being attached to the phenomenon in the dream. As Tilopa told Naropa: "Appearances don't bind you to samsara, but attachment to them does. Get rid of your attachment, Naropa!"

Once we truly recognize the nature of mind, we'll realize everything is empty in nature and nothing exists inherently. Recognizing that a dream is a dream is actually awakening. This enables us to stop being attached to appearances and thinking of them as reality in itself. By then, we will understand the nature of the two truths: they are not independent of one another but are two aspects of one unity in reality, like two sides of the same coin.

That Which Is in Accord with Reality

In Tibetan, ultimate truth is *dondam denpa*. *Dondam* refers to the "ultimate level" that is not refutable by any conceptual arguments, and again *denpa* means "reality." Therefore, ultimate truth is "that which is in accord with reality." As Chandrakirti said, "The ultimate truth is what is seen correctly."

As previously mentioned, there is also "truth" in the relative world. Although everything is an illusion, for ordinary "dreaming" beings everything appears real and unmistakable.

If we tell worldly people that everything is just an illusion devoid of inherent nature, most of them will laugh aloud. "How silly!" they will say. "I am running a business, living a life, and raising my kids. This is my real life. Where is the illusion? What is empty?"

Some Buddhists also believe that everything inherently exists, even at the ultimate level. As a result, no matter what they are doing, be it meditating or running errands, they believe, "This should be real. Even if its nature is emptiness, its appearing mode still acts as a symbol, or a representation of its existence."

Sometimes people simply reject core Buddhist teachings, such as the two truths, and replace them with their own views. They somehow reinvent the Buddha and his teachings based on their own prejudices, preferences, and speculations so as to conform to their distorted views. How regrettable that, in so doing, they are unable to truly embark on the path!

THE STUDY OF THE MIDDLE WAY

The Middle Way and the Two Truths

For many years I have been advocating the studies of the Middle Way. The Middle Way system describes the two truths in the greatest depth. After several years of studying the doctrines of emptiness and the analytical approaches of the Middle Way, Dharma students can fully accept that the Buddha's 84,000 teachings are based on the two truths, and their own understanding of the two truths will penetrate to a deeper level.

Allow me to reiterate: the importance of the two truths, in a nutshell, is that without a comprehensive understanding of them, one is incapable of understanding the profound teachings of the Buddha.

Without the foundations of the Middle Way, we won't fully comprehend the highest Buddhist teachings in Sutrayana such as the *Shurangama Sutra*, the *Diamond Sutra*, the *Sutra of Perfect Enlightenment*, the *Lotus Sutra*, the *Vimalakirti Sutra*, and others. The foundations can help us better understand profound Vajrayana teachings as well.

A practitioner lacking in-depth understanding of the Middle Way teachings will encounter great challenges when listening, contemplating, and meditating on the Dharma. "Before understanding the two truths, when attending Dharma teachings, I looked at the teacher like a deer in headlights," one of my disciples once told me. "My eyes were wide open; I listened but didn't hear. I was so confused that my mind stayed in a pseudo-meditation. Gradually I fell asleep and started to dream in my 'meditation.'"

Many Dharma teachers and practitioners have developed unwavering faith in the doctrine of the Middle Way, and have thus gained deep understanding of emptiness. Therefore, they are very proficient in studying and teaching the Dharma and benefiting beings.

Studying the Middle Way

Here are the core texts (also listed in the bibliography) for the Middle Way studies that most institutes of Tibetan Buddhism (*shedras*) put in their curricula:

1. Chandrakirti's *Introduction to the Middle Way*. This work refutes the four theories of production—self-production, other-production, production from both self and other, and uncaused production—from the standpoint of the two truths. Anything produced cannot go beyond these four kinds, and since none of the production is possible, nothing can arise or be produced, so nothing can inherently exist. Quite a few teaching transcriptions and commentaries are available.

2. Nagarjuna's *The Root Stanzas of the Middle Way*. This work describes the content of the Buddha's central teachings of dependent origination and emptiness. It covers the supreme teachings on great emptiness.

3. Aryadeva's *Four Hundred Stanzas on the Middle Way*. This work covers the teachings of relative truth in the first eight chapters, and ultimate truth in the rest. It acutely examines and analyzes the three times, and refutes the existence of the past, present, and future. Also, it refutes the four "upside-down" views of permanence, pleasure, self, and purity.

4. Shantarakshita's *The Adornment of the Middle Way*. This work synthesizes the views of the Mind Only School and the Middle Way School into a single system, thereby unifying the two great streams of Mahayana Buddhism. The text focuses on the "neither one nor many" argument to refute the inherent existence of all phenomena, which is most succinctly presented in the first verse:

> The entities that our and other schools affirm,
> Since they exist inherently in neither singular nor plural,
> In ultimate reality are without intrinsic being;
> They are like reflections.[16]

Mipham Rinpoche's commentary on this text articulates unique Nyingma views and has been described as one of the most profound examinations of the Middle Way.

Dharma students who haven't yet studied Buddhist logic might sometimes find the texts on the Middle Way quite challenging to understand. Do not become discouraged if you are struggling with the teachings. Studying the Middle Way is not the same as reading a novel. Novelists write under the influence of their habitual patterns, conceptual thoughts, and emotional obscurations, which resonate with ours. This is why we can easily immerse ourselves in their stories.

The views of the Middle Way are diametrically opposed to our conceptual thoughts, as we are exposed to words of transcendental wisdom based on the doctrine of emptiness. As emptiness is the most difficult of all Buddhist teachings to understand, it is no surprise that beginning students of the Middle Way struggle with the teachings.

While monastics are required to study the Middle Way as part of their education, many laypersons prefer easier Buddhist teachings such as the law of karma or else, and they want to skip to the highest Vajrayana teachings. Even when laypersons show some interest in Middle Way teachings, they are typically more interested in Vajrayana for its supremacy and extraordinary power.

Mahayana Buddhists, especially younger ones, shouldn't be satisfied with studying only "easier" Buddhist teachings such as the stories, legends, and biographies of masters. If you don't establish a proper foundation for understanding emptiness, you cannot truly internalize the Dharma, making you more likely to flounder whenever unfavorable conditions in life or practice arise.

You can study the Middle Way with a sangha or alone, but at the very beginning, it's best to follow a Dharma teacher's course. If you read the study texts on your own, you may not understand the most profound views correctly.

When you study the Middle Way texts under the guidance of a qualified teacher, it seems that your understanding of the Middle Way has arisen. However, without long-term study and practice to make it second nature, this understanding can be easily dissipated by mundane life encounters. What a great pity!

Therefore, I urge most Dharma students to embrace the spirit of lifelong learning. While in worldly life most people would stop studying once they receive their graduation certificates, this doesn't apply to most Dharma students and practitioners who seek enlightenment. Given our level of faculties, we have to continue long-term sequential study of the two truths and the Middle Way.

Understanding and Realizing the Middle Way

After systematic study, Dharma students gain intellectual knowledge of the two truths. The questions answered include:

- How are the two truths explained in different schools, including the Great Exposition (Vaibhashika), the Sutra School (Sautrantika), the Mind Only School (Chittamatra), and the Middle Way School (Madhyamaka)?
- Within the Middle Way School, how do the two sub-schools—Autonomy (Svatantrika) and Consequence (Prasangika)—differ from each other?
- How do the major traditions within Tibetan Buddhism—Nyingma, Geluk, Kagyu, Sakya, Jonang, and others—differ in their analysis of the two truths?
- How are the two truths established differently in the outer Vajrayana classes and the inner ones?[17]

Intellectual study should be followed by contemplative and meditative experience, through which we'll start to uncover transcendental wisdom. Thus, it is essential for us to experience the meaning of the Middle Way teachings by means of valid reasoning. As wisdom develops, we'll be less likely to regress because of distorted views, and also less likely to succumb to temptation. In the end, we'll attain the purity of mind and the wisdom that Chandrakirti described in his *Introduction to the Middle Way*:

> Whatever is perceived with dimmed, defective sight
> Has no validity compared with what is seen by healthy eyes.
> Just so, a mind deprived of spotless wisdom
> Has no power to contradict a pure, untainted mind.[18]

Mipham Rinpoche explained the verse in his commentary:

The illusion of black lines seen by people suffering from cataracts has no validity, compared with the experience of someone with healthy eyes. In the same way, the consciousness of someone who has not realized stainless wisdom has no validity, compared with the perception of one who has.[19]

Once we realize wisdom, we are blissful even when trapped in a prison cell. I heard that a monastic member of Larung Gar had been in charge of cleaning toilets for four or five years. Regardless of his task, he was always joyful.

This shows how important a person's attitude is. If a person keeps a pure attitude, that person won't be weary of helping others, and also won't be weary of hearing, contemplating, and meditating on the Dharma. It is just as Longchenpa said in his *Special Prayer of Aspiration*:

May I teach the sacred Dharma to beings wandering in samsara,
And never tire or grow weary of working to help others.

As we more deeply understand emptiness, our motivation to benefit beings will strengthen.

Compassion and the Middle Way

As you will soon read in chapter 6, at relative level, karma governs our life. For ordinary beings, because of our karmic propensities, none of us in samsara is free from suffering. Understanding emptiness can help us reduce suffering, and cope with life's challenges and hardships.

Through blessings of the guru and the Three Jewels, the mind that comprehends emptiness will disclose wisdom and courage beyond those of ordinary persons. As a result, even if an individual doesn't have beauty, talent, wealth, and power—the symbols of worldly success—that person will still feel blissful, nevertheless.

While the primary goal of studying the Middle Way is to realize emptiness, make sure not to leave your compassion on the back burner. In fact, when realizing emptiness, intense compassion for sentient beings will arise spontaneously, as Shantarakshita described in the last two verses of *The Adornment of the Middle Way*:

Those who have the mind to follow this tradition
Will strongly feel intense compassion
For those who have the mind to trust
The tenets of mistaken teachings.
Those rich in wisdom, who perceive
To what extent all other doctrines lack essential pith,
To that extent will feel intense devotion
For the Buddha, who is their protector.[20]

When we realize that everything is an illusion without inherent existence, our compassion for sentient beings naturally arises. We think, "Although I still wander in samsara, I'm starting to gradually understand the truth of emptiness. Compared to me, those beings who know nothing about emptiness are truly wretched!"

When we see people achieving success according to cultural standards, we may rejoice at their achievements, but we also clearly know we are not aiming at the same goals. It's just as Jigme Lingpa said:

The so-called success and prosperity in this world arouse no desire in me; it is only the enlightened beings—who have attained supreme stainless wisdom, who are free from the cycle of birth and death, whose enlightened activity of benefiting innumerable beings is spontaneously present—that are worthy of my admiration.

In summary, the most important thing is to fully understand that the relative world is an illusion or a dream—vivid but without any inherent existence. I wish that all of us will realize ultimate truth, which is obscured by mistaken appearances. Shantarakshita said in *The Adornment of the Middle Way*:

Those who ride the chariot of the two approaches,
Who grasp the reins of reasoned thought,
Will thus be adepts of the Mahayana
According to the sense and meaning of the word.[21]

The union of relative truth and ultimate truth is like a chariot, and the valid methods of reasoning that investigate the two truths are like two reins that a Mahayanist charioteer holds in his hand. With only one rein, a charioteer cannot drive the chariot straight on the lane. Similarly, if focusing only on the valid reasoning of one of the two truths, a Buddhist is not an authentic Mahayanist.

Many Buddhists are adept at teachings concerning the postulates of relative truth, including karma and rebirth, so they are meticulous in engaging positive actions with body, speech, and mind—they hold the rein pertaining to relative truth tightly; however, when it concerns the postulates of ultimate truth, they simply equate emptiness with nothingness—the rein pertaining to ultimate truth is not yet in their hands. In contrast, some other Buddhists hold the rein pertaining to ultimate truth tightly, and completely let go of the rein of relative truth; hence, they strive to "discover emptiness" elsewhere from their present being and doing, and pay little attention to vices and virtues in life. In both cases, these Buddhists are like a single-winged eagle that can never fly, let alone soar high, into the sky of reality.

We should hold on to the reins pertaining to both relative truth and ultimate truth on the path to enlightenment, and understand that all phenomena are just projections of our own mind, and essentially their nature is emptiness. I hope every one of us can adeptly drive the chariot of the two truths, and eventually recognize the wisdom that is primordial, unchanging, innate, and in us all along, including in the moment in which you are reading this very line.

6. REBIRTH AND KARMA

Actions for the Future

UNDERSTANDING REBIRTH deeply matters to all of us, Buddhist or not. But sadly, for many the idea of contemplating death and rebirth arises rarely, if ever, or is avoided out of fear or indifference. People are too absorbed in daily living. Many people, in the East and in the West, place success in the external material world above peace in the internal spiritual world. Because of this, headlines are crowded with news about wars, political campaigns, Wall Street's hedge funds, Chanel's new runway fashions, new residential skyscrapers, and the richest billionaires in Silicon Valley. We are daily bombarded with information in this digital age. While it is good to be informed, when we are overloaded, we are less likely to pause and reflect on life and death. When did you last ask yourself, "Why am I here?" or "Where am I going?"

Understanding rebirth is very important. If there is no afterlife, we can arguably live this life any way we prefer, in vice or in virtue, with no consequences to worry about. If death brings nothingness, living as Adolf Hitler or Mother Teresa makes no difference when the body ceases to function.

However, rebirth does exist. No one has successfully refuted rebirth, and there's much evidence suggesting that consciousness does continue beyond this life. Some of the evidence is offered in this chapter.

Many people may wonder, "If rebirth exists, why do so many people reject the concept?" Well, as the old saying goes, "Truth always rests with the minority." Denial of an understanding despite supporting evidence is not uncommon in history. For example, the heliocentric theory—that the earth and planets revolve around the sun at the center of the solar system—was not accepted for more than 1,000 years after it was first proposed. The resistance was so widespread that seventeenth-century heliocentric scientist

Galileo Galilei was put on trial and convicted. Given this, it is not perplexing that people don't accept the idea of rebirth. Nevertheless, their disbelief does not in itself disprove rebirth.

The Buddhist view is that the cycle of rebirth is determined by karma—actions done through body, speech, and mind. Good intent and good deeds contribute to good karma and then favorable rebirths, while bad intent and bad deeds contribute to bad karma and then unfavorable rebirths. From this viewpoint, we must prepare for future death and rebirth, which can happen at any minute, by avoiding bad intent and deeds and by engaging in good intent and deeds. These are the choices of a wise person.

Rebirth is integral to the Buddhist understanding of life and to the path to awakening. Without accepting rebirth, we may not be fully motivated to pursue a spiritual path. If we don't want to understand samsara and suffering in samsara, then how can we truly renounce our desire and attachment? Also, there can be no bodhichitta without renunciation. Without accepting rebirth, how can we view all beings as our mothers and fathers in past lives, and from this generate genuine bodhichitta? Bodhichitta is essential because without it, as described in chapter 3, there is no path to full enlightenment.

Many Buddhists who don't accept rebirth still aspire to reach the Pure Land or even to realize the Great Perfection. From a Buddhist viewpoint, this is impossible.

Buddhism without accepting rebirth isn't Buddhism. I will explain what rebirth is, how rebirth takes place, and why rebirth is possible. The main takeaway from this chapter is that you establish and hold a right view of rebirth.

THE BASICS OF REBIRTH

What Is Rebirth?

I was born into a nomadic family that practices in the Nyingma tradition of Tibetan Buddhism, in a small valley of a Tibetan region called Kham. Belief in rebirth, which is a vital part of my upbringing, was instilled in me from childhood. However, during my school years from elementary to normal school,[1] I was exposed to philosophical views about atheism and materialism that diverge from my convictions about rebirth. "Why do others believe that death is like extinguishing the light of a lamp?" I thought to myself, "like a dark void, no thoughts, no consciousness, nothing?"

After I took ordination and began to study Dharma systematically, the first question I wanted to answer was: "Does rebirth really exist?" As I pursued an answer, I studied many sutras and shastras, as well as related publications from around the world. In addition, I debated rigorously with sangha members who are very learned on the topic. After some time, I became fully convinced rebirth is true, and I had no lingering doubts at all.

Rebirth says that what survives the death of the physical body is not a permanent self or soul, but a form of impermanent continuity like the flowing stream of a river. There is a continuity, yet there is never the same substance in the stream. Buddhists deny there is anything unchanging, either physically or mentally, in rebirth. That is, rebirth is the state of being born again as another living being. I primarily use the term "rebirth" in this book to describe this continuity.

The terms *reincarnation* and *rebirth* are often used interchangeably in Buddhist writings and translations in English, but the two are not identical. Reincarnation often has the connotation of a solid nonphysical essence of a living being, a permanent self or "soul," after biological death transmigrating into another body to start a new life. Put simply, reincarnation is often about the same soul going to a different body in the next life. There are occasions when a Buddhist mentions "reincarnation" but actually means "rebirth."

What Buddhism focuses on is the rebirth of the mind, or consciousness, instead of the reincarnation of a permanent soul. Mind comes into existence because of a preceding moment of mind, and it is the continuum that carries on before and after the present life between different states of existence or lifetimes through the six realms of existence. As a human being, for instance, wrongdoings may cause rebirth in the three lower realms of animals, hungry ghosts, and hell beings. Virtuous deeds cause rebirth in the three higher realms of gods, demigods, and humans. The transcendental practices of Buddhism can free beings from entrapment in this cyclic existence of suffering. This process is taught extensively in the sutras.

In Buddhist cosmology, each of us has been reborn innumerable times in the past and very likely will continue this process in the future. Buddhists consider that our state of being includes the body and mind, with body commonly divided into gross body and subtle body, and mind divided into gross mind and subtle mind. At the time of death, the gross body—our relative, physical body that is composed of the four great elements of water, earth, air and fire—can no longer function as a foundation of the gross mind. The gross body dies and merges into the subtle body during the bardo,[2] or intermediate stage, after death. Similar to the dream body that appears in our dreams, the subtle body is weightless and volatile, so that bardo beings can immediately go where their minds bring them.

The gross mind—the five-sense consciousness and the mental consciousness—dissolves into the subtle mind that is called the "all ground" or *alaya* consciousness, which is the storehouse of our karmic imprints and the ground of our erroneous notion of duality.

If you want to know exactly how the subtle mind carries karmic imprints from previous lives and transmigrates into another existence, you can consult Vajrayana texts, or tantras, such as the *Kalachakra Tantra* when appropriate. I am not covering the process in depth here because the explanation belongs to tantric teachings, which are only accessible to those who have received the empowerment.

Rebirth and Emptiness

Some Buddhists like to quote verses from the *Heart Sutra*, such as "form is emptiness, emptiness is form, form is no other than emptiness, emptiness is no other than form," or from the *Diamond Sutra*, such as "all conditioned phenomena are like a dream, an illusion, a bubble, a shadow, like dew or a flash of lightning; thus shall we perceive them."[3] Without understanding the true meaning of these teachings, some people claim the Buddha's teaching that everything is empty means that everything is devoid of existence, therefore rebirth and karma don't exist at all. This wrong view emerges because of their incorrect understanding of the doctrine of two truths. They haven't yet understood that emptiness—the ultimate truth of all phenomena—is not equal to nothingness or nihilism.

As covered in the last chapter, Mahayana Buddhism explains that all phenomena, sentient beings and objects included, subsist in the manner of the two truths—relative and ultimate. The existence of rebirth and karma is within the scope of relative truth, which is the mere appearance of everything—how we perceive things familiar and unfamiliar to us—ranging from the vastness of divine beings and the billion-fold universes called *trichiliocosm* to the tininess of ants and dust particles. Ultimate truth is the empty nature of everything—how things really are—which is beyond any conceptual fabrication. As nothing inherently exists, those who realize ultimate truth are free from the bondage of cyclic rebirth. Therefore, ultimate truth is the final state of realization, the goal of a Buddhist practitioner's aspirations.

The two truths are not independent of one another but are two different aspects of what is an inseparable unity in reality. As you may already have figured out from chapter 5, one of the most important elements of Buddhism is "union": the union of ultimate truth and relative truth, the union of emptiness and appearance, and the union of appearance and reality. Without accepting the notion of union, we won't be able to understand and appreciate the profound Dharma.

In the case of rebirth and karma, at the ultimate level they are neither inherently existent nor nonexistent; but at the relative level, karma and the suffering of rebirth appear true to the dualistic and deluded minds of ordinary beings. Those who accept the concept of emptiness yet reject the tenets of karma and rebirth haven't yet understood the *union* of the two truths.

Rebirth and Science

A solid comprehension of the two truths makes it easy to understand that what is covered in Buddhism is far broader and deeper than what is covered in science. Buddhism covers both relative truth and ultimate truth, while science covers only relative truth and, more specifically, only *part* of relative truth.

Science, according to the commonly accepted definition, is a systematic and logical approach to discovering how things in the universe appear and function. Most science is built around the notion of proof; it aims for measurable results through testing and analysis—the scientific method. If scientists cannot measure something, they cannot study it. The mysteries of life, death, and rebirth cannot be examined by looking through a microscope, put simply; even Albert Einstein realized some realities couldn't be explained by science.

Thus, although science has advanced significantly in understanding materiality, it cannot verify the appearances and mechanisms of all phenomena, especially in the spiritual and transcendental world. Therefore, it is important for people holding the materialistic view that all phenomena, including consciousness, are the results of material interactions[4] to acknowledge the limitations of science.

When materialists reject the concept of rebirth because of what they consider a lack of scientific empirical proof, they should recognize the logical fallacy here: the absence of proof on rebirth is not the proof of its nonexistence; so it is not a valid argument to disprove rebirth.

Some scientific research findings and theories offer substantial support for rebirth. For example, Max Planck, widely considered the father of quantum mechanics, considered the material world as derived from mind, not the other way around. If consciousness doesn't completely depend on the material medium of the body to exist, it will survive after the body dies and continue in a new form.

THE LAW OF KARMA

Karma and Rebirth

Unlike Bodhisattvas who deliberately choose to take rebirth through the power of compassion and aspiration, ordinary beings are bound to the ever-turning wheel of rebirth involuntarily under the sway of karma. The word *karma* means "action" in Sanskrit. The law of karma, or the law of cause and effect, is not something made up or invented by the Buddha. The Buddha simply revealed it.

Karma encompasses the fundamental natural law of causation that governs our lives: every action brings a certain result. For example, when a seed is planted, provided there is sufficient water and sunshine, its result—the sprout from the seed—will certainly appear. Or, as Buddhists like to say, when causes and conditions ripen, our positive actions will yield a higher rebirth in a positive place such as the gods' realm, even if we don't really want to go; our negative actions will produce rebirth in a lower realm such as hell, no matter how reluctant we are to go there.

The Buddha teaches that our sufferings in samsara are caused by the ignorance of not knowing the true nature of reality, so our rebirths are the karmic results of actions from past lives as well as this life. Owing to our not knowing the truth of reality, we choose actions that inevitably bring about negative karmic consequences. As a result we deluded beings remain deeply trapped in our defilements and mental afflictions, cycling in the wheel of life, death, and rebirth throughout the six realms of existence.

At the relative level, every being is within reach of the law of karma, including the buddhas and bodhisattvas. As the Pure Land patriarch Master Yinguang (1861–1940) said,

> Tathagatas attaining the perfect enlightenment,
> Sentient beings falling to the three lower realms,
> Neither is beyond the law of cause and effect.

The Buddha teaches that karma is carried from moment to moment and lifetime to lifetime. No matter how long ago our karma was generated, the resultant karmic imprints don't get lost or disappear without reason.[5] When causes and conditions meet, these karmic imprints will ripen and generate corresponding karmic fruits.

Two kinds of causal conditions, or antecedent causes, lead to karmic results. The first are immediate causes that are coarse, obvious, and visible. The second are remote causes such as actions in previous lives that are subtle, latent, and invisible. For example, sickness may be caused by both kinds of antecedent causes. Exposure to cold temperatures or bad food would be the immediate causes for sickness, while wrongdoings from past lives such as killing or beating others would be remote causes. Thus, from a Buddhist viewpoint, nothing in life happens only by chance. Everything happens for karmic reasons resulting from past actions.

Remote karmic causes are very subtle and hard to identify, so most ordinary people don't even have a glimpse of them. Ordinary people can only identify immediate causes. The law of karma is so hidden and profound that it is incomprehensible to people who rely solely on their intellectual understanding.

Those who embrace materialistic views tend to disagree about the immutable law of karma. "It is superstitious," they say, "I believe in neither karma nor rebirth." I have to say they are holding a distorted view. As mentioned before, at the ultimate level all things are devoid of inherent existence, including karma and rebirth. Yet the empty nature of things doesn't impede their dreamlike or illusory appearance. It is because of this empty nature that everything happens, including appearances, karma, and samsara. As Chandrakirti states in his *Introduction to the Middle Way*:

> Empty things, reflections and the like,
> Dependent on conditions, are not imperceptible.
> And just as empty forms reflected in a glass
> Create a consciousness in aspect similar,
> So too all things, though empty,
> Strongly manifest within their very emptiness.[6]

Things do appear even though they are inherently empty. At the relative level, the law of karma is infallible: causes undeniably lead to effects. The *Sutra of a Hundred Actions* says:

Even hundreds and thousands of kalpas later,
Karma will not vanish;
When causes and conditions meet,
Karmic fruit will surely ripen.

Gaining conviction in the law of karma is a prerequisite for becoming a genuine Buddhist. This conviction empowers an individual to abstain from committing wrongdoings, which makes realization possible. Rejecting the law of karma will preclude a practitioner from attaining realization, regardless of the practice that person engages in, including the Great Perfection.

Karma and Destiny

The Buddha taught that because of karma, beings are bound to cyclic rebirth. It is a pitfall to deny the existence of destiny and to think that our life is only governed by free will. But the law of karma is not purely deterministic, so we shouldn't mistake karma for the notion of a fixed destiny. Buddhists believe that we make our own destiny through karma, so we can also change destiny through karma.

To be more specific, karma means that past actions shape the present, and present actions will shape the future, but it doesn't mean that experiences in this life are solely determined by the actions committed in past lives such that there is nothing we can do about the conditions we find ourselves in. In fact, what happened today is the result of not only our actions in previous lives but also the causes and conditions in this lifetime. To help you understand this, let me briefly describe the four types of karma, categorized by the time when the karmic imprint ripens:

1. *Karma experienced within this life*: actions committed in this lifetime ripen within this very life.
2. *Karma experienced after taking rebirth*: actions are certain to ripen in the next life.
3. *Karma experienced in subsequent lives*: actions will ripen in future lifetimes, other than the next life.
4. *Karma not certain to be experienced*: although actions are accumulated and stored, it is not certain they will eventually ripen. For example, bad actions may not ripen if the doer has earnestly

repented through Vajrasattva practice, whereas undedicated good actions may be destroyed by the rise of anger and hatred.

Knowing this, we will easily understand why some conditions in this life cannot be changed while others can. It's like this: among all our "karma" trips in this life, sometimes we are on a scheduled "karma" flight with an airline, so we can hardly change the route and destination unless extreme conditions occur; and sometimes we are in a "karma" taxi, so it is much easier for us to make changes.

It is possible that today's actions may change some of tomorrow's conditions in this very lifetime. And, if we zoom out our "karma lens" to get the widest possible view of the process of our cyclic rebirth, we will realize that even if the "karma" flight cannot change within this lifetime, it can change its route and destination in a future life. To eventually halt the cycle of rebirth, we have to change today's "causes" from the root, thus altering the "results" of our near and distant future.

When we fully understand and accept the law of karma, we will believe in ourselves: we have the power to change our karma to change our future, including the rest of this life and the rebirth yet to come.

You may then ask: what, exactly and fundamentally, should we change? The answer is: our mind. The Buddha says in the *Dhammapada*: "All things are preceded by the mind, led by the mind, created by the mind."

Everything the Buddha teaches is meant to free us from the ceaseless cycle of death and rebirth, and that only happens through the mind. Mind can create karma; mind can also change karma. Change comes from mind.

Buddhists understand that when the mind changes, all that we are and that we experience also changes. Thus, our destiny—the joys and sorrows of this life and many lives yet to come—is dependent upon ourselves. Then, what change is the right change? The answer is simple: following the law of karma. As the Buddha says in the *Nirvana Sutra* (*Mahaparinirvana Sutra*):

> Knowing that good causes lead to good fruits,
> And bad causes lead to bad fruits,
> One will stay away from wrongdoings.

If we turn our mind in a positive direction, we won't engage in actions that cause negative karmic consequences, and we'll be motivated to conduct positive actions; therefore we will eventually end the cycle of rebirth and attain liberation.

THE PROOF OF REBIRTH

Logical Inference

We can validate the existence of rebirth through the inference of Buddhist logic (*pramana*).[7] In his *Commentary of Valid Cognition*, Dharmakirti (c. sixth or seventh century) explains that mind continues from life to life owing to its unceasing and everlasting nature of luminous clarity. Mind is unlike a physical object in the material world, such as a light bulb, which ends when it "dies." Mind carries on. In essence, Dharmakirti's validation examines the cause of mind. To do this we first need to validate the existence of mind.

What is mind after all? Traditionally, scientists have tried to define mind as the product of neural activities in the brain, and nothing more. Buddhists disagree on this view of mind-body materialism. One thing I want to reiterate is that the Buddhist understanding of mind centers on the doctrine of no-self. That is, mind is empty of inherent existence. As you've already learned, being empty doesn't mean it does not exist; at the relative level, mind exists as momentary consciousness that is an active agent of knowing. To Buddhists, mind goes far beyond the physical workings of the brain, and the purview of mind isn't just mental, intellectual, and psychological. Buddhist philosophical texts define mind as *that which is clear and knowing*, with "clear" referring to the entity of mind and "knowing" to its function.

Now let's start the validation process. When we were born into this life, was there any prior cause for our first moment of mind? No is an illogical answer to this question, because if no prior cause was needed mind could arise anytime from anywhere, and this is not in accordance with the observable truth. Therefore, the definite answer to the question is yes, that there was a cause for our first moment of mind in this life.

Then we proceed further and ask: Is this cause permanent or impermanent? "Permanent" refers to something that has inherent existence and never changes. If a cause is permanent, be it an ultimate creator or an almighty god, such a cause cannot produce results. This is because cause and effect function only in relationship to impermanent phenomena. You may examine phenomena occurring in your life: Is anything the effect or result of a permanent cause? It is evident that no result can be produced from a permanent cause!

If you insist that a permanent cause can produce a result, ask yourself further: Does a cause remain the same or does it change after the result is produced? If it remains the same, then there's no evidence that this cause produces the result, or, in other words, "a preceding cause produces a subsequent effect" has never really occurred. If it becomes different, this implies that the cause changes over time, so it is no longer a permanent cause. Through this logical examination, we now know that permanent causes cannot produce results, so we can refute the existence of a permanent creator.

If there were such a creator who created everything, that creator would not have a cause because that cause would have preceded all of existence. But without a cause, how could the arising of such a creator be explained? If the creator didn't arise owing to a cause, it would be permanent, which would mean it could not create results such as the creation of things and beings. A permanent creator cannot change, but creation requires change, so the existence of such a permanent creator cannot be proven.

In addition, we can also refute the existence of a permanent cause by analyzing the creation of mind. If there is a permanent creator, all beings' minds would have been created either simultaneously or subsequently. If they were created simultaneously, this doesn't match the reality that beings, including humans and animals, appeared in this world not all at once but over millions of years. If beings' minds were created subsequently, we can further examine whether or not a creator consciously created beings' minds. If a creator consciously created beings' minds, that creator would have thought, "I will create this bad person, or I will create that good person," yet no religious or spiritual system has agreed upon such a process of creation. If a creator acted unconsciously, such a creator has never been proclaimed.

The logical analysis laid out above tells us the cause of mind can only be impermanent.

Having read thus far, some people might want to bring back the argument that mind is from the body, in particular from the brain. "Mind is in the brain," they say, "and there's evidence that specific brain areas correspond to certain functions of the mind." Dharmakirti analyzes why this view is fallible and refutes it in the second chapter of his *Commentary on Valid Cognition*, which offers logical proofs for the existence of rebirth.

Here is Dharmakirti's logical inference on the mind-body issue in brief, and here we replace "body" with "brain" for your better understanding. Let's examine a brain; is it permanent or impermanent? If the brain is permanent, it is unable to generate the mind; and even if the mind is generated from such a brain, then the mind must be permanent as well, which is definitely not true. From this, a logical fallacy will inevitably occur, creating the extreme view of permanent existence.[8] As we see by observation, the brain changes and so does the mind. Now that we all agree that the brain is impermanent, then, is the mind generated from the whole of the brain or parts of it? If the mind comes from the whole brain, then when a fragment of the brain is missing, the mind will accordingly be incomplete. However, this is not true. If the mind comes from a key part or parts of the brain, then since the brain is composed of countless particles, there should be countless number of minds. However, this also is not true.

A case described in the *Lancet* in 2007 provides evidence that mind cannot be confined to the brain.[9] The case is about a French civil servant who lives normally with damage to 90 percent of his brain. An X-ray shows that his brain is mostly filled with fluid, leaving just a thin outer layer of actual brain tissue, with the internal part of his brain almost totally eroded away, yet it doesn't impair his ability to carry out tasks at a local tax office.

This remarkable story created a great buzz in the media, but it is not the only one. In 1980, *Science* already published research findings that reported cases of individuals with only a thin layer of brain cells that functioned as normally as others. One of the individuals has an IQ of 126, gained a first-class honors degree in mathematics, and is conventionally socially competent.[10]

Such cases puzzled scientists and challenged materialistic view on the mind. According to Buddhism, mind does not arise from the body or specifically the brain, and that mind is not the brain. The brain is not the primary cause of the mind but just an external condition for its existence. Then what is the primary cause of mind? It is the previous moment of the mind. As Dharmakirti says: "The preceding moment of the mind is indeed the cause of the present moment of the mind, therefore the cause is present at all times."

Thus, the first moment of our mind in this lifetime is caused by its last moment in the bardo stage of the previous life, and the last moment of our mind in the bardo stage of this lifetime is the cause of the first moment of the mind in the next life. The preceding moment of the mind was impermanent and neither completely the same nor completely different from its result—the present moment of the mind. Thus, at the relative level, the succession of moments of mind, also called mind-stream, continues from life to life, so rebirth continuously occurs.

Past-Life Recollections

There are many stories of rebirth, among Buddhists and non-Buddhists, in which people can vividly recall past lives with details that are difficult for rebirth-deniers to explain. Anyone's past-life recollections originate from their own mind-stream, which is hard to invalidate definitively. Similarly, when a sober and honest person retells an event that happened the day before or describes a paragraph from a book the person read thirty seconds ago, it's difficult to assert that person is talking nonsense.

If anyone thinks recollections are insufficient to validate the existence of rebirth, this standard of proof invalidates most life experience, because "remembering" from yesterday or thirty seconds ago is also recollection. People may disbelieve past-life recollections, but they are unable to prove that rebirth doesn't exist.

In the *Ten Stages Sutra*, the Buddha clearly states that some people can recall a past life, or even many of their past lives. In the Tibetan region where I live, many eminent masters have remembered specific past lives. For instance, when giving Dharma teachings my root guru the great Jigme Phuntsok Rinpoche often remembered his life as Nanam Dorje Dudjom (c. eighth–ninth century), meaning "indestructible subduer of Mara," who was one of Guru Rinpoche's twenty-five main disciples.

Once the great Jigme Phuntsok Rinpoche was invited to teach at Tibet's oldest temple, Samye Monastery, which was built in the late eighth century. While offering teachings to the sangha, Jigme Phuntsok Rinpoche retrieved his own past-life memories of watching Guru Rinpoche teach tantras to him and fellow disciples at that very monastery. "The memory was so vivid," Jigme Phuntsok Rinpoche said, "it was as if Guru Rinpoche gave the teachings just yesterday." As he shared his memories to the audience, myself included, Jigme Phuntsok Rinpoche appeared sorrowful and shed heavy tears.

I also know a rebirth story about a monk from Batang county near Larung Gar who held the *geshe* degree[11] and was reborn in Lhasa. Several years after the geshe died, his sister traveled to Lhasa on pilgrimage. While she was passing a kindergarten, a six- or seven-year-old boy approached and held her tight, exclaiming, "You are my sister!" The woman was in a state of joyful awe, suspecting the boy was the rebirth of her brother. Two monastics from the geshe's monastery, who happened to be in Lhasa also, went to visit the boy a few days later. The boy immediately recognized the two monastics,

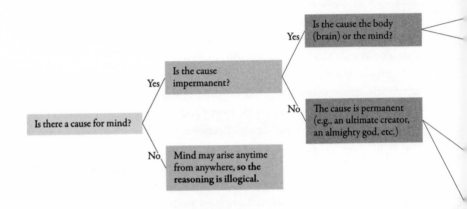

Is there a cause for mind?

Yes — Is the cause impermanent?

Yes — Is the cause the body (brain) or the mind?

No — The cause is permanent (e.g., an ultimate creator, an almighty god, etc.)

No — Mind may arise anytime from anywhere, so the reasoning is illogical.

FLOWCHART FOR THE LOGICAL INFERENCE
ON THE EXISTENCE OF MIND

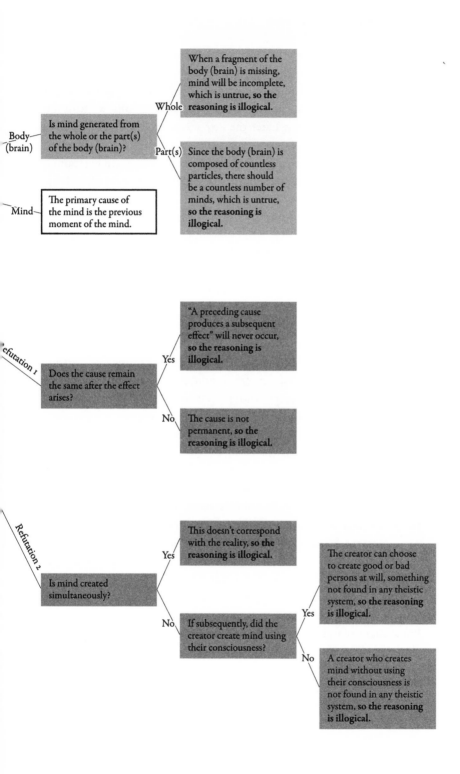

Body (brain) — Is mind generated from the whole or the part(s) of the body (brain)?

Whole — When a fragment of the body (brain) is missing, mind will be incomplete, which is untrue, so the reasoning is illogical.

Part(s) — Since the body (brain) is composed of countless particles, there should be a countless number of minds, which is untrue, so the reasoning is illogical.

Mind — The primary cause of the mind is the previous moment of the mind.

Refutation 1

Does the cause remain the same after the effect arises?

Yes — "A preceding cause produces a subsequent effect" will never occur, so the reasoning is illogical.

No — The cause is not permanent, so the reasoning is illogical.

Refutation 2

Is mind created simultaneously?

Yes — This doesn't correspond with the reality, so the reasoning is illogical.

No — If subsequently, did the creator create mind using their consciousness?

Yes — The creator can choose to create good or bad persons at will, something not found in any theistic system, so the reasoning is illogical.

No — A creator who creates mind without using their consciousness is not found in any theistic system, so the reasoning is illogical.

who then brought him back to his original monastery as a *tulku*. Since the boy had been the head of the monastery's three principal teachers, upon entering the Dharma hall he went directly to the highest Dharma seat and sat down. For some reason the monastery didn't hold an official enthronement ceremony for the boy. Later the boy was sent to a shedra in Lhasa for his training. He easily exceeded his monastic peers in memorizing and interpreting Buddhist texts, and a few years later he continued his training in India. There he was recognized as the rebirth of the geshe by several realized eminent masters.

In addition to great Buddhist masters, some ordinary people show evidence of recalling previous lives. For example, there was a young girl from a village close to Larung Gar who, before she was five or six years old, could clearly describe her past lives. Puzzled, her parents managed to verify the details of her statements by visiting people mentioned by the girl and found compelling evidence that the girl was telling the truth.

People who recall their past lives are not necessarily Buddhists. The best-known evidence is the work of the late Dr. Ian Stevenson, a psychiatrist in the School of Medicine at the University of Virginia. During forty years of research, Stevenson collected data from more than three thousand people primarily from Asia and Europe who spontaneously recalled past lives. His empirical research offered considerable evidence for rebirth.

Dr. Jim Tucker, the research heir of Dr. Stevenson, now investigates rebirth cases among American children. Using a rigorous scientific approach like his predecessor, Tucker has accumulated many cases in which children tell stories about past lives with persuasive evidence in support of their memories. The cases suggest that it's not unreasonable to conclude rebirth is true.

People today generally accept the scientific method, so providing evidence is very important. Some people argue that while the purported past-life recollections collected by Stevenson and Tucker are persuasive, the researchers' logic is flawed. These skeptics say Tucker and Stevenson used inductive reasoning—a logic of evidential support—to draw conclusions about rebirth from specific and isolated cases, which they believe is not proof.

But as many of us have learned in school, refuting a scientific theory only requires one negative piece of evidence. For example, to refute the statement "No swans are black," only one observation of a black swan is needed.

Therefore, the landmark work of Stevenson and Tucker is the "black swan" of rebirth for materialists who contend "rebirth doesn't exist." In other words, science cannot unequivocally assert there is no rebirth as long as there is one irrefutable case of rebirth, or substantial evidence validating rebirth.

In a related area, people sometimes ask, "If I've had other lifetimes, why don't I remember anything about them?" Owing to their lack of recollection, they then conclude rebirth is a speculation. Failing to remember past lives, or not perceiving them, does not prove past lives do not exist. In a similar way, dark matter, of which roughly 70 percent of the universe is made, exists even though we cannot see it; buried treasure is there, even if people can't find it or don't know where it is; and our personal potentials in music, painting, or mathematics exist, whether we discover them or not.

That you don't recall past lives doesn't mean you don't *have* past lives. Events from past lives cannot be perceived directly by our sense organs; they cannot be seen directly by our eyes or heard directly by our ears. It is like most details of our childhood—we cannot travel back in time to see what happened then, but does that mean we didn't have a childhood? No. Thus, it is unreasonable to conclude the existence or nonexistence of things based merely on our human perceptions.

We're already limited in the phenomena we can detect through our ears, eyes, nose, mouth, fingers, and mind. For example, without a telescope we can't see details of other planets in the solar system; without a microscope we can't see the details of bacteria or the nuclei and chromosomes of cells. Similarly, without attaining yogic perception through meditation, most of us cannot see the scenes of our past lives. Therefore, it is somewhat irrational to disbelieve rebirth for no reason, especially when there is abundant evidence suggesting that rebirth exists.[12]

Why is it that most people don't recall past existences? According to the Buddha's teaching, for most people, when their wandering consciousness enters a mother's womb, the trauma of yet again coming into physical existence makes them lose memory of all past lives. Rebirth blocks memory, much like a Wi-Fi-free zone prevents a laptop from connecting to the Internet.

We don't remember all our childhood events or even yesterday's meals, let alone our experiences in our past lives! Only a very few people, through the power of meditation or because of special causes and conditions, can remember their past lives.

I understand that conviction about rebirth and karma doesn't come easily to many people. Very often, we deluded beings only see what we *want to* see, and only hear what we *want to* hear. Therefore, many people reject the concepts of rebirth and karma, regardless of the solid logical inferences and compelling empirical evidence.

Nevertheless, I urge you to live as if rebirth is fact, even if you're not convinced that this basic tenet of Buddhism is correct. In the *Kalama Sutra*, the Buddha suggests the benefits of living as if rebirth is true, whether or not one accepts its veracity:

> Suppose there is a hereafter and there is a fruit, result, or deeds done well or ill. Then it is possible that at the dissolution of the body after death, I shall arise in the heavenly world, which is possessed of the state of bliss.
>
> Suppose there is no hereafter and there is no fruit, no result, or deeds done well or ill. Yet in this world, here and now, free from hatred, free from malice, safe and sound, and happy, I keep myself.

At the very least, if you act as if rebirth is true, you will cultivate mindfulness of your thoughts and actions. You will refrain from wrongdoing and instead act virtuously. This will not bring harm or suffering to your life. It will only make your life more meaningful (please also refer to the appendix on how to prepare for death).

7. The Spiritual Teacher

Guiding Us on the Path to Enlightenment

I N *The Words of My Perfect Teacher*, Patrul Rinpoche highlighted: "No sutra, tantra or shastra speaks of any being ever attaining perfect buddhahood without having followed a spiritual teacher."[1]

A qualified spiritual teacher is indispensable on our Dharma path to enlightenment, from beginning to end. All Buddhist traditions celebrate the teacher, who helps us awaken and realize our true nature, thus putting an end to our suffering.

In this chapter I will primarily refer to teachings from *The Words of My Perfect Teacher* to explain why we should follow a spiritual teacher, how to examine a teacher, how to properly follow a teacher, and how to emulate the teacher's realization and actions.

WHY FOLLOW A SPIRITUAL TEACHER?

Without the guidance of a qualified teacher, you cannot master the Dharma, even if you possess superior intellectual capacity and have read every Buddhist scripture. Many Dharma students develop right attitudes for following a teacher by clearly knowing the benefits of doing so.

The *Great Treatise on the Stages of the Path to Enlightenment* (*Lamrim Chenmo*) discusses nine attitudes a good disciple should have.[2] Given the extensive work available, I will not repeat the explanations of these nine correct attitudes. Instead, I will present eight types of wrong attitude, or erroneous reasons, for following a teacher and upon which you can reflect. We may find traces of these eight types of wrong attitudes within ourselves.

The Eight Wrong Attitudes

1. The Attitude of Seeing the Teacher as a Superstar

Nowadays many people are fans of movie stars, famous singers, or sports celebrities. Likewise, people become "fans" of Buddhist teachers for various reasons. They may follow a teacher who is charismatic, good-looking, cutely chubby or slim, or has a contagious smile. Sometimes Buddhist "fans" choose a teacher based on their gut feelings, instead of from careful examination.

2. The Attitude of Compensating for Lack of Love

Those who feel emotionally insecure may see the teacher as a deputy parent, family member, or significant other. The student doesn't rely on the teacher because of the teacher's compassion, loving-kindness, and transcendental wisdom. Instead, the student obtains a sense of security from having a teacher, which compensates for the lack of love and affection in their life. Seeing the teacher as the most important person in life helps fill this missing piece in the student's heart.

3. The Attitude of Seeing the Teacher as a Useful Tool

Some students see the teacher as a service provider or a "tool" that they can use when needed. They mostly use this "tool" for casting divinations (*mo*), receiving blessings, or chanting prayers during offering ceremonies (*puja*). The student might contact the teacher saying, "I need you to do this and that for me," or "I need your blessings on so and so." The teacher is treated like a staff member of the "Buddhist customer service center."

4. The Attitude of a Bee

A bee visits many different flowers for nectar or pollen, rarely staying with one specific flower for long. Similarly, there are beelike Dharma students who don't rely on a teacher for a long period of time, and as a result, they rarely practice the Dharma steadily with any teacher.

There is no rule in Buddhism that says you should not rely on more than one teacher. However, if the Dharma student follows a teacher but soon leaves or even slanders that teacher and then moves to another, this is not beneficial. Constantly changing teachers can exhaust a student so that they gain nothing substantial in the Dharma.

5. The Attitude of a Jealous Concubine

The popular Chinese television series *Empresses in the Palace* featured a very jealous imperial concubine named Consort Hua who often stopped other concubine members from visiting the emperor. Some Dharma students consciously or subconsciously seek more attention, blessings, and inspiration from their teacher than others, and thus they find ways to prevent other students from getting closer to the teacher. As a ruse, they might claim their real intention is to stay by the teacher's side continuously to "serve the teacher and propagate the Dharma."

6. The Attitude of a Controlling Executive

The executive-like student, often also a big donor or fundraiser for the sangha, likes to interfere in the teacher's public and private life. This donor may arrange every bit of the teacher's schedule, including whom the teacher sees and where the teacher appears.

7. The Poisonous Attitude

Poison is a substance capable of causing sickness or death when ingested. The poison-like student causes chaos by slandering his or her own teacher or others' teachers. This student often gossips about nonexistent wrongdoings of teachers in an effort to belittle them. Dharma students should watch out for peers with poisonous attitudes because their behavior may cause pain and disharmony in the otherwise congenial community.

8. The Attitude of Seeing the Teacher as a God

Some religions are based on the existence of a single almighty god. Some Dharma students adopt this belief, making no personal effort to practice but instead relying on the teacher's blessing, power, and precious qualities for their liberation from samsara. These students believe the teacher will toss them up into the heavenly realms as if throwing a pebble. But in fact, the Buddha said, "I have shown you the methods that lead to liberation. But you should know that liberation depends upon yourself."

The Right Motivation

The true reason we follow a Buddhist spiritual teacher is to attain liberation from rebirth and samsara.

Parting from the Four Attachments, the well-known short teaching from the great Sakya master Sachen Kunga Nyingpo, which you already briefly encountered in chapter 4, says:

> If you are attached to this life, you are not a true spiritual practitioner;
> If you are attached to samsara, you do not have renunciation;
> If you are attached to your own self-interest, you have no bodhichitta;
> If there is grasping, you do not have the view.[3]

If a student is relying on a teacher only for the eight worldly preoccupations[4] of hopes and fears in this life, or for clinging to the three higher realms within the domain of samsara, that student is not a true practitioner. Each Dharma student and practitioner should self-reflect: Why am I following my teacher?

I've noticed that some Buddhists think, "It is unnecessary to rely on a teacher. I can study the Dharma by myself." This view is not correct. As Patrul Rinpoche said, nobody has ever developed the accomplishments of the stages of a bodhisattva and the path to buddhahood through their own ingenuity and prowess. Even Shakyamuni Buddha followed teachers such as Dipankara in his past lives and listened to their teachings at various places before he eventually attained enlightenment. The Buddha said in the *Flower Ornament Sutra:*

> Just like a jewel in the dark
> Cannot be seen if there is no lamp,
> With no one to explain Buddha's teachings
> Even the intelligent cannot comprehend it.

Even if a Dharma student knows the Buddha's teachings in theory, without receiving the guidance in how to practice from a teacher, the student will never achieve realization, as stated in the *Nirvana Sutra*:

> By not being able to get close to a good spiritual advisor,
> Despite the fact [that each of them] has the buddha-nature,
> They cannot see it.

Since Shakyamuni Buddha is long gone, who can we rely on to help us attain enlightenment? The Buddha said to his disciple Ananda in the *Sutra of the Great Drum*:

> Don't feel sad, Ananda,
> Don't lament, Ananda,
> In future times I will
> Take the form of spiritual teachers,
> To help you and others.

Scriptural evidence suggests that after his parinirvana the Buddha repeatedly appears as spiritual teachers to benefit beings. These teachers hold and confer the Dharma of transmission and the Dharma of realization. The former is indicated by words and letters in the three collections or "baskets" (Skt. *tripitaka*; Tib. *denö sum*) of the Buddha's teachings that the teachers verbally teach to Dharma students, and the latter is the teachers' individually experienced wisdom that is passed on to the disciples. A Dharma student must rely on a qualified teacher to understand the Buddha's teachings, attain insight and experience, reach a state of realization, and eventually obtain full enlightenment.

The path to enlightenment is completely new to most ordinary Dharma students. It is similar to climbing an unknown high mountain. Before reaching the summit, an inexperienced climber has no idea what to expect. Where to start? Where will it end? What will they encounter in the middle? Is it dangerous, and if yes, then where are the dangerous spots? Every step requires guidance from a guide who has already walked the path. With their experience, qualified teachers can lead us with full confidence, so we won't get lost. If we choose to walk alone, even if we hold a map or the most advanced GPS device, there is no guarantee we will be on the right track.

The Dharma is so profound and wondrous that we must rely on a qualified spiritual teacher to reach the summit of liberation.

Even if we are aware of the importance of walking on the right path, doing so is easier said than done. As Patrul Rinpoche said in *The Words of My Perfect Teacher*,

> Indeed, all beings, ourselves included, show particular talent in discovering wrong paths to take—while when it comes to following the path leading to liberation and omniscience we are as confused as a blind person wandering alone in the middle of a deserted plain.[5]

Adventurers cannot bring back jewels from treasure islands without guidance from experienced navigators, just as ordinary people cannot attain liberation without guidance from qualified teachers. To attain ultimate liberation, we must follow a teacher, and we must follow that teacher wholeheartedly.

HOW TO EXAMINE A TEACHER

The *Sutra of the Collection of the Original Acts of the Buddha* (*Abhiniskramana Sutra*) recorded a story about Nanda and the Buddha.

After Nanda received ordination, he still showed no interest in virtuous conduct, despite the Buddha's repeated entreaties. Instead, he befriended misbehaving bhikshus and engaged in empty talks and gossip all day long.

One day, the Buddha brought Nanda to a fish market and asked him to pick up a handful of straw upon which had lain more than a hundred rotten stinky fish. The Buddha asked Nanda to keep the straw in his hand for a while, and then to throw it away.

The Buddha asked: "Do you smell something in your hand, Nanda?"

"Yes, teacher. It smells very strongly of fish. It is stinky."

"Well, it is the same when you are with unqualified teachers and friends. Even if you don't stay too long with them, you will be contaminated with the bad odors. You will be polluted with bad habits and become notorious."

Then, the Buddha brought Nanda to an incense store and asked him to hold an incense bag in his hand for a while, then put it away.

The Buddha asked: "Do you smell something in your hand, Nanda?"

"Yes, teacher. It smells of a pleasant aroma."

"Well, it is the same when you are close with qualified teachers and friends. If you rely on a perfect teacher full of good qualities, you will be permeated by the perfume of those qualities. You will grow the precious qualities within yourself and become renowned."

From this story we know that a Dharma student must examine a teacher thoroughly before following them. In our daily lives if we want to collaborate with someone, we must get to know the candidate very well before signing any contract. Similarly, before relying on a teacher, we need to examine them from various perspectives to see whether they are a qualified teacher or a charlatan.

A Qualified Teacher to Follow

When we examine a teacher, the following characteristics are not determining factors: clairvoyance, good looks, eloquence, wealth, prestige, and fame. The key is to see whether the teacher can guide beings to abstain from unwholesome deeds and to perform wholesome ones. The *Nirvana Sutra* says:

> Why do we say "a good spiritual advisor"? The good spiritual advisor teaches beings to refrain from the ten non-virtuous deeds and to engage in the ten virtuous deeds. That is why we say "a good spiritual advisor."

To describe the specific qualities of a qualified teacher, I will borrow teachings from Patrul Rinpoche. Bear in mind that a vajra guru who bestows empowerments and gives tantric pith instructions should be examined on more qualities than other teachers (see chapter 9). It's like when we evaluate a university professor, we apply more criteria than we do for an elementary school teacher.

Checklist of the Teacher's Qualities according to Patrul Rinpoche

1. *The teacher should be pure.* The teacher should have never broken any of the three sets of vows: the vows of individual liberation, the bodhisattva vows, and the *samaya* vows—the tantric commitments.

If the teacher is an ordained monastic member, they should at least uphold the vows of Buddhist monastics. If the teacher is a householder, they should at least uphold the vows for laypeople. If no vow is upheld, any great quality and state of realization would be rootless.

During this degenerate age, even if teachers cannot meticulously uphold every item on the lists of the three sets of vows, they—at the minimum—must uphold the root precepts with the attitude of bodhichitta (renunciation at the very least) and not commit any root downfall of the three types of vows.

2. *The teacher should be learned.* If the teacher is poorly trained and knows little—for example, they know few Buddhist scriptures, let alone have studied them in depth—they are not a good teacher to follow. The teacher should master the fundamental knowledge of the sutras, tantras, and shastras.

3. *The teacher should demonstrate great compassion.* The teacher should love each one of the innumerable beings like their own child—have an impartial compassion for all beings. It's not appropriate if a teacher loves and cares for family and friends and answers their requests generously, while ignoring and disdaining someone who appears hostile. A teacher who acts with such distinctions doesn't even possess worldly compassion and kindness, let alone the great compassion and bodhichitta of Mahayana Buddhism.

4. *The teacher should be well versed in ritual practices.* If a teacher only talks about the teachings yet never puts them into practice, it is impossible for that teacher to guide Dharma students through Buddhist liturgies.

5. *The teacher should have attained freedom and realization.* The teacher should have followed their own teacher's practical instructions and the teachings in sutras, shastras, and tantras, and practiced diligently in person. As a result, this teacher has actualized the extraordinary achievements of freedom and realization—they have cleared their afflictions and obscurations, and have realized emptiness.

At a minimum, even if the teacher hasn't realized emptiness, they should be capable of suppressing or transforming afflictions and attaining certain state of realization. Otherwise, if Dharma students are faithful and experienced in their practice, while the teacher is clinging to the eight worldly preoccupations and unable to exceed the students in diligence and precious qualities, it is truly laughable.

6. *The teacher possesses the four ways of attracting beings.* First, the teacher should be generous. The teacher benefits beings through three kinds of generosity: material giving, giving Dharma, and giving protection from fear.

Second, the teacher's language should be pleasant. The teacher delivers the Buddha's teachings with appropriate words in an appropriate manner, so that living beings are willing to accept and follow the teaching. Some people think "pleasant language" refers to talks that cater to Dharma students' preferences, but this is not the case. For example, if a Dharma student likes anger-inducing situations, it would not be helpful for the teacher to tell that student war stories every day. According to the *Ornament of the Great Vehicle Sutras*, pleasant language refers to instructions related to Dharma practice.

Third, the teacher should teach everyone according to their individual needs. Through this way of attracting beings, the teacher can benefit Dharma students and transform their mind. The teacher should truly care about the students' needs. The "care" that worldly people refer to includes giving wealth or praise and having frequent contact. However, a true caring teacher encourages Dharma students to practice the six transcendent perfections that, unlike worldly care, offer ultimate benefits to the student.

Fourth, the teacher should act in conformity with what they teach. It doesn't make sense if the teacher only talks the talk; they must also walk the talk. For example, if a teacher tells students, "You must practice no-self and bodhichitta; make sure you don't get lazy and sluggish," while the teacher sleeps until noon, never practicing no-self and rarely thinking of freeing all living beings from suffering, then the teacher is only paying lip service to the Dharma.

The list of a teacher's qualities mentioned in other Buddhist texts is mostly consistent with Patrul Rinpoche's list. For example, the *Ornament of the Great Vehicle Sutras* suggests ten qualities of a teacher that are summarized in one stanza:

> One should serve a (spiritual) friend who is disciplined, tranquil, serene, outstanding in good qualities, energetic, rich in (knowledge of) scripture, awakened to reality, skilled in speech, compassionate, and indefatigable.

When I first followed the great Jigme Phuntsok Rinpoche on the pilgrimage to the sacred Mount Wutai in China's Shanxi province in 1987, I put the page containing this stanza in my scripture folder and read it from time to time. Jigme Phuntsok Rinpoche often cited this stanza in his teachings.

If you find a teacher has the above-listed qualities, confidently follow

140 — TIBETAN BUDDHISM

that teacher. If some of those qualities are lacking, remain cautious before proceeding to following them.

Bodhichitta

If you feel the qualities listed by Patrul Rinpoche are a bit hard to pinpoint, you may check for one essential quality in a Mahayana teacher: bodhichitta. Examining a teacher could be condensed into a single question: Does that teacher have bodhichitta or not?

A teacher with bodhichitta will do whatever is best to benefit students for their present and future lives, leading them along the path to liberation. It is stated in Ithe *Great Jewel-Heap Sutra*:

> The person with Bodhichitta can be followed,
> Because he is praised by all the wise men.

If a teacher has bodhichitta, follow them, regardless of how the teacher appears externally—they may be a householder or monastic member, dress like a derelict or rich heir, gulp an entire bottle of hard liquor or just a glass of water while teaching. Nevertheless, follow such a teacher who always demonstrates skillful means to teach students. Khyentse Yeshe Dorje (1800–1866) shot guns aimlessly in the air, a seemingly bizarre action that enabled his fortunate disciples to realize emptiness then and there.

In fact, teachers with genuine bodhichitta will be welcomed warmly wherever they live and travel, so they will naturally attract many students. As Jigme Lingpa said in his *Treasury of Precious Qualities*, a teacher with great qualities is like a brilliant flower that attracts fortunate disciples to gather like bees. Likewise, Gungtang Tenpe Drönme (1762–1823) stated in his *Water and Wood Shastras*:

> Around a compassionate and altruistic teacher,
> A crowd of people will gather naturally.

In contrast, if a teacher lacks bodhichitta, do not follow them. However profound their Mahayana and Vajrayana teachings appear to be, however prestigious their Dharma throne seems, however dignified demeanors they display, however long they can meditate, however abundant the ceremonial scarves and alms they have received, however impressive their self-promotion sounds, a teacher without bodhichitta still has selfish desires and is entangled by worldly concerns. This teacher might at most plant the seed of merit in students.

People may initially approach such a teacher on account of good first impressions. But, as the Chinese proverb "Distance tests a horse's stamina and time reveals a man's heart" suggests, gradually people will uncover the teacher's lack of good qualities and stay away from them. The *Great Jewel-Heap Sutra* says:

> Don't get close to inferior persons;
> When seeing a non-righteous person,
> Move away from this person immediately,
> As if you are avoiding a venomous snake.

It is important to be cautious because people can mask their real selves with pseudo-bodhichitta. When witnessing a suffering being, a teacher may appear very compassionate and immediately recite "May all beings attain buddhahood." However, the recitation does not necessarily reflect genuine bodhichitta. The ego can be very cunning, and it can be hard to tell whether great compassion has arisen in the teacher's mind.

It's not easy to find a teacher who has genuine bodhichitta because bodhichitta is difficult to achieve. The foundation of genuine, uncontrived bodhichitta is a mind with the four boundless qualities (discussed in chapter 3)—love, compassion, joy, and equanimity. Generating boundless compassion, for instance, is not as easy as we would expect. Feeling sorry for a suffering being may be a form of compassion, but it is not sufficient to constitute "boundless compassion." Why? If your parents or beloved friends are sick, you may earnestly wish they get well soon, while you may not generate the same intense wish about a sick stranger. If you don't feel the same compassion for strangers as for your parents or friends, this lack of treating everyone equally indicates your compassion is not yet boundless. Instead, it is still bound and conditioned by "my" family, "my" friends, and "our" human species.

Examination Tips

Someone may wonder, "Since we should refrain from judging a teacher just by appearance, how can we really tell whether that teacher has genuine bodhichitta or not?" It says in *The Buddha Speaks of the Ten Dharmas of Abiding in the Mahayana Path Sutra*:

> Just as one infers the presence of fire by seeing smoke,
> Or the presence of water by seeing aquatic birds,
> The presence of the intelligent bodhisattvas' disposition
> Can be understood from certain signs.

One can approximately determine whether a teacher has bodhichitta from their activities, including propagating the Dharma and benefiting living beings. But a novice Dharma student is best off relying on someone who is already recognized as a good teacher by reliable sources.

Just knowing a teacher for a few days or months may not be sufficient to decide whether they can be relied upon. According to Tsongkhapa's commentary on the *Fifty Verses of Guru Devotion*, certain tantras recommend that examination between a disciple and a guru go on for as long as twelve years. It took Kublai Khan (1215–1294) of the Mongol Empire six years to closely examine Drogön Chögyal Phagpa (1235–1280) before the emperor decided to follow the Sakya master.

Some learned masters suggest the following step-by-step examination of a teacher. Before following a teacher, one should from afar ask those who are close to the teacher; then one should go near and investigate the teacher's actions in person; lastly, one should make direct contact with that teacher to have a close examination, as Kublai Khan did.

One challenge to following this procedure arises when a Dharma student has not finished examining a potential teacher, yet the teacher believes the student has a karmic affinity and proposes bestowing an empowerment or offering an instruction. This can put the student in an awkward situation. I once heard that a Dharma student was reluctant to receive empowerment from a probationary teacher, so he hid in the bathroom until the empowerment was over.

Since it is difficult to distinguish whether a teacher is qualified or not, what should we do? Patrul Rinpoche suggested:

> The greatest of all teachers is the one with whom we are linked
> from former lives. With him, examination is superfluous. Simply
> to meet him, simply to hear his voice—or even just his name—

can transform everything in an instant and stir such faith that every hair on our bodies stands on end.[6]

This was true for many past prominent masters. For example, Jetsun Milarepa (1052–1135) felt extraordinary faith from the very depths of his mind after just hearing the name of Marpa. When Milarepa finally saw Marpa in person, in an instant, all his restless conceptual thoughts ceased, and he stood transfixed.

I certainly cannot say I've had a similar experience as Milarepa, but when I first heard the name of my root guru the great Jigme Phuntsok Rinpoche, I experienced great faith. In the early 1980s, when I was still a student at a teacher-training school in Garze, my Tibetan language teacher often wore a fox-fur hat and taught us while smoking tobacco and drinking tea—a true maverick. Once he said in class, "I personally don't acknowledge some existing so-called lamas, but there is a great lama called Jigme Phuntsok Rinpoche who gives teachings to over fifty monastic members at Larung Gar in Sertar. I really admire him!" Upon hearing his name, I was overwhelmed with great faith toward the great Jigme Phuntsok Rinpoche. I was transfixed and my heart skipped a beat, and I kept him in my mind and heart ever after.

It wasn't until I was twenty-three years old that I first saw Jigme Phuntsok Rinpoche and started to follow him at Larung Gar. Although I am just an ordinary monk, the wisdom and power my root guru gave me is beyond the reach of anyone in the world, including my parents. In my life, no one can compare to my root guru.

Unfortunately, I have noticed many Dharma students blindly pursuing this feeling rather than thoroughly scrutinizing the potential teacher. While it is possible for students' mind-streams to instantly change by hearing the names of teachers with whom they were linked in former lives, this is not the case for everyone. Students must be careful not to rush to claim a charlatan as their teacher in this life and their lives to follow, not to force the arising of reactions like tears falling, hair standing on end, and body twitching.

A Charlatan to Avoid

Several years ago, I watched the documentary *Kūmāré* about a made-up guru and his phony religion. Filmmaker Vikram Gandhi was born in the United States of parents from India. He found out that gurus and yoga were becoming popular among Americans, but many yogis were charlatans. That led him to transform himself into Kūmāré, an allegedly enlightened Indian guru, by growing a long beard and a ponytail, donning orange robes, and adopting a fake Indian accent modeled from his grandmother. He hired an expert to teach him yoga and a public relations person to promote him as a guru. Gradually he attracted sincere followers in Arizona. He delivered teachings on yoga and even invented mantras that his disciples would chant earnestly.

Many of Kūmāré's followers believed him without question. They shared their deepest secrets with him, and some claimed their lives had been transformed. One day he told his followers the time had come for him to leave them. He went back to his home in New Jersey, cut his hair, shaved his beard, and sent a video back to his followers: "I am not who you think I am." The truth brought sadness and disappointment to some followers, as well as insightful reflections to others.

Nowadays some Kūmāré-like teachers are fully aware they're unqualified but encourage students to follow them and demonstrate unalloyed faith in their "wisdom." Both teacher and followers are trapped in the same sham experience. In the documentary, Kūmāré said, "It is you real gurus that make us fake gurus so necessary."

After describing the qualities of a real teacher in the previous section, it is necessary to explain the characteristics of a charlatan. Some Dharma students follow teachers for decades before discerning the teachers are con artists. By then, the students have exhausted their energy and faith. Even worse, they have no time left to seek a new teacher, as they are at the end of their lives. What a great pity! Such a student may eventually abandon and even slander the teacher. If the teacher is a pure charlatan who knows little about the Dharma, who is not eligible to bestow empowerment and transmission, and who acts pretentiously just to attain wealth and fame, it might not matter too much if the student abandons them. However, if the charlatan has transmission from previous hearing of the Dharma, then the Dharma the charlatan gives is at least partly an authentic teaching from the Buddha, even if the teacher has their own agenda. In such a case, the student should still refrain from slandering the teacher.

Some Dharma students want to follow a teacher as soon as possible, claiming they're in a hurry and don't have time for a thorough examination. Alas! It's not like they are having acute appendicitis, so why are they out of time? In the past twenty or thirty years, even seventy to eighty years, they've chosen to do anything but the Dharma, so why are they suddenly in such a hurry that they cannot find time to examine the teacher?

Patrul Rinpoche listed the following types of teachers we should avoid.

A Teacher Who Is Like a Millstone Made of Wood

A wooden millstone may look real, but it cannot grind any grains despite the loud noise it generates; it only damages itself. In a similar manner, these teachers act sanctimoniously and might become better known than many qualified teachers, but they are deceiving others. Such teachers have no trace of the qualities arising from hearing, contemplating, and meditating on the Dharma. They boast of being superior to everyone because they are residents of a sacred place, the offspring of a great lama, or the descendants of a sublime being.

Some people are easily fooled and may consider charlatans *mahasiddhas*[7]—practitioners who have attained supreme spiritual accomplishment. These people may exclaim, "Really? You are from the sacred place? Then I must follow you!" Then they call around and tell others that a certain teacher has just arrived, and that they should all go to receive empowerment or listen to the teachings.

Dharma students may also be convinced by a teacher introducing themself as the child, sibling, or grandchild of a renowned lama. Even if a lama is a highly accomplished master, the family members don't necessarily possess similar qualities. For example, Devadatta, the cousin of Shakyamuni Buddha, was prone to arrogance, anger, and jealousy, exactly the opposite of the Buddha's qualities.

A Dharma student who follows such teachers will not only be devoid of the qualities arising from hearing, contemplating, and meditating but will also eventually fall to the lower realms. This is very dangerous. As recorded in many sutras, the Buddha taught that neither the caste nor the fame of the teacher is important. What is most important is the *sikkhapada*, which means both "moral rules" and "states of realization."

Some so-called teachers have neither good characters nor real qualities arising from studying and practicing the Dharma, yet they believe they are superior to everyone else. Some others may have a few qualities, yet they've never thought of liberation from samsara. They appear very dignified in front of people merely to attain status and wealth. Please avoid such charlatans, who bring harm to themselves and to their students.

A Teacher Who Is Like a Frog in a Well

Teachers who are shortsighted like a frog in a well lack competence to teach and guide students. They don't have special qualities distinguishing them from ordinary people: no great compassion, no wisdom of realizing emptiness, no skillful means to help free beings from suffering, or even worse, they are not even a moral person.

This kind of teacher knows very little about the Dharma. But some Dharma students out of blind faith might hold such teachers in high regard, carelessly addressing them with titles including *tulku* or guru and seeing them as the only guide capable of liberating everyone from samsara. Puffed up with pride and bolstered by the profits and honors received, these teachers become arrogant. Even if they don't mean to fool students, they themselves can become so blinded by their arrogance that they believe in their own nonexistent competence. A Dharma student must avoid such teachers!

A Mad Guide

Mad-guide teachers have never tried to follow a learned master. They have not diligently studied the Buddhist texts nor attained any meditative wisdom. They often have more mental afflictions and negative emotions than ordinary people, throwing temper tantrums and startling disciples. Wrapped up in anger and jealousy, these teachers break the lifeline of loving-kindness and compassion.

Such people lack mindfulness and belittle the law of karma, becoming vow-breakers and, even worse, samaya-breakers. They commit wrongdoings including stealing, eating meat,[8] sexual misconduct, and even killing. They act like great enlightened beings with "crazy wisdom"—a sort of divine madness with wisdom at its core—and claim their views and actions are higher than the sky. They will lead any students who follow them down the wrong path. It is terrifying!

These mad guides don't behave in accordance with the principle of cause and effect, and their bad behavior has nothing to do with Buddhism itself. The precepts that an authentic Dharma practitioner should follow are listed clearly in Buddhist texts. When faulty teachers trample on the precepts and behave wrongly, some people generate wrong views toward Buddhism or are repelled by Buddhism. It is the faulty teachers, not Buddhism, that should take the blame.

A Blind Guide

Such teachers don't possess qualities superior to those of their disciples. They themselves don't know what should and should not be done, so they are unable to teach disciples what to do and what not to do. They lack the loving-kindness and compassion of bodhichitta. They attract others by boasting of their fame. As a result, they are not competent to guide students and will lead them to the wrong path.

I read a Chinese book called *In Search of the Mind*, in which the author depicted many charlatans who acted pretentiously as tulkus. One of these fake tulkus would come to mainland China and tell a young female follower: "You were a renowned *dakini* in a previous life, so we have very auspicious affinity with each other. If you and I have a tulku son together, he will propagate the Dharma and benefit beings." Some women believed him and introduced more people to this "tulku." As Jigme Lingpa said in *Treasury of Precious Qualities*, having such frauds as your blind guides is a huge mistake because you'll wander deeper into darkness.

In summary, spiritual teachers are those we firmly follow and place trust in for this life and all future lives. Teachers offer authentic teachings so that we can achieve ultimate freedom from samsara. If a Dharma student relies on a charlatan because of a lack of prior careful examination, their merit and precious opportunity for spiritual practice will be squandered. *Treasury of Precious Qualities* has a verse explaining the harmful effect of bad teachers:

> By not examining a teacher with great care
> The faithful waste their gathered merit.
> Like taking for the shadow of a tree a vicious snake,
> Beguiled, they lose the freedom they at last had found.[9]

Please be aware that it is not totally random that we encounter a charlatan in this life. In the *Wish-Fulfilling Treasury*, Longchenpa said Dharma students with no merits often encounter teachers with no true wisdom. Without affinity from past lives, we may not have accumulated enough merit in this life to meet a qualified teacher.

Without a pure mind, even if we happen to meet the real Shakyamuni Buddha in person, we may fail to see him as a teacher with great qualities.

It is recorded in the *Sutra on the Ocean-Like Samadhi of the Visualization of the Buddha*:

> Five hundred Shakya[10] descendants see the Buddha's body in the color of charcoal; one thousand bhikshus see the Buddha's body in the color of red clay soils; sixteen upasakas[11] see the Buddha's body in the color of a black elephant's foot; twenty-four upasikas[12] see the Buddha's body in the color of ink. Thus, these four groups have their different perceptions of the Buddha's body.

Why did they fail to see the true golden color of the Buddha's body? As explained in the sutra, it is because in past lives the Shakya descendants slandered the Buddha and Dharma with ill intentions, the bhikshus generated wrong views toward the Dharma and the teacher, the upasakas followed bad teachers and believed in the wrong Dharma, and the upasikas seduced and insulted well-behaved monks.

Thus, the teachers we meet are determined by the karmic power of our past actions, as well as by the purity or impurity of our perceptions. The qualified teacher we meet in this life is the most important of all, far more important than winning a billion-dollar lottery.

How to Follow a Teacher

After examining a qualified teacher, Dharma students should firmly follow them for as long as they can.

Here is an analogy in a tantra: when a swallow wants to build a nest, it will first examine a possible spot from many different angles, and once the bird chooses a spot, it will build a nest and then remain in it without wavering. Similarly, once a Dharma student decides to follow a teacher, that student should remain respecting and obeying the teacher while steadfastly seeking the authentic Dharma.

The longer the Dharma student follows a teacher, the more likely that student is to attain the teacher's qualities. Following a teacher for just a few days or months is insufficient. Some Dharma students act like they are collecting "Dharma stamps." They like to receive empowerments, transmissions, and teachings given by the teacher from time to time, and then they go back to their nine-to-five jobs without reviewing or practicing what they've received. They naively think they are all set with the "Dharma stamps" collected from the teacher.

It is possible for a student to quickly attain the supreme state of realization if the teacher has impeccable blessing power and the student has abundant merit from past lives as well as extraordinary faith. There are many stories of such awakenings. The great Jigme Phuntsok Rinpoche, for example, relied on his root guru, Thubten Chöpel Rinpoche, for a mere six years, yet he attained all the great qualities of his guru.

Nevertheless, most of us are ordinary practitioners, so we're better off steadily following a teacher for as long as possible. Then, when the time with the teacher is over, the separation will be carefree and joyful since the student has nothing to regret.

Follow the Teacher through the Dharma

Following spiritual teachers should be primarily through the Dharma. According to sutras and shastras, it is only when teachers transmit the Dharma to students that the teacher-disciple relationship is truly established. Therefore, students should listen to teachings directly from teachers, and teachers should offer teachings to students. However, many people hold a different view. They think following a teacher means a Dharma student asks a teacher, "Can you take me as your disciple?" and the teacher happily nods in agreement, saying, "Okay, you are my disciple." Students who receive this permission are thrilled and cannot wait to share the news with friends. For them, following teachers simply means receiving verbal consent, like signing a worldly agreement.

On rare occasions, the teacher's nodding in agreement may be sufficient to transform Dharma students, because the realization of some awakened masters is inconceivable. Through their immeasurable blessings and wisdom, such great teachers are able to swiftly bring students with superior faculties onto the path to liberation.

Some Buddhists have received empowerments, heard teachings, and obtained pith instructions from a Dharma master, yet refuse to admit the master is their teacher. Instead, they visit a lama from whom they have never received any teachings, and declare, "I am your disciple, and you are my teacher." Speaking of such a declaration, it is worth mentioning a story of Mahakashyapa:

After Mahakashyapa renounced his lay life, he and the Buddha exchanged declarations of commitment. Mahakashyapa said to the Buddha, "You are my teacher, I am your disciple." The Buddha replied to Mahakashyapa: "Just so, Kashyapa. I am your teacher; you are my disciple." The declarations established the teacher-disciple relationship between the Buddha and Mahakashyapa.

Unless you have faculties as sharp as Mahakashyapa's, which most ordinary beings don't, following a teacher doesn't count if you haven't heard their Dharma teachings. The *Sutra of the Right Mindfulness of Dharma* (*Saddharma-smrity-upasthana Sutra*) says:

> The person who teaches one verse of the virtuous Dharma to others
> Is considered a virtuous teacher and
> Shall be respected by all living beings.

If someone taught you at least one verse of the authentic Dharma, that person can be considered your teacher. From then on, you should adjust your attitude to show respect to that teacher. Establishing a teacher-disciple relationship through anything other than the Dharma is not consistent with Buddhist doctrines.

Consider the Teacher as a Doctor

What should Dharma students bear in mind to properly follow teachers? The similes in the *Flower Ornament Sutra* provide good hints. The sutra says:

> Noble one, think of yourself as sick,
> and think of spiritual benefactors as physicians;
> Think of their instructions as medicines,
> And think of the practices as getting rid of disease.

We should see ourselves as patients with a severe disease, qualified teachers as experienced doctors, the Dharma taught by teachers as the remedy, and following the teachers' instructions as taking the medication. Without practicing the Dharma, it is very unlikely that we can eradicate our afflictions in the same way a patient who refuses to take the medicine prescribed by a doctor will not recover.

When we are sick, we should consult the right doctor and take the right medicine. For example, if we suffer from pneumonia, seeking help from a silversmith or taking a pill for anemia will be as futile as "milking a bull." In the same way, space scientists and academics are not optimal candidates for curing the "illness" of our tormenting mental afflictions. Instead of seeking a teacher, some people seek relief from afflictions through outer activities— yoga, running, knitting, gardening,which provide only temporary relief and happiness. These individuals still haven't learned how to completely uproot the ubiquitous sufferings of samsara.

To cure ourselves of the diseases of karma, mental afflictions, and negative emotions, we must follow the prescriptions of an experienced doctor— the authentic teacher—by taking the medicine of the Dharma. This alone can bring ultimate liberation through training our minds.

While in this degenerate age it may not be possible to find a teacher equivalent to Shakyamuni Buddha, but as long as the teacher has certain levels of compassion, wisdom, and power, and can help tame our minds and transform us, this person is a qualified teacher for us.

Can We Follow a Teacher We've Never Met in Person?

Even if some people have successfully identified a qualified teacher, they may have circumstances that prevent them from hearing the teacher's teachings in person. Under this circumstance, watching the teacher on videos and reading their books, then practicing accordingly, can be a legitimate manner of following the teacher.

My root guru the great Jigme Phuntsok Rinpoche never met Mipham Rinpoche in person but developed great faith in him from a young age. Through reading Mipham Rinpoche's works and praying earnestly to him, eventually my root guru received all his blessings. After that, he always paid homage to Mipham Rinpoche at the beginning of his own compositions.

Likewise, Jigme Lingpa generated great faith in Longchenpa after reading his writings, and started to see him as a buddha, although they lived almost five hundred years apart and never met. Through praying to Longchenpa earnestly and practicing his teachings diligently, Jigme Lingpa received all the blessings of the wisdom mind of Longchenpa and eventually recognized the nature of mind.

From the stories of these achieved masters, we see that some practitioners can indeed attain realization through indestructible faith in a teacher they've never met in person. Following a teacher doesn't imply a Dharma student has to physically follow that teacher. It doesn't mean the student has to always stay with the teacher—when the teacher takes a walk, sits down, or has dinner, for example.

Even when the Buddha was giving teachings, he didn't require his disciples to always stay beside him. At the most, there were 1,250 people surrounding the Buddha, and it was impossible for every disciple to stay close to him. Usually only a few of his primary disciples were physically close to him, such as Ananda, Mahakashyapa, and Katyayana.

The real manner of following teachers is that Dharma students master the teachings of sutras, shastras, and tantras from the teachers, contemplate the teachings, integrate the Dharma in daily life, and take on the teachers' wisdom and compassion as their own. From this, they can gradually attain the same precious qualities the teachers attained, through the three higher trainings[13] of discipline, meditation, and wisdom.

Following One Teacher versus Many Teachers

Some Dharma teachers tell their students, "You should only follow one teacher and engage in one specific Dharma practice; otherwise, the more teachers you follow and the more teachings you hear and contemplate, the more mental afflictions will arise and the less wisdom you will attain. In the end, you may not get enlightened." Some masters refuted this argument with scriptural evidence, such as the text in the *Flower Ornament Sutra* regarding Sudhana's visits to fifty-three teachers.[14]

Which view is right? My opinion is that it depends. I once met a Dharma student who, after following many teachers, is constantly worried about whether he would upset this teacher or that one. Inevitably, he became very exhausted. One day, he exclaimed, "I don't want to follow any teacher anymore. I would be better off staying independent and alone like a pratyeka-buddha who is always in solitude." Alas!

Buddhist practitioners differ in faculties and predispositions. When someone is deeply immersed in his or her own afflictions and conceptual thoughts, one teacher's effort alone may not be sufficient; therefore more teachers may be helpful. Another practitioner may feel perplexed and overwhelmed when following multiple teachers, so following just one teacher is better for that person. As long as our goal is to attain liberation from samsara, we can follow either one teacher or many teachers.

Do Not See the Teacher as an Ordinary Person

When we follow a qualified teacher, although we may exceed them in certain worldly things—we may be taller, stronger, more attractive, or have earned a higher degree or more certificates—we won't exceed them in their vast wisdom, great compassion, skillful means, and altruistic activities.

When I was young and had just started my study and practice at Larung Gar, I felt like I was as good as, if not better than, some Dharma masters who taught us novices. As I grew older and more experienced in life, I gradually realized the masters teaching me the Dharma all had extraordinary qualities that have proven out of reach for me.

Here is a story that I heard during my earlier years at Larung Gar:

One day Atisha was asked a question by his chief disciple Dromtonpa: "In Tibet there are many people who try to meditate, but it seems they do not achieve the supreme qualities. Why is that?" Atisha answered, "All the qualities of the Mahayana, be they great or small, arise from reliance upon the teacher. These Tibetans see their teacher as an ordinary person, then how could they achieve the supreme qualities?"

Hence, we should see our qualified teacher as someone with great transcendental qualities. Only in this way can our faith arise naturally, and our body-speech-mind be conducted in a proper manner.

No one can follow their teacher for infinite years. The time spent learning with one's teacher is very precious. Often it is not until the teacher passes into parinirvana that students start to realize the teacher's precious qualities and to see that teacher is not an ordinary person. By then it may be too late. This is a common mistake among Dharma students!

In the trichiliocosm, Shakyamuni Buddha is the only one with perfect qualities who is devoid of any faults. However, some people may fail to recognize it, just like Sunaksatra did. Sunaksatra was the personal attendant of the Buddha for twenty-four years, and he knew by heart all twelve categories of teachings in the Tripitaka, the collected teachings of the Buddha. Sunaksatra saw everything the Buddha did as deceitful, so one day he told the Buddha:

Apart from that light around your body six feet wide, never have I seen, in twenty-four years as your servant, even a sesame seed's worth of special qualities in you. As for the Dharma, I know as much as you—and I will no longer be your servant![15]

After saying this, Sunaksatra left the Buddha.

There are many Sunaksatra-like disciples who have been seeing their teacher as an ordinary person. What a pity!

Follow the Teacher with Pure Perception

After carefully examining a qualified teacher and then following them, wise students should never abandon and slander the teacher. It is important not to take the teacher's actions in the wrong way. Dharma students, especially vajra disciples, should train to have pure perception toward a qualified teacher.

Some qualified teachers adopt low lifestyles, such as being a butcher or a hunter, or appear mischievous such as drinking or stealing. There are many stories of such teachers in Taranatha's (1575–1634) historical work on the lives of the Indian mahasiddhas.

It says in Nagarjuna's *Discourse on the Ten Stages* (*Dasabhumika-vibhasashastra*):

> Internally, he has qualities and wisdom;
> Externally, he appears having no proper demeanor;
> To ignorant walkers,
> He is like a fire covered by ashes.

The verse explains that a person who disdains and slanders such a qualified teacher is like someone sitting on a fire covered by ashes; soon that person will catch fire.

It is easy to make mistakes if one measures a qualified teacher's inner states of realization through that teacher's outer behaviors. In Nagarjuna's *Letter to a Friend*, he said there are individuals who are similar to four types of mango fruits: unripe, but seemingly ripe; ripe, but seemingly unripe; unripe appearing as unripe; and ripe appearing as ripe. The second type—ripe but seemingly unripe—represents mahasiddhas who, while free from samsara themselves, appear to engage in morally inappropriate conduct with the intention to liberate certain beings. The secret meaning of mahasiddhas goes beyond the understanding of ordinary people. Some students remain convinced even on their deathbeds that a teacher was immoral, when in fact that teacher was an incarnation of a buddha or a bodhisattva.

Even if we haven't yet developed unwavering pure perception toward our teachers, we should always respect them and acknowledge their kindness in teaching us authentic Dharma. We respect our parents because they gave life to us and raised us. Likewise, we should respect, even more so, our teachers who have taught us even just one verse of the Dharma because they uplift the wisdom of our Dharma life.

The Dharma teacher–disciple relationship is unlike the workplace relationship between supervisor and subordinate. As long as there is no serious conflict in the workplace relationship, the subordinate can still function well. In contrast, a Dharma teacher and disciple are connected by an inconceivable affinity, linked to the disciple's liberation in this life and in many lives to come. For those who show no respect to their Dharma teachers, no matter how many teachers they've followed, the Buddha's teachings won't benefit them. Thus, enlightenment is very hard for them to attain.

If Dharma students respect and appreciate their teachers, and see them with pure perception, the Dharma will be integrated into their mindstreams naturally. As a result, their minds will resonate with the Dharma, and realization will gradually arise.

It's Not a Personality Cult

Some people, especially Westerners, believe that respecting and appreciating Buddhist teachers is a form of personality cult, so they denounce following teachers. But, while many Westerners grew up in a different educational and value system from Easterners and thus perceive things differently, there is always a common ground for discussing this topic.

I don't think following a teacher equals cult behavior. When students attain levels of realization through the guidance of their Dharma teachers, faith and devotion arise naturally. No teacher who gives worldly knowledge is comparable. I've encountered many Buddhist practitioners in the West, including scholars, scientists, doctors, professors, and others, who have strong devotion and unshakable faith in their Dharma teachers.

During a trip with the great Jigme Phuntsok Rinpoche to the United States, Canada, and France in 1993, I met some disciples of a great Dharma teacher and was deeply moved by their guru devotion. The teacher passed into parinirvana in the 1980s, so when we visited the Dharma centers, he had already been gone for several years. Nevertheless, when his disciples heard their teacher's name, they appeared struck by the "electric shock" of their own impeccable devotion to the teacher; many of them shed tears.

Rational people may be more likely to see faults in teachers' behaviors. But, this rationality doesn't obstruct them from following a teacher, and in fact can further strengthen their faith and devotion. Several years ago, I revisited several centers of that teacher, and was again impressed that although the teacher had left more than thirty years prior, some of his disciples had never stopped passing on his legacy with their strong guru devotion. This can truly be called "following a teacher."

My root guru the great Jigme Phuntsok Rinpoche drew around him many disciples, myself included, who continue to have impeccable devotion and gratitude toward him. Whenever we hear the name "Jigme Phuntsok Rinpoche," we lineage disciples are always touched deeply by an inconceivable power. The great Jigme Phuntsok Rinpoche passed into parinirvana in 2004, and every day I miss him even more. Because he is in my heart and mind all the time, I often meet him and listen to his words in my dreams.

Götsangpa Gönpo Dorje (1189–1258) once said:

> High devotion leads to high realization;
> Medium/low devotion leads to medium/low realization;
> So one must cultivate and preserve sufficient devotion.

Your level of realization depends on the level of your devotion. Among all the factors that lead to enlightenment, blessings from a teacher play the most important role. The more devotion we have toward the teacher, the more blessings we receive from the teacher, and the more realization we attain. We should always pray to the teacher wholeheartedly. Devotion to a teacher is the essential path to enlightenment. It is far more profound and enriching than any personality cult.

A Novice Should Not See the Teacher as the Buddha

Many Buddhist texts[16] say that Dharma students should have such fervent devotion that they see the teacher as the Buddha, namely, as a fully enlightened being. In fact, this teaching does not appear in all Buddhist texts, but mostly within the scriptures of the highest yoga tantra. According to the tantric view, the mind of a qualified teacher is no different from the Buddha's mind, and the teacher's nature embodies the nature of all buddhas and bodhisattvas. To skillfully guide living beings on the path, this supreme teacher looks no different from a worldly person, but ultimately their mind is always aligned with the Buddha's. As Jigme Lingpa said in *Treasury of Precious Qualities:*

> But teachers who are rich with every perfect quality,
> Who from the sphere of all the Buddhas' primal wisdom and
>   compassion
> Come in human form to worlds where there are beings to be
>   trained—
> Such teachers are the supreme root of all accomplishments.

In the tantric practice of guru yoga, you imagine your being is non-dual with the teacher's wisdom mind. You see the teacher as the Buddha and all sentient beings, yourself included, as buddhas. Bring to mind the qualities and blessings in the guru's body, speech, and mind and imagine they have merged with your own body, speech, and mind. This seeing corresponds to the pure perception cultivated through the skillful means of Vajrayana, where everything is perceived and experienced purely in its true nature.[17]

I strongly suggest that novice Buddhists should NOT try to see the teacher as the Buddha when they first embark on the path. This is very important because most ordinary people lack the required levels of diligence, devotion, and faculties to correctly see the teacher as the Buddha; they are unlike Milarepa, Sadaprarudita, or the eighty-four Mahasiddhas of India, whose supreme faculties allowed them to generate fervent devotion toward their spiritual teachers almost immediately.

When we first start following a qualified teacher, it is better to take the teacher as a friend, coach, or supervisor. If at a certain point the teacher appears to act inappropriately, a novice Buddhist won't feel betrayed and even quit the path because they know that a friend or coach is not immune to making mistakes.

Without sufficient examination of the teacher and cultivation of pure perception, a disciple could start by seeing the teacher as the Buddha but end by seeing the teacher as a demon. The qualified teacher bears some responsibility if this happens. It can be avoided if the teacher uses the Buddha's teachings to adequately prepare disciples for pure perception.

Respect Other Followers of the Teacher

The sangha plays a crucial support role on our Dharma path. Therefore, it is important that sangha members help one another. The most important support is not financial but helping people enter the Dharma door and reinforcing their faith in the Dharma. For example, while practicing the demanding preliminary practices (ngöndro) of Vajrayana Buddhism, some Dharma students need others to push them to finish, lest those students procrastinate and give up. We should also respect the teacher's entourage and our Dharma peers, especially our vajra brothers and sisters. No matter how much time we spend with our peers, we should never feel wearied or irritated by them. Patrul Rinpoche used three similes to explain how a Dharma student should approach Dharma peers. Here are detailed explanations of the three:

Be Like a Belt

A good Dharma student should be easy to be with, like a belt. When wearing traditional Tibetan clothing as well as monastic wear, a belt is a must. I have been using the same belt every day for more than a dozen years. It never happens that I use the belt today and discard it the next day.

We should refrain from loving new friends and loathing old ones. Some people treat their Dharma peers the same way they do teachers—they are on good terms with a Dharma friend today but will discard that person rather quickly. They do not treat Dharma peers like they treat their belts. Instead, they treat them like toilet paper. How very sad.

Be Like Salt

In our daily lives no matter what we are experiencing, we should swallow our self-importance and get along with others. We should mix easily with others like salt in food. Whichever meal we prepare, be it veggie stir-fry, quiche, or ratatouille, a pinch of salt is always necessary. Salt easily mixes with any food.

Similarly, some Dharma students are comfortable with any assigned task. They have a can-do attitude and always get along with people around them. The great Jigme Phuntsok Rinpoche told us many times, "If one cannot be a good person, one can never become a Buddha." According to Jigme

Phuntsok Rinpoche, one of the very important characters for being a good person is to "always be in harmony with friends in attitude and deeds," as said in his vajra song called *The Song of Victory*.

Be Like a Pillar

We should be ready to bear anything untiringly, like a pillar. There are occasions when people speak harshly to us for no reason, or when we have to assume greater responsibility. No matter how heavy a roof, strong pillars will always bear the weight and support the whole building.

In summary, when following teachers, good students should also respect their peers and act like a belt, salt, and pillar. Students should avoid being like chili peppers who don't get along easily with others and often scare people away, or like spiky trees who hurt others' feelings with cutting and intimidating remarks. To successfully uphold the teacher's Dharma activities, disciples should act in solidarity and harmony.

HOW TO EMULATE THE TEACHER'S REALIZATION AND ACTIONS

It says in *Treasury of Precious Qualities*:

> In the beginning, skillfully examine the teacher;
> In the middle, skillfully follow him;
> In the end, skillfully emulate his realization and action.
> A disciple who does that is on the authentic path.

I will briefly explain how to emulate teachers' realization and actions— by carefully examining the way they behave and doing exactly as they do.

Patrul Rinpoche said the practice of Dharma is to imitate the buddhas and bodhisattvas of the past. Imitation leads to perfect actions, so when disciples follow teachers, they are assimilating these teachers' realization and way of behaving. Whenever your teacher is engaging in Dharma activities, make sure you try your best to participate through offering materials, time, and expertise, or just rejoicing in the teacher's actions.

This participation, according to Patrul Rinpoche, will bring you as much merit as springs from your teacher's own unsurpassable intention. Make sure you do whatever the qualified teacher suggests, without ever feeling bored or tired.

As Patrul Rinpoche said, disciples should be like molded clay votive tablets (*tsa-tsa*)—made from the "mold of the teacher." Just as tsa-tsas faithfully reproduce all the patterns engraved on the mold, disciples should make sure they acquire qualities identical with, or at least very close to, those of their teacher. If the teacher demonstrates wisdom and compassion like that of the Buddha, yet the disciples demonstrate none of those qualities or even have many unwholesome qualities, they cannot be considered the teacher's disciples.

Faith and Devotion

As Dharma students learn to be like their teachers through assimilating their realization and actions, it is very important that the disciples have strong faith and fervent devotion toward the teachers. Once Dharma students have strong faith in the teacher, guru devotion will arise naturally; with this devotion, precious qualities in the guru's wisdom mind also will arise in the student's mind naturally. As shown in the biographies and stories of past eminent masters, such as Sadaprarudita following Dharmodgata and Naropa following Tilopa, success in fulfilling the path to enlightenment depends upon great faith and devotion.

When following qualified teachers, Dharma students should pray to them fervently with great faith and devotion. Praying to teachers is very important. If Dharma students pray often and visualize all the qualities of their teachers merging into their own mind, as in the practice of guru yoga, gradually their mind will be tamed and transformed. Whatever Dharma students do, it is always beneficial to ask teachers for advice. The student should put into practice whatever the teacher suggests and rely on the teacher totally, as mentioned in the *Sutra of Skillful Veneration*:

> The teacher doesn't ask, do not speak out;
> Whenever the teacher gives instructions, do not disobey.

If a Dharma student does whatever the teacher says, without feeling bored or tired, with this fervent faith and devotion this student can surely attain all the great qualities from the qualified teacher, just like the contents of one pot being poured into another. This is possible even if the student receives the teacher's instruction once. Here is a story I'd like to share with you:

Once, when Katok Dampa Deshek (1122–1192), a well-known Tibetan master of the twelfth century, was bestowing a high-level empowerment, three beggar-like Dharma practitioners in shabby clothes arrived. The monastery was so crowded that even the rooftop was full of people. There was not even a niche left for a newcomer. Since they were late and couldn't squeeze in the monastery, they had no choice but to climb onto the highest branch of a nearby tree, looking in the direction of the monastery, and receiving the empowerment and the teaching from Dampa Deshek. All three of them had fervent faith and devotion toward the teacher. After the empowerment, none of the audience members sitting inside the monastery awakened, but these three practitioners attained realization.

As long as a Dharma student has faith and devotion, that person can receive great benefit from hearing the Dharma even though the student sits far away on top of a tree. Without faith and devotion that student can barely receive the benefit of the Dharma, no matter how close the student is to the teacher physically.

Mind-to-Mind Transmission

The goal of following a qualified teacher is to obtain the great qualities of their wisdom mind. Particularly in the highest teachings such as the Great Perfection, great emphasis is placed on mind-to-mind transmission. There are two ways to attain the wisdom mind of the teacher. One is through systematic studies of the Dharma: a student follows the teacher properly and studies the Buddha's teachings with the teacher's guidance. The other is primarily through faith and devotion. The teacher's blessings enter the student's mind through the student's earnest prayer, veneration, and devotion, and by personally serving the teacher. In the second way, all the precious qualities in the teacher's mind merge completely with the student's mind, like the contents of one vessel pouring entirely into another, so the student receives the authentic blessings of the teacher's wisdom.

The second way also includes the practice of guru yoga, in which you cultivate faith and devotion through bringing to mind the presence of the guru. You should end each session of guru yoga by abiding in the state where your mind completely merges with the wisdom mind of the guru. If it is too challenging for you to abide in such a state, you may think, "Whatever I think and whatever I perceive is my guru's very essence." In a nutshell, whenever you think of the guru, this thought itself is the very essence of the guru's wisdom mind.

In my own case, I often chant prayers to my root guru, the great Jigme Phuntsok Rinpoche:

> In the pure realm of the great sacred site, the Five-Peaked Mountain,
> The blessings of Mañjuśrī's wisdom ripened in your mind.
> Jigme Phuntsok, at your feet I pray!
> Inspire me with your blessings: transmit the realization of the wisdom-mind lineage![18]

Whenever I chant my root guru's name, "Jigme Phuntsok," I feel the supreme power of his blessing, which is incomparable to any mantra. Whenever I chant this prayer for dispelling obstacles or for abiding in the nature of mind, the experience is inconceivable and beyond any verbal expression. This is a sign of receiving the teacher's blessing.

In addition to the outer guru—the qualified teacher we follow—Buddhist texts such as the *Prajnaparamita Sutra* and the *Ornament of Clear Realization* also talk about the inner guru, which refers to the view of emptiness and the great compassion. According to Vajrayana teachings when a Dharma practitioner merges their mind completely with the guru's mind, this state is the ultimate guru, or *rigpa*—the innermost nature of the mind. When we receive all the blessings of the guru, our mind is inseparable from the guru's wisdom mind. Then we are able to spontaneously benefit innumerable living beings.

Whether we successfully attain this state of realization or not primarily depends upon ourselves. If a disciple never puts the teachings into practice, however great the teacher is, the disciple can barely attain any state of realization. Devadatta and Sunaksatra failed to attain enlightenment when following Shakyamuni Buddha because of their lack of faith and internalization of the teachings. To attain realization a disciple must follow the teacher's instructions and guidance and practice the Dharma with diligence and devotion.

When we eventually attain higher levels of realization, we can live unfettered by fear of life and death, as the great Jigme Phuntsok Rinpoche expressed in his vajra song entitled *A Yogi's Song of Happiness*:

> In life, I am joyful because I serve the teachings and beings.
> In death, I shall be joyful too, as I shall surely go to a Pure Land;
> So whatever karmic experience arises, whether positive or
>   negative,
> I have let go of mental agitation based on hopes and fears![19]

8. HEARING, CONTEMPLATION, AND MEDITATION

How to Study and Practice the Dharma

NOW THAT WE know how to examine and follow a qualified teacher, the next question is how to study and practice the Dharma. The answer is that we need three ways of developing wisdom: hearing, contemplating, and meditating.

To develop wisdom from hearing, we listen to teachings from qualified teachers or study sutras, shastras, and tantras. During contemplation, we process and reflect upon content learned during the hearing stage, so that we achieve an embodied understanding. For the third kind of wisdom, we gain practical experience of what we have understood through meditation, so that certainty is born from within.

Through proper hearing, contemplating, and meditating, we can generate the wisdom of hearing, the wisdom of contemplation, and the wisdom of meditation, which enable us to recognize, control, and uproot our afflictions, respectively. Among them there exists a causal relationship, that is, the wisdom of meditation arises from the wisdom of contemplation, which arises from the wisdom of hearing.

Without wisdom of hearing and contemplation, there can be no wisdom of meditation; hence, no enlightenment is possible. Thus, a Dharma practitioner aspiring to attain buddhahood cannot skip or shortchange any of the three.

My root guru the great Jigme Phuntsok Rinpoche always told us: "Nothing in Buddhism outweighs the importance of hearing, contemplation, and meditation." In *The Heart Essence: My Heart's Advice,* Jigme Phuntsok Rinpoche stressed that hearing, contemplation, and meditation are the essence of Buddhism. "Without them," Jigme Phuntsok Rinpoche said, "Dharma cannot penetrate our hearts and minds."

According to Jigme Phuntsok Rinpoche's legacy, a new refuge-vow taker or a novice Buddhist practitioner should not engage in intensive meditation practice right away. Instead, they should first conscientiously take time to hear and contemplate the Dharma. In particular, they should practice preliminary practices (ngöndro) if they aim to take the tantric path, and study the *Five Great Treatises*[1] when applicable. It is not until these stages are finished that a Dharma practitioner may take a further step to engage in intensive meditation practice as one does in a solitary retreat. By then, the meditation practice will be able to disclose its heart essence. Otherwise, it can be very harmful to go straight to meditation practice without establishing a solid foundation through hearing and contemplation.

BUDDHISTS AND THEIR DHARMA TRAININGS

Status Quo

To truly accept Buddhism, you need both an open-minded attitude and the wisdom developed through hearing, contemplation, and meditation. Given my encounter with Buddhists from both the West and the East, I've noticed there exist some differences between the two groups. I don't mean to make sweeping generalizations here. My goal is just to give all of us food for thought.

I've noticed that some people, especially Westerners, who frequent Dharma centers are mostly interested in meditation, and less interested in systematically hearing and contemplating the Sutrayana and Vajrayana teachings. If someone isn't interested in the Dharma and isn't motivated to get out of the mire of samsara to enlightenment, but simply considers meditation a way to calm the mind, then not hearing and contemplating the Dharma is fine. But anyone seeking liberation must start with hearing Dharma teachings. This is similar to the study of worldly knowledge. If one wants to become a competent researcher in physics, chemistry, or biology, one should first listen to the teachings from a professor. Without this, one may deviate from the right path of knowledge.

The Western Buddhists I've met seem to have steady personalities, and many have been following their teachers for ten, twenty, thirty, or even forty years. Despite these years some of them lack significant training in the foundations of Buddhism—few have finished all the studies of the Five Great Treatises or repeated several times the whole cycle of *ngöndro*.

Except when they're also Buddhist academics, some Western Buddhists I know are reluctant to systematically hear and contemplate the Dharma. They are usually very rational and science-driven, so it is hard for them to accept some Buddhist teachings. Yet they also seem unwilling to utilize systematic study to clarify their doubts and suspicions about the Dharma.

Buddhism has its own unique study system. Therefore, those studying the Dharma should refrain from falling into the trap of a scientific, materialistic, and inflexible attitude, and should instead cultivate open-mindedness.

Many Eastern Buddhists are willing to take time to delve into hearing and contemplating, but they need to apply themselves more to meditation. It would be a great pity for these practitioners to die without developing meditative practices, although they have been hearing Buddhist teachings for their entire lives.

Compared to their Western counterparts, it seems to be easier for many Eastern Buddhists to accept the Buddha's teachings. Some Eastern Buddhists easily generate faith when they first encounter the Dharma and enthusiastically start their practice and study, but their faith proves transitory as their enthusiasm dissipates over time. In my view, this wavering faith is the weakness of some Eastern Buddhists. They can be less steady than some of their Western counterparts, who rely on a teacher or stay in a Dharma center for many years.

Buddhists should aim for a lifetime of steady study and practice. Going to this Dharma center today and that center tomorrow and following this teacher today and that teacher tomorrow renders little benefit for real progress in practitioners' studying and practicing the Dharma in this life.

Retreat

Buddhists with an interest in meditation often like the idea of taking a "retreat" to engage in intensive meditation practice. An authentic Buddhist retreat must involve practices that lead to liberation from the cycles of rebirth and thus toward attaining enlightenment. After engaging in an adequate level of hearing and contemplation, Buddhists in retreat know that they can find the best solutions to their own liberation from texts[2] written by learned masters that cover all possible situations one might encounter during a solitary retreat.

Beginning practitioners must be careful because, owing to their limited hearing and contemplation of the Dharma, they might be easily persuaded to join a "retreat" program that will not facilitate real progress on their spiritual path. People often seek things that are of little value but expensive and forego things that are of great value and possibly even free. I noticed that there are some "teachers" or "counselors" who mix up yoga and solitary retreat, packaging them into an efficient moneymaking program. Some of these retreat counselors might not have enough personal retreat experience based on rigorous training in Dharma, or may have never even been a practitioner. They give eager attendees gibberish instructions such as "your consciousness should go up . . . then go down . . . and now please relax your mind. . . ." It only sounds like meditation guidance, but the attendees blindly follow the counselor: "Ah! I am up now; Ah! I am down; Ah! So, this is it. . . ." Alas! Then, the counselor announces, "Now that you've reached the required state, I am going to give you the highest teaching tomorrow. Since the program is so packed, tomorrow's teaching will be charged at a premium price. No worries, your practice itself is fine!" For example, there exists some sort of "fasting" retreat that claims to help detox the body and destress the mind. A seven-day retreat would charge US$1,200 for no eating in a week. But one could simply fast at one's own home, free of charge. There is also a costly "solitary dark retreat." Traditionally, the Buddhist dark retreat is a restricted practice only for advanced practitioners under appropriate spiritual guidance. In the popularized version of the so-called dark retreat, attendees enter a room completely absent of light and stay inside alone for seven or twenty-one days. In some cases, the retreatants don't receive any practical guidance, so they may do whatever they like, including sleeping longer hours and partying in the mind. How does this experience differ from staying in a dark solo prison cell? Some retreatants find the retreat offers a spa-like experience for the mind, protected from the stressors of daily life, while others may have gained deeper insight. I was told that many people were looking forward to the dark retreat, and some were even put on a waiting list for years.

If you were or are one of the attendees of one of these so-called retreats, you may feel a bit offended or embarrassed reading my comments. But many of these retreat programs have zero connection with renunciation, bodhichitta, and non-dual transcendental wisdom—the objectives of an authentic Buddhist retreat. To just suppress discursive thoughts or have a spa-like experience in the mind is not the real purpose to engage in a retreat. Patrul

Rinpoche exclaimed, "When practicing without renunciation and bodhi-chitta, even if one has remained in a retreat for nine years, nothing will be attained, not even a seed of liberation being sown." So, I seriously doubt whether some of those abovementioned retreat programs are worthwhile for the attendees!

With a solid foundation built through hearing and contemplation, a retreat practice is not difficult at all. In so doing, we can practice meditation on our own. It is not wise to overly depend on a guru or a meditation center for constant guidance. I feel so sad when I see Buddhists go to completely unknown centers and blindly participate in so-called retreats. I wish they had carefully scrutinized the retreat programs before making any decision. That said, if the centers are indeed of help to their spiritual practice, it's totally fine wherever they go. Keep in mind that paid retreat programs are not the only option.

Empowerment

For practitioners who want to enter the tantric path, it is essential to receive empowerments. Those who've completed *ngöndro* must receive an empowerment to proceed to receive tantric teachings of the main practices such as the Great Perfection. It is said in a tantra:

> In Vajrayana, there can be no accomplishment without
> empowerment,
> For that would be like a boatman without oars.

Some Buddhists, especially those from the East, like receiving empowerments (Skt. *abhisheka*; Tib. *wang*). It is indeed extremely fortunate if you can receive an empowerment from a qualified vajra teacher, as stated in a verse quoted by Patrul Rinpoche in *The Words of My Perfect Teacher*:

> To rule over the universe
> Is nothing compared to receiving a tantric empowerment.[3]

Empowerment has two meanings. The first one is "pouring," which refers to pouring a special blessing that brings to maturity the capability for enlightenment to arise. Our inherent buddha-nature can be discovered, but without us receiving the "pouring"—a sort of power—and with us just relying on our own capacity, it is hard for us to discover the primordial state that is present within us from the very beginning. In the course of "pouring," our dormant buddha-nature is awakened, in the same way that watering activates a seed's innate sprouting capacity.

The second meaning of empowerment is "dismantling," which refers to dismantling obscurations that prevent us from discovering our buddha-nature, including our karmic obscurations, emotional obscurations, cognitive obscurations, and obscurations of habitual tendencies. This "dismantling" enables the activation of our ever-increasing wisdom.

Empowerment produces special transformative effects in the mindstream of the recipients. So, it is understandable that some Buddhists like to receive empowerments. However, without adequately hearing the Dharma, contemplating the teachings, and engaging in preliminary practices, a recipient might not be well prepared for fully receiving the empowerment. As a result, such a Buddhist attending an empowerment ritual might simply follow the formality without understanding its heart essence and thus not really be empowered to follow a particular tantric practice.

Has any practitioner attained enlightenment solely through receiving empowerments? The answer is yes. There are some practitioners with the sharpest faculties who, because of their faith and devotion as well as blessings from their gurus, swiftly recognized the nature of mind during an empowerment. Such swift realization occurred in the past and present, so empowerment itself does carry supreme blessing power. Yet, after receiving an empowerment, you need to start the corresponding tantric practice. This practice requires the foundations of a good understanding of tantric doctrines and the preliminary practices, followed by applying these tantric doctrines to real practice.

Hearing

Great Buddhist masters are unanimous that hearing and contemplation are essential before the main practice of meditation. The *Sutra of the Right Mindfulness of Dharma* has covered extensively the benefits of hearing the Dharma. For example, the sutra states: "Because of hearing the Dharma, one's mind can be tamed."

People who haven't heard or internalized the Dharma will still be engaged with the afflictions of desire, aversion, and ignorance, making it harder for them to enter the path of transcendent liberation. Thus, it is very important that we start by hearing the Dharma. Through hearing and understanding the Buddha's teachings taught by a qualified teacher, we can recognize the afflictions that, otherwise, are undetected or even mistakenly considered favorable.

Identifying the problem is the first step in solving any problem. The cause that keeps us trapped in the mire of samsara is the three poisons—the afflictions of desire, aversion, and ignorance. The problem is that very often we don't recognize that the three poisons are the root of suffering. Hearing the Dharma allows us to pinpoint the problem—this is the wisdom of hearing.

Sakya Pandita Kunga Gyeltsen (1182–1251) once said that a practitioner who meditates without hearing teachings might gain some experience, but the experience will soon dissipate. Nowadays some teachers, including achieved masters, don't put special emphasis on hearing and contemplation during their teachings. Instead, they teach more advanced meditation techniques and the main practice right away. This might be their skillful means of attracting people to the Dharma path, but without a solid foundation the disciples' practice may eventually collapse into ruin.

At the very beginning of my Buddhist training at Larung Gar, I was taught: "One should hear the teachings broadly, then contemplate over and over again, and in the end meditate day and night."

In many legendary enlightenment stories still told today, Tibetan yogis seemed to start solitary retreat without receiving any formal teachings. While nobody can deny these stories, most of us don't have faculties as sharp as those yogis had. For us, the most reliable and safest approach is to follow the sequential order that I was told at Larung Gar.

As told by some Buddhist masters, when we first encounter Dharma the Buddha is as close as our own heart, but by the tenth year the Buddha can be as distant as the horizon. This fading is common among Buddhist practitioners lacking systematic study and practice. If we start to systematically study the Dharma in the first year, then ten years later our faith will have become very steady, and we will never regress.

In Tibetan Buddhist tradition, higher-level meditation practice requires very solid foundations built from hearing and contemplation.[4] One can practice meditation safely and surely only with well-established foundations. Longchenpa said in the *Treasury of Word and Meaning*: "The primordial purity of mind's original nature in the Great Perfection can only be realized by those who have sufficient hearing and contemplation."

Hearing Is a Must

Nowadays it is very rare to find someone like Huineng, the Sixth Patriarch (638–713), or Jetsun Milarepa, both of whom had extremely sharp faculties. Neither of them heard teachings extensively, but they attained enlightenment after receiving their gurus' supreme blessings. We modern practitioners normally don't have such sharp faculties. Worse yet, we are often preoccupied with conceptual thoughts that tightly block us from recognizing the nature of mind. To dissolve those conceptual thoughts we must systematically study the corresponding doctrines in Buddhism.

Many Buddhists wonder whether hearing the Dharma will reinforce their conceptual thoughts. The answer is definitely not. When done properly, hearing won't backfire. The meanings of the Buddha's words cannot be compared to the conceptual thoughts of a worldly person. The Buddha always spoke from his wisdom, which means his words never increase obscurations or defilements.

What about the words of the great masters after Shakyamuni Buddha, such as Nagarjuna, Vasubandhu, Asanga (c. 300–c.370), Ashvaghosha (c. 80–c.150), and Xuanzang (602–664)? It's equally impossible that the words of such great masters would backfire. Owing to their great compassion and wisdom, whatever these masters said—even their jokes—are beneficial and counter the conceptual thoughts of deluded beings.

Our right views are largely established through hearing the Dharma. When we were born, were we able to hold correct Buddhist views? Definitely not. Except for a few reincarnated spiritual children who can recall their past lives, ordinary people don't have any worldly knowledge when they are born, let alone knowledge of the Dharma. Ordinary people begin to generate right views in their mind-stream only after listening to Dharma teachings from qualified teachers.

The world is filled with areas of study and knowledge, among which we are fortunate enough to have encountered the Dharma. This is surely due to good karma from our past lives. Each time I visit a bookstore and see piles of books from different disciplines, I feel so lucky to be able to study the Dharma. I think there must exist a supreme cause and condition, otherwise how could I have encountered the great Dharma amid the vast ocean of knowledge?

How to Hear Properly

The opportunity to hear and practice the Dharma is rare. When listening to the Dharma, we should meticulously concentrate on the teachings. The Indian sage Padampa Sangye (d. 1117) said, "Listen to the teachings like a deer listening to music." When a deer hears the sound of a veena, an ancient Indian musical instrument, it stops moving and becomes deeply entranced by the music, noticing nothing else. We should behave like such a deer when hearing the Dharma.

Moreover, we should listen to the teachings of a sutra or a shastra entirely, from the beginning until the end. Some Buddhists don't act like this. Without any scrutiny of the teacher, they join a teaching carelessly. They sometimes discontinue following one teaching to follow another, sampling teachings here and there, the opposite of Padampa Sangye's suggestion.

Some Buddhists complain that listening to teachings takes too much time and will slow the progress of their Dharma practice. While systematically listening to teachings may seem slow at first, ultimately it speeds realization. Whereas starting immediately with meditation practice may seem like the faster way, this so-called practice often quickly collapses into failure. This is easy to understand. To master worldly knowledge, we start by listening to instructions. From kindergarten through elementary and secondary school to an undergraduate program and then graduate school for a master's or doctorate—the whole process is centered on "listening and study." Given that one must spend up to twenty years in the worldly educational system, it seems ridiculous that one might skip hearing the Dharma teachings, which are much more profound than worldly knowledge, and dive directly into the main practice of meditation.

How Long Should the Engagement of Hearing Be?

Hearing is a lifelong engagement. In the *Sutra of the Right Mindfulness of Dharma*, the Buddha said: "Therefore, a wise man should always listen to the Dharma as long as he is alive."

Sakya Pandita also stressed the importance of lifelong hearing in his *Precious Treasury of Elegant Sayings*:

> Knowing tomorrow brings another death,
> Today one must learn even if wisdom does not arise in this life,

By entrusting in future lives,
Just as one obtains wealth.

Even practitioners expecting to die tomorrow should study the Dharma today. While such practitioners may not attain wisdom in this life, when studying Dharma again in the next life, they will more easily grasp the teachings and be able to retrieve what they've deposited in the mind.

Some Dharma students left Larung Gar after listening to my teachings on just one shastra. When I asked about them, their peers told me they were in a solitary retreat somewhere. "I've already listened to the teachings of one shastra! That is enough for me," said some. "Now it is time to focus on the meditation!" Sadly, this is not uncommon. These days many Buddhists enter retreat after receiving a few teachings. At least the Dharma students who left Larung Gar have heard one shastra. Others don't listen to any teachings at all and go straight to a solitary retreat. This doesn't make sense to me. One verse from the *Flower Ornament Sutra* addresses this point:

When pursuing the Dharma,
[The practitioner] shall be more and more diligent,
Listen to teachings day and night,
And never grow weary of hearing.

Many great masters share the same opinion on hearing the Dharma. For example, Sakya Pandita said:

It is not by rivers that the ocean is quenched.
It is not by wealth that the king's treasury is satisfied.
One is not satisfied by the enjoyment of sensual pleasures.
The wise are not satisfied by eloquent sayings.

The verse says a wise person can always absorb and master more Dharma teachings, just as an ocean can always absorb more water. Many Buddhists don't recognize the importance of hearing the Dharma, so they flip through Buddhist texts once and claim they understand everything.

Buddhist studies are not like academic coursework, in which second-year students don't have to revisit first-year courses. Many great masters and achieved practitioners practice for their entire lives one or more of the four common preliminaries, such as the impermanence of life or the defects of samsara, and never stop revisiting them in a similar way that worldly professions require annual recertification and continuing education.

Patrul Rinpoche, a master who had already attained great wisdom, still chose to hear twenty-five times the teaching of the preliminary practices of the *Longchen Nyingtik—The Heart-Essence of the Vast Expanse*, a spiritual treasure discovered by Jigme Lingpa—while sitting before his root guru Jigme Gyalwai Nyugu (1765–1843). *The Words of My Perfect Teacher* is a completely faithful written record of the oral teachings Patrul Rinpoche received directly from Jigme Gyalwai Nyugu.

It's worth repeating that hearing and contemplation should be a lifelong endeavor. Some Dharma students start hearing devotedly, then gradually become indifferent and eventually weary. They start by frequently attending Dharma classes, dwindling to periodic appearances until they vanish completely.

We should meet the standard set by the great masters of the past, who spent many years hearing, contemplating, and meditating. Let me share my personal experience of listening to the teachings at Larung Gar. I don't say this out of self-praise, but from 1985 when I started to follow my root guru the great Jigme Phuntsok Rinpoche, I never missed any of his teachings without a reason, right up to his parinirvana in early 2004. During my early years at Larung Gar, I often stayed up late to study the Dharma, so a few times I felt sleepy in class and struggled to concentrate. Other than that, I always came to the Dharma hall for his teachings and listened attentively. At one point Jigme Phuntsok Rinpoche set up an internal radio system so Dharma students could listen to the teachings in their dwellings. While this was far more convenient and comfortable—no excursion of climbing up and down the Larung valley to the Dharma hall anymore—I still chose to listen in the Dharma hall, where I could see my guru in person. Not once did I listen to my guru's teachings by radio at home. I deeply felt how precious it was to have encountered my guru and the Dharma, and I deeply venerated him.

What to Hear

It is not easy to find a Buddhist who has listened to Dharma teachings for twenty or thirty years. But real bodhisattvas persevere by listening to the Dharma, appreciating the Dharma, loving the Dharma, following the Dharma, and practicing the Dharma, as described in the *Flower Ornament*

Sutra. Shakyamuni Buddha, in his previous lives before he awakened, was willing to sacrifice his life to receive the teaching of just one verse. Nowadays we don't have to risk our lives in the same manner. Why are we so reluctant to hear the teachings?

Of course, hearing the Dharma doesn't mean one randomly picks up any sutra or shastra to start with. We must follow a sequential order along the path to enlightenment, not neglecting the foundations or preliminary practices. We cannot choose to start from the highest teachings right away. According to the legacy of the great Jigme Phuntsok Rinpoche, as indicated in *The Song of Victory*, one should start by building virtuous characteristics, followed by arousing renunciation, then generating bodhichitta, and lastly attaining non-dual wisdom.

The hearing should follow this sequential order accordingly. I often suggest lay practitioners first study Mipham Rinpoche's *The Way of Living: The Precious Jewel That Attracts Divinity and Excellence*, a great teaching on how to be a good person. They then build their foundations through studying texts such as *The Way of the Bodhisattva* and *The Words of My Perfect Teacher*, which prepare them for advancing further on the path. In the meantime, they practice *ngöndro*, which consists of the common preliminary practices—the analytical meditations on the four thoughts that turn the mind away from samsara, and the uncommon preliminary practices—taking refuge, generating bodhichitta, meditating and reciting on Vajrasattva, mandala offering, and guru yoga. Only after these foundations are well established, will they start Vajrayana studies and main practices.

Dharma practitioners with few conceptual thoughts, who hold strong devotion toward Vajrayana and the guru, may not have to broadly study. After finishing *ngöndro* they can start Vajrayana practice right away. However, in this degenerate era most Dharma practitioners are laden with various discursive thoughts. Therefore, it's better that they study the Five Great Treatises to eliminate discursive thoughts and "unlearn" their conceptual thoughts. With this foundation, they then can more effectively practice Vajrayana to attain buddhahood in this very life.

Contemplation

Once we've heard the teachings, it's not enough to intellectually understand the words in the Buddhist texts and commentaries. In addition, as Patrul Rinpoche said in *The Words of My Perfect Teacher*, we need to internalize the knowledge. We need to review the teachings back and forth in our minds, clearly establishing the meaning through reflection, examination, and analysis, asking questions about what we do not understand.

Our habitual tendencies and karmic obstacles stemming from ignorance—the main obstacles to our liberation—are deeply rooted since beginningless time. This rootedness is so deep that it's hardly possible to uproot these obstacles simply by hearing the teachings every now and then. A Dharma student once said to me, "I have been hearing the teachings for almost seven months; why do I still have conceptual, clinging, and discursive thoughts?" Seven months—not to mention seven years—of listening to teachings may not result in the needed changes if one doesn't contemplate and meditate deeply.

When contemplating the Dharma, it is not enough to make believe we understand the teachings. We must master the subjects with solid and accurate understanding so that the wisdom of contemplation will arise. Then when the time is right to practice in solitude, we will be able to manage on our own, without needing anyone to clarify anything. The *Commentary on the Flower Ornament Sutra* says: "The wisdom derived from reflection is the great wisdom, because it arises through logical reasoning, so one becomes absolutely sure about its meaning."

To generate such wisdom, in addition to individual contemplation, we should engage in group discussions and debates, take exams, and attend symposia. This means most Dharma practitioners will benefit from staying in the sangha during the stages of hearing and contemplation. It is very difficult to be a solo practitioner during the stages of hearing and contemplation; this is well illustrated by the simile of the solo yak.

Some Tibetan yaks retain traces of the wildness of their ancestors, which among other things means they like to wander off solo, beyond the control of their herders. Once separate from the herd, these yaks enjoy their freedom. However, this freedom also shortens their lives because eventually they're eaten by wolves. It is the same with people on the path. A solo practitioner who leaves the sangha early may fail to attain achievement regardless of hard practice because that person lacks the protection and support that the sangha brings.

Padampa Sangye said practitioners should contemplate the teachings "like a northern nomad shearing sheep." By this, he meant that after listening to teachings a practitioner should reflect upon them word by word, phrase by phrase, and sentence by sentence, leaving nothing out. This attention to detail parallels how nomads shear sheep. When spring arrives on the sparsely populated, high-altitude Tibetan Plateau, sheep start to shed their old wool and grow new. A nomad will then carefully shear off all the sheep's wool, leaving nothing untouched. In the same way, we should meticulously contemplate the teaching in its entirety, rejecting nothing.

It's said that the Dharma is like a piece of honeycomb; every bit of it is sweet, whether the sides, the middle, or the four corners. We should not be like Buddhists who think some parts of the teachings can be accepted, some rejected, and the rest put on hold. For example, after hearing teachings on the preciousness of human life we should reflect on each point and analogy, like the improbability of a blind turtle putting its head through a yoke floating on the ocean. In so doing we will internalize the teachings.

An example is the sequence of teachings that comprise the preliminary practices. These teachings allow us to contemplate starting from the preciousness of human life, followed by the impermanence of life, the defects of samsara, the principle of cause and effect, taking refuge, arousing bodhichitta, and so on. If we steadily practice in this sequential order, step by step, by the end when we receive the main teaching on the ultimate truth, we will be well prepared to recognize the luminous nature of mind, realize emptiness that is beyond mental fabrication, and eventually abide in the Great Perfection's non-duality of awareness and emptiness.

Thus, it is very important to contemplate the teachings thoroughly and extensively. If we fall asleep like a log after Dharma teachings, the teachings will benefit us little. In contrast, if we reflect on the teaching's meaning, and try our best to understand and digest the content, then this contemplation will change our mind and will also accumulate great merits. The Buddha addressed this in the *Jewel Rain Sutra* (*Ratnamegha Sutra*),[5] where he said, "An impeccable contemplation in itself is the offering to all the tathagatas."

Meditation

Once you establish the meaning of the teachings through contemplation, you may focus on meditation. The goal of meditation is to gain practical experience of what you have intellectually understood. As Patrul Rinpoche said in *The Words of My Perfect Teacher*, it is through meditation that true realization of the nature of mind eventually arises, without any mistake. Through meditation, certainty about *the natural state* will be born from within. We will be disentangled from the web of doubts and hesitations, and eventually recognize the true nature of everything. Attaining such wisdom through meditation is the resultant state of our Dharma practice.

The Importance of Meditation

If we rely on a teacher, listen to their teachings, and contemplate a bit but never meditate on them, we won't cut off our afflictions. It is like eating: watching others eat or hearing them slurp will not fill our stomachs. Without gaining practical experience of what you study through hearing and contemplation, the Dharma cannot turn your mind away from samsara. The Buddha uses several similes to address the importance of meditation in the *Flower Ornament Sutra*, saying that the person who is learned but doesn't practice the teaching is like the poor person who counts the treasures of the rich day and night but remains penniless; the sick doctor who gives prescriptions to patients but refuses to take medicine himself; the deaf person who plays a catchy melody but remains immune to sound. In the same manner, no matter how eloquent we are in talking about the Dharma, without practical experience through meditation, our suffering will remain. As Longchenpa urged:

> If realization does not dawn from within, dry explanation and theoretical understanding will not bring the fruit of awakening. To put it simply, unless we blend our own mind with the Dharma, it is pointless merely to adopt the guise of a practitioner.

At the end of our lives, nothing but the Dharma that we have practiced can be of help; without it we will find ourselves helpless on our deathbeds. Even if we verbally pray for the blessings of our teachers every day, we won't be able to eliminate the seeds of our afflictions without our own meditation practice. Thus, broadly compared to hearing and contemplation, meditation practice is more important because we all have to face our death sooner or later, and it is meditation practice that enables most of us to attain liberation at the moment of death. When the moment of death arrives, our fame, wealth, social status, friends, and other worldly achievements will not help us. None of them can accompany us into our future lives; they are all left behind. Consequently, as mentioned in chapter 7, we should always apply the four metaphors: "I am someone who is sick, the Dharma is the remedy, the teacher is a skillful doctor, and diligent practice is the way to recovery." If we don't meditate on the Dharma, we're like a patient surrounded by innumerable remedies who refuses to take them. The doctor knows what to prescribe to cure the patient's disease, but that's useless unless the patient takes the medicine. Meditation practice is a must to heal the sickness of samsara.

What to Expect

Some Buddhists have unrealistic expectations about meditation practice. They say, "I've received the highest empowerment and have been practicing for over a month; why haven't I attained any realization?" or "I received my ordination three years ago, but why do I still have desire? Is there something wrong with my meditation?" You need to recalibrate your expectations. Let me tell you why. Our afflictions and habitual tendencies are deeply rooted because we have been practicing them life after life in samsara. The time we practice the Dharma is far less than the time we have spent repeating the afflictions. Reversing our habitual tendencies is as difficult as recovering from a chronic disease. If a patient has been confined to bed rest for years, it's unlikely that one pill or injection will effect an immediate cure. Once when I was sick and hospitalized, my doctors told me they would give me injections three times daily plus intravenous therapy. I believed in my doctors and followed their instructions. Likewise the more Dharma remedy we receive and absorb, the more likely our psychological struggles will be cured.

Many people consider the Dharma a panacea, hoping their afflictions will vanish after one or two Dharma classes, or that they will achieve realization after receiving the guru's empowerment or blessings. Some even hope they will be transformed from ordinary practitioners into first-stage bodhisattvas simply by seeing their gurus. These thoughts may sound inspiring, but the Dharma doesn't work instantly like this. Without continuously drinking the Dharma nectar for a long time, most ordinary people will not achieve enlightenment quickly, if ever. Thus, we must come to the practical experience of meditation after hearing and contemplation. As Patrul Rinpoche said, "If you don't practice, what use are Buddhist texts at the time of your death?"

What Is Meditation?

I've noticed that some Buddhists primarily think of meditation as calm-abiding meditation. For them meditation means burning incense, sitting on a cushion, and looking like a quiet Buddha with thoughts stilled. But the truth is that meditation covers a much broader range than that. Generally speaking, there are two types of meditation: *shamatha* and *vipashyana*.

Shamatha, stabilizing meditation or concentration meditation, means one-pointed concentration on a chosen object. This reflects the fact that our minds are always distracted like restless monkeys, running ceaselessly after forms, sounds, smells, tastes, and sensations. Shamatha practice is to still an active mind and bring us calm.

Vipashyana, clear seeing or insight meditation, means developing deep insight into the true nature of all phenomena. It is the wisdom of seeing things in a direct and clear way, which can be classified into analytical meditation and settling meditation. Because our minds are filled with confused thoughts and beliefs, we need to deconstruct those thoughts and beliefs by employing vigorous reasoning and analytical methods, such as actively examining the concepts or emotions we cling to and questioning whether they ultimately exist or not. This is called analytical meditation. Whenever we reach a conclusion through analysis and reasoning—for example, impermanence or selflessness—we remain settled on that conclusion. Or if we achieve a certain level of realization on the genuine nature of reality, we rest our mind in that realization. This is called settling meditation.

Through these two types of practice, logic becomes more sustainable, and understanding gains force, eventually leading to wisdom, the direct cause of full enlightenment. As Nagarjuna said in his *Letter to a Friend*:

> Lacking wisdom, concentration fails,
> And without concentration, wisdom too.
> For someone who has both, samsara's sea
> Fills no more than the print left by a hoof.[6]

The capabilities and forms of meditation differ among worldly practitioners, Common Vehicle practitioners, and Mahayana practitioners. Especially for bodhisattvas, concentration yields abundant happiness for themselves and for others. Maitreya said in the *Ornament of the Great Vehicle Sutras*:

In the cases of worldly practitioners and Common Vehicle practitioners, their concentration yields little happiness and personal happiness, and these are subject to deterioration, exhaustion, and delusion. The case is the opposite for bodhisattvas.

Maitreya also said:

Endowed with meditative absorption, bodhisattvas practice all forms of concentration. Abiding in the highest bliss of meditation, they establish all beings in the three kinds of enlightenment. And since their concentration is embraced by the wisdom of emptiness, it remains inexhaustible in the world.

As we follow meditation instructions in a Mahayana context, we realize that everything in our lives is an opportunity to apply meditation practice to train our minds. We find a perfect way to integrate our practice into life and work and increasingly appreciate the amazing functions of the mind.

How to Meditate

Padampa Sangye said we should meditate "like a person unable to speak savoring food." Padampa Sangye's point is that when such a person tastes food and savors it, that person is absorbed and engrossed in the experience; they have a complete immersion in the mouth sensations but cannot verbally describe the flavors to others. In the same way, we should remain immersed in the course of meditation. By doing so, we are able to attain the direct experience and deeply understand why the taste of true meditation is beyond words.

For example, when we practice analytical meditation on the subject of "the precious human life," we won't gain any practical experience if we just sit on a cushion with eyes closed and think of nothing. Instead, we should immerse ourselves in the practical guidance of the lineage masters and concentrate our mind over and over again on the preciousness of our human life—with its many freedoms and advantages—until we gain conviction and experience. Until then, we finally start to taste the true flavor of the Dharma. As a result, we'll be more motivated to practice the Dharma with great diligence.

Practitioners should delve deeply into their practice. Serious practice of the common preliminaries such as "the precious human life" or "the principle of cause and effect," not to mention the more profound Mahamudra and the Great Perfection, will help us attain in-depth practical experience. It is through meditation practice that a practitioner can truly "own" the Dharma. Here is a story I want to share with you:

In the Buddha's age there were two bhikshus. One practiced meditation after fulfilling the stages of hearing and contemplation and thus achieved arhatship. The other focused on hearing and contemplation but paid no attention to meditation, and eventually became a renowned Tripitaka master owing to his broad knowledge of the canonical texts.

Once the Tripitaka master was about to challenge the arhat with a hard-to-answer question in public, so he could belittle the arhat and boost his own image. The Buddha was aware of the Tripitaka master's intention and wanted to protect him from the karma of such a wrongdoing, so he appeared and earnestly praised the arhat.

The puzzled disciples of the Tripitaka master asked among themselves why the Buddha had only praised the arhat, who knew so much less about the texts than their teacher. Knowing what they were thinking the Buddha said, "Your teacher is like a herder hired to tend the cattle; while the arhat is like the cattle's owner." From this, the disciples understood that meditation is indispensable.

Meditation in a Solitary Retreat

Practitioners who have attained the wisdom of hearing and contemplation are capable of solitary retreat. I oppose novice Buddhists entering solitary meditation retreat too early. I have encountered people who wanted to enter solitary retreat the day after taking refuge. A retreat initiated so precipitously is an empty exercise that brings little benefit to one's liberation from samsara. According to the legacy of my lineage masters, a practitioner should mainly focus on hearing and contemplating for five to ten years before going into a solitary retreat. It's true that some Buddhists, whether from old age or lack of foundational knowledge, may not be able to study the Five Great Treatises intensively. Nevertheless if causes and conditions permit, it is better that one finishes studying the Five Great Treatises before proceeding to Vajrayana's generation stage (Kyerim), completion stage (Dzogrim), and the Great Perfection (Dzogchen) in a solitary retreat.

Some Dharma students worry they won't know how to practice in a solitary retreat unless their teachers guide them in person. But if the teacher has already provided all necessary teachings during the hearing and contemplation stages, and the student has heard and contemplated those teachings, that student will manage on their own when entering the solitary retreat.

The Buddha said: "I have shown you the methods that lead to liberation. But you should know that liberation depends upon yourself." Even the Buddha didn't guide his disciples individually in their solitary retreat. He didn't say to the lead disciple Shariputra, "Let me meditate with you." The Buddha gave meditation instructions to his disciples, and they then knew what to do.

In a retreat, a practitioner can follow guides such as the 141 meditation practices[7] in Longchenpa's *Finding Comfort and Ease in the Nature of Mind*. The instructions cover the fundamental and essential meditation practices to attain the ultimate realization of the Great Perfection. Longchenpa said a diligent practitioner can achieve enlightenment after just six months of fulfilling these meditation instructions.

As early as 1992, some of my disciples started following Longchenpa's meditation instructions. In one of my teachings, I told the story of a Chinese *bhikshuni* at Larung Gar who attained enlightenment after six months of these practices. I have no doubt about her spiritual achievement.

In his *Treasury of Pith Instructions*, Longchenpa suggested six types[8] of retreat that a practitioner should establish:

1. *Outer retreat* is established when a retreatant stays in a place free of the stimuli that result in attachment, anger, and ignorance. Ordinary people are easily influenced by external stimuli such as interpersonal conflicts and hedonic experience, so it is good to distance oneself from these distractions.

2. *Inner retreat* is established when the retreatant neither amasses external wealth nor holds on to any internal desires. Whether it is their family and friends, or faithful devotees, the retreatant should cut off attachment to them and focus on the practice with great diligence. Through inner retreat, the retreatant reduces negative emotions such as desire, hatred, jealousy, and arrogance, and increases positive factors such as faith, devotion, compassion, wisdom, and bodhichitta.

3. After the outer and inner retreats are well established, it is time to establish a *secret retreat*, in which the retreatant recognizes that the nature of mind is free from any conceptual grasping and abides in the state of inseparable union of luminosity and emptiness. At this time, no matter what

kind of thoughts arise—be they negative or positive—the retreatant won't indulge them or reject them, but settle, without adulterating them, in the very mind where the thoughts arise.

Some meditation centers instruct their novice participants to remain in a state of thinking-of-nothing at the very beginning of their practice. This is a bit dangerous. Some of their participants have zero experience in meditation and in Buddhism at large, and even if they have some experience, they haven't done any preliminary practices. Asking these students to "think of nothing" or "just sit still" in meditation is therefore not a good idea because they haven't yet reached that level of preparation.

4. An *upper retreat* is established when the retreatant neither prays for clairvoyance, nor hopes to be blessed or foretold the future by deities. The retreatant just remains in the meditative state.

5. A *lower retreat* is established when the retreatant neither has concerns and doubts about the Buddha's teachings that they are practicing, nor is worried that demonic obscurations and sickness will arise. Thus, the retreatant isn't bounded by fear. During the meditation practice, the retreatant prays for blessings from their guru, the Three Jewels, and the Dharma protectors.

6. A *peripheral retreat* is established when the retreatant does not overly cling to their own practice. If good dreams or other auspicious signs appear, the retreatant won't feel ecstatic and think, "Bravo! I am close to enlightenment! My retreat practice is a great success!" When nightmares, physical health problems, bad moods, and loneliness emerge, the retreatant won't be too concerned.

Some people's moods swing like the unpredictable weather in spring. At one moment, their mood is high-spirited, and they seem happier than the laughing Buddha. The next moment their mood becomes downhearted, and they appear more miserable than hell beings. In fact, all phenomena, good or bad, are dreamlike and illusory. Understanding this is very important to our practice and daily life; we won't feel overly attached to anything, any event, or any person.

When examined from the viewpoint of the Middle Way and the Great Perfection, there is nothing for us to grasp on to because all phenomena have no substantial entity—they are empty at the ultimate level and dreamlike at the relative level. Knowing this, the retreatant will gain practical experience. This view is extremely important!

Some practitioners ask me, "Is my meditation retreat on the right track? Is there something wrong with my retreat?" How should we evaluate whether a meditation retreat is working or not? In his *Beacon of Certainty*, Mipham Rinpoche said that whether a practitioner has realized emptiness and attains the realization of *siddhis*[9] depends on whether he takes the principle of cause and effect seriously, as well as whether his afflictions are diminishing. You'll know the answer after checking your faith in the law of karma, and the intensity of your afflictions. If during or after retreat your compassion toward sentient beings is diminishing, your faith in the law of karma is wavering, your view on rebirth is sliding toward error, your devotion toward the guru is failing, your afflictions are increasing, and you're more easily angered, then something is very wrong with your meditation retreat. If your compassion is increasing, your faith in karma is growing, your afflictions are diminishing, and you're slower to anger, then something is going right.

To conclude, hearing, contemplation, and meditation are interconnected—they support and complement each other. Patrul Rinpoche quoted the peerless Dagpo Rinpoche (1079–1153) on this point in *The Words of My Perfect Teacher*. Dagpo Rinpoche said: "To churn together hearing, contemplation, and meditation on the Dharma is an infallible essential point."[10]

Hearing more teachings results in better understanding when contemplating, which in turn leads to more authentic experience during meditation. Thus, a solid basis in hearing and contemplation will help a practitioner eliminate afflictions and defilements, so their realization will steadily increase.

Eventually this will be, as Padampa Sangye described, "like the sun coming out from behind clouds." When the sun is out, its rays shine upon everything unstoppably. Likewise when true realization is attained, its precious qualities arise effortlessly.

9. THE GREAT PERFECTION

The Pinnacle of Nyingma's Vajrayana Practice

VAJRAYANA, also known as Tantrayana or Tantric Buddhism, offers simple and straightforward methods for swiftly eradicating the poisons of our very deep-rooted greed, anger, and ignorance. Lineage masters including Jigme Phuntsok Rinpoche, Penor Rinpoche (1932–2009), Dilgo Khyentse Rinpoche, and Kyabje Dudjom Rinpoche (1904–1987), all called Vajrayana a "shortcut" to enlightenment.

Pema Dündul (1816–1872), a vajra master who attained rainbow body—the level of realization in which his physical body dissolved into light—said about Vajrayana:

> The more dismal the darkness of the five degenerations is,
> The brighter the moon of Padmasambhava's blessings shines.

As our afflictions intensify when we move further into the degenerate age, Vajrayana's blessings grow in vibrancy because the more intense the affliction, the more powerful is its energy available to be transformed into enlightenment through Vajrayana practices. It's like when there's a lamp fire, a gale can easily blow it out, but when it's a wildfire, a gale can build it up until the fire burns over the whole forest. Vajrayana is the gale to the wildfire of our afflictions.

Drawn by this vibrancy more and more, people are developing strong commitments to Vajrayana. Western seekers immersed in quick-fix culture long for the most effective practices to promptly eradicate afflictions, and therefore many choose Vajrayana.

Tantric literature says Vajrayana encompasses all practices of the 84,000 teachings of the Buddha, and it can lead one to buddhahood in a single lifetime. For example, the *Collected Tantra of the Ultimate Meaning* says:

> Those who generate faith in this (Vajrayana) and uphold it
> Will receive the blessings from all the buddhas,
> Will attain the inexhaustible treasury of merits and virtues,
> Will obtain the fruition that would otherwise mature in the
> future within this life.

While it may take someone ten million eons to attain liberation from the cycle of rebirth by following the Sutrayana tradition, through the blessing of Vajrayana a person can fast-forward to enlightenment in this very life.

The view, meditation, action, and fruit of Vajrayana practice are incredibly profound. Even if you cannot completely assimilate tantric teachings, you can nevertheless accumulate inconceivable merit by trusting Vajrayana and accepting tantras and tantric rituals with veneration. The *Tantra of Vast Open Space* says:

> Whoever generates faith in Vajrayana
> that conveys the ultimate teachings,
> And further assimilates its doctrines,
> Even if he hasn't ever put it in the real practice,
> Not even as little as a particle of dust,
> The fruition he attains is buddhahood.

Therefore, "lazy" practitioners can still receive incomparable merit, just by receiving Vajrayana teachings and empowerments.

The Great Perfection (Dzogchen), the highest and innermost teaching of the Nyingma School, is the pinnacle of the Vajrayana vehicle. Mipham Rinpoche, a great spiritual leader of Tibetan Buddhism's Nyingma School whom I've mentioned several times in the book, wrote:

> Sentient beings in a degenerate age are deeply entrapped by
> afflictions. Other Dharma practices are hard-pressed to
> tame their minds, whereas the supreme Great Perfection can
> completely uproot all afflictions.

Guru Rinpoche Padmasambhava, who brought Vajrayana to Tibet, similarly prophesied: "As five degenerations aggravate, the blessing of the Great Perfection will have an even greater effect."

The Great Perfection is the ultimate teaching in that it explicitly and directly reveals true reality, which is only explained implicitly and indirectly in Sutrayana. Therefore, the practice of the Great Perfection is swift and effective. It's like paddling downstream, which is much speedier than against the current. Relying on the pith instructions of the Great Perfection, even an ordinary practitioner can generate extraordinary conviction about the nature of mind. Nevertheless, except for a very few who have extremely sharp faculties or who have reached sudden realization, most Vajrayana practitioners follow a steady sequential order. This starts with preliminary practices and then proceeds to the main practice, until the practitioners recognize the luminous nature of mind. A gradual path is a safer approach. In fact, Vajrayana beginners should start by learning the history, tenets, liturgies, and maybe some simple mantras. It is very important that practitioners establish this foundation in order to delve deeper.

SUTRAYANA AND VAJRAYANA

Sutrayana Is the Foundation

The Vajrayana path is built on the foundation of the Sutrayana, which can be explained by the following two perspectives.

The first is from a historical perspective. Tibetan Buddhism, which includes Vajrayana, began with the introduction of Sutrayana Buddhism into Tibet in the fifth century by King Lha-Thothori Nyentsen (374–unknown). He was the twenty-eighth king of the Chogyal Dynasty. One day, in the king's later years of life, a set of sacred objects, including several Buddhist scriptures, appeared on the roof of his Yumbu Lakhar Palace. The king then received a prophecy that the meaning of the scriptures would be revealed five generations later. In accordance with the prophecy, the Tibetan alphabet was introduced during the seventh-century reign of King Songtsen Gampo (c.605–c.650), allowing people to understand the sutras for the first time. It was also during King Songtsen Gampo's reign that the Dharma took root in Tibet. The Sutrayana texts provided a solid foundation for Vajrayana that was introduced later and continues to thrive today.

The second is from the perspective of bodhichitta. Vajrayana is based on the foundation of Sutrayana because renunciation and bodhichitta—essential aspects of Sutrayana teachings—are also the fundamental prerequisites of Vajrayana. In Tibetan Buddhism, almost every liturgy of Vajrayana practice starts with taking refuge and generating bodhichitta.

As previously mentioned, in *The Song of Victory*, my root guru the great Jigme Phuntsok Rinpoche delineated the stages of the Dzogchen path, with each stage being the prerequisite for the next:

- ▶ First, a practitioner should be a good person because virtuous characters are essential to becoming a real Buddhist.
- ▶ Second, the practitioner develops genuine renunciation, not clinging to any worldly concerns.
- ▶ Third, the practitioner generates bodhichitta, aspiring to attain complete enlightenment for others' sake.
- ▶ Fourth, upon these foundations, the person may practice Dzogchen, and achieve the union of emptiness and luminosity.

These stages clearly show that it's not appropriate to reject the Sutrayana teachings while grasping at the highest Vajrayana teachings. Practitioners who disdain Sutrayana must adjust their views.

The Same Ultimate Goal

Great masters of Tibetan Buddhism, including Tsongkhapa and Mipham Rinpoche, have repeatedly asserted that Sutrayana and Vajrayana use different methods but share the same goal for the practitioner whose goal is attaining enlightenment. Shakyamuni Buddha said in *Chanting the Names of Manjushri* (*Arya-manjushri-nama-samgiti*):

> According to the skillful means of each successive vehicle,
> The Three Vehicles[1] are classified for the benefit of beings,
> And ultimately, they are all incorporated into
> The definite and unique resultant vehicle.

The Buddha says the three paths of shravakas, pratyekabuddhas, and bodhisattvas in the Sutrayana, or the Causal Vehicle, can all be incorporated into the Vajrayana, or the Resultant Vehicle. The Buddha offered 84,000 different teachings, each providing antidotes to specific afflictions in response to sentient beings' varied needs and temperaments. The intention of the teachings is to guide every being to eventually attain buddhahood.

We could say Vajrayana practitioners are like people speeding to the destination of enlightenment by airplane, utilizing the tradition's many skillful means, while Sutrayana practitioners are arriving later because they take a slower train. While these practitioners have chosen different modes of transport, their final destination is exactly the same.

The Extraordinary Features of Vajrayana

Vajrayana is exceptional and effective because of its four distinguishing features pertaining to view, action, meditation, and practitioners' faculties. These are summarized in the *Torch of the Three Methods*:

> It has the same goal but is free from all confusion,
> It is rich in methods and without difficulties.
> It is for those with sharp faculties.
> The Mantra Vehicle (Vajrayana) is sublime.[2]

First, the Vajrayana *view* is "free from all confusion." As covered in chapter 5, Buddhist views are based on the two truths: relative truth and ultimate truth. As for ultimate truth, Sutrayana, via the doctrine of the Middle Way, recognizes the empty aspect of all phenomena, which is devoid of any conceptual proliferation. However, Sutrayana, unlike Vajrayana, doesn't explicitly expound another aspect—the luminous aspect of our buddhanature—while Vajrayana explains the union of both aspects. As for relative truth, Sutrayana perceives all phenomena as illusions and dreams lacking any inherent existence, while Vajrayana further sees all appearances as the essence of the five aspects of our primordial wisdoms[3] that are embodied in the deities of the five buddha families.[4]

Second, Vajrayana is "without difficulties" in terms of *actions*. Through supreme pointing-out instructions, Vajrayana practitioners can realize that the experience of the five senses—seeing, smelling, touching, hearing, and tasting—is and has always been enlightenment. Such practitioners can swiftly attain enlightenment without giving up or rejecting anything, including negative emotions. The Vajrayana path requires few ascetic practices to reach enlightenment. For example, King Indrabhuti recognized the nature of the mind while pursuing hedonistic pleasures.

Third, Vajrayana is "rich in methods" of *meditation*. It consists of many uncommon methods, including the generation stage, the completion stage, and the Great Perfection of the Nyingma tradition. The Vajrayana path also includes abundant pith instructions from the gurus. These methods are only brought up indirectly and covertly in Sutrayana.

Fourth, Vajrayana is for "those with sharp *faculties*." Practitioners develop five spiritual faculties: faith, diligence, mindfulness, concentration, and wisdom. For Vajrayana practitioners the most fundamental faculty is faith. With fervent faith in the guru and Vajrayana, such practitioners can swiftly realize the nature of mind, as repeatedly shown over the history of Vajrayana Buddhism.

It is worth stressing that all Vajrayana teachings are subsumed in the view of the great purity and the great equality of appearance and existence. This central principle of Vajrayana embraces the nature of all appearances. It is elaborated exquisitely in Mipham Rinpoche's *Essence of Clear Light*—his overview of the *Guhyagarbha Tantra*. To be more specific, the great purity is the pure-appearance aspect of enlightenment, and the great equality is the non-dual wisdom of emptiness. Put in other words, purity is the superior relative truth in all phenomena, and equality is the ultimate truth. Purity and equality are present indivisibly in each and every phenomenon. It is totally normal that few people can realize the profound view of Vajrayana because the teachings on purity and equality are of a very high level. Even the Buddha's foremost-in-wisdom disciple Shariputra couldn't understand the teachings upon first hearing them.

In the first chapter of the *Vimalakirti Sutra*, "Purification of the buddha-field," Shariputra said the buddha-field appeared to be impure because he saw "this great earth, with its highs and lows, its thorns, its precipices, its peaks, and its abysses, as if it were entirely filled with ordure." Brahma Sikhin disagreed, saying the buddha-field of Shakyamuni Buddha was equal to the splendor of, for example, the abodes of the highest deities. Then the Buddha touched the ground with his big toe, and the universe suddenly was transformed into a display of splendor. The Buddha said, "Shariputra, this buddha-field is always thus pure; it is just that you failed to see the purity of my buddha-field."

As for Vajrayana practices, the pith instructions are extremely effective for experienced practitioners. Sutrayana practitioners have to exert effort, such as engaging in breathing meditation or practicing patience, to counteract the negative emotion of anger. By contemplating the harm of anger and the benefit of patience, the negative emotion gradually dissolves, and peace of mind returns. In comparison, Vajrayana practitioners need no deliberate means to stop or transform difficult emotions such as anger. Following the guru's pith instructions, they just look at the true nature of anger, then anger dissolves right away.

Inexperienced beginners cannot yet realize the fullest potential of this Vajrayana approach. But, once we grasp the pith instructions, through looking at the true nature of arising afflictions, we realize how laughable the negative emotions are: they are simply illusions in our self-clinging minds. This experience is fascinating! I have strong faith in Vajrayana and aspire to devote my entire life to it. I am so grateful to my lineage gurus who, through devotion and practice, keep intact this spiritual jewel so future generations may encounter authentic Vajrayana teachings. I consider myself extremely lucky to have encountered Vajrayana, so in this degenerate age an ordinary practitioner like me can embark on this simple yet most profound path of Vajrayana.

Now that you are aware of the exemplary features of Vajrayana, you should also know that Vajrayana is extremely demanding on practitioners in terms of their characters and actions. As Guru Rinpoche said: "Even if my view is higher than the sky, the attention I pay to my actions and their effects is finer than flour."

If the great master Guru Rinpoche Padmasambhava had to pay meticulous attention to his own actions, we ordinary practitioners should definitely pay much more attention. Unless a Vajrayana practitioner has reached the state beyond cause and effect, they must carefully discern in their actions between what is beneficial or harmful and what is good or bad.

Vajrayana in Different Traditions

The practice of Tibetan Buddhism, including Vajrayana, includes within it the eight major practice lineages.[5] The differences among these lineages are neither contrasting nor incompatible like fire and water; they all fully incorporate the Buddha's teachings, so they are in essence the same. The differences reflect the way the Buddha tailored his teachings to the needs and capacities of different people, so all of us can find the very thing we need in the treasury of Dharma.

After the Buddha's parinirvana the great masters who truly propagated the Dharma were emanations of Shakyamuni Buddha, therefore their teachings are in accordance with those of the Buddha. The fourth Panchen Lama Lobsang Chökyi Gyaltsen (1570–1662) said:

> The enlightened Padmasambhava with supreme wisdom,
> The Emanation of the glorious Dipamkara, the Lamp Bearer
>   (Atisha),
> And Lobzang Drakpa (Tsongkhapa),
> Beside whom I don't have other refuge objects.

In a similar manner the second Dalai Lama Gedun Gyatso (1475–1542) said:

> The enlightened *vidyadhara* Padmasambhava,
> The pinnacle of five hundred (pandits) Atisha,
> The Buddha *vajradhara* Tsongkhapa,
> I prostrate myself before you, the emanations of the same deity.

The major Tibetan Buddhist schools agree that their lineage founders are the same emanation. These include Guru Rinpoche Padmasambhava of the Nyingma lineage, Tsongkhapa of the Geluk lineage, Atisha of the Kadampa lineage, Gampopa of the Dagpo Kagyu lineage, and Sakya Pandita Kunga Gyaltsen of the Sakya lineage.

Patrul Rinpoche prayed:

> Sakya Pandita—the illuminating teacher who was proficient in
>   the Five Sciences,
> Lama Tsongkhapa—the source of virtuous Sutrayana and
>   Vajrayana teachings,
> Longchenpa—the holder of all the Buddha's teachings,
> I prostrate myself before you, the three Manjushris of the Snow
>   Land.

Renowned masters of Tibetan Buddhism consider Sakya Pandita, Tsongkhapa, and Longchenpa to be emanations of Manjushri. Thus, the teachings from each lineage represent the authentic Dharma.

THE GREAT PERFECTION

The culminating Vajrayana teaching of the Nyingma lineage is Dzogchen or "the Great Perfection." The practice is primarily based on tantric texts such as the *Seventeen Tantras of the Great Perfection* (Tib. *dzogchen gyü chu dün*), the *Seven Treasuries* (Tib. *dzö dün*), and the *Four Parts of Heart Essence* (Tib. *nyingtik yabshyi*). Transmission of the Great Perfection teachings has been passed down the lineage, through the guru's pith instructions.

In the Nyingma tradition, the highest yoga tantra corresponds to the three inner tantras of Mahayoga, Anuyoga, and Atiyoga. In Atiyoga the prefix *ati* means the "topmost," "utmost," or "summit," and Atiyoga is synonymous with the Great Perfection. Therefore, this is the highest teaching, the ultimate teaching, the pinnacle of the teachings of all the buddhas.

The Great Perfection is especially effective and relevant for wandering beings of this degenerate age. According to tantras, the cycle of time is divided into four sequential vast periods (Skt. *yuga*): the accomplished age (Krta Yuga), the threefold-life age (Treta Yuga), the twofold-life age (Dvapara Yuga), and finally the current dark age (Kali Yuga).

During the accomplished age, people were honest, vigorous, virtuous, and free from mental afflictions. Because of this, the action tantra (Skt. *kriyatantra*; Tib. *ja gyü*)—the first of the three outer classes of tantra—was sufficient for beings to awaken.

During the threefold-life age, virtue diminished while mild mental afflictions increased, so people started to commit misdeeds including sexual misconduct and theft. This meant the second of the three outer classes of tantra, the conduct tantra (Skt. *charyatantra*; Tib. *cho gyü*), was needed for awakening.

During the twofold-life age, people suffered from more serious mental afflictions, so the yoga tantra (Skt. *yogatantra*; Tib. *nal jor gyü*), the third of the three outer classes, was sufficient.

During the last of the four stages, namely the dark age—the stage that we are currently in—people are spiritually bankrupt, mindlessly hedonistic, and immoral owing to their exceptionally intense mental afflictions. Because of these deep obscurations, only the highest yoga tantra can subdue their minds—the Great Perfection is the most powerful and effective teaching that corresponds to the current degenerate age. The *Reverberation of the Sound Tantra* says: "It is the Great Perfection that can subdue the minds of wandering beings of the degenerate age."

As quoted in the beginning of this chapter, Guru Rinpoche prophesied: "As the five degenerations aggravate, the blessing of the Great Perfection will have an even greater effect." Nowadays many people have enormous faith in the Great Perfection, so this prophecy has already become a reality.

Regarding the superiority of the Great Perfection, the great Jigme Phuntsok Rinpoche wrote in *The Song of Victory*:

> The Great Perfection, profound and luminous,
> Upon hearing its verses alone, one can break the roots of samsara,
> Through committing six months of its essential practice, one can attain liberation,
> May all engrave this in the heart!
> Those who are fortunate to encounter this supreme teaching,
> Must have accumulated merits in their previous lives through numerous eons,
> And share the same affinity with Buddha Samantabhadra,
> May all Dharma friends be blissful!

In this vajra song Jigme Phuntsok Rinpoche referred to the Great Perfection as the quintessence of sutras and tantras, the pinnacle of all the vehicles. The Great Perfection is so profound that it's difficult for ordinary people to fully grasp its heart essence. Nevertheless, those who hear only a few words of the teachings, even without engaging in the actual practice, may eradicate the roots of samsara.

The first human Dzogchen master Garab Dorje says, "The Great Perfection enables liberation through seeing, on hearing, and by touching." This means every Vajrayana practitioner of this highest yoga tantra can attain liberation, as long as they uphold samaya vows.

In fact, it says in tantras such as the *Heart-Essence of Chetsun* (Tib. *chetsun nyingtik*) that a practitioner of the Great Perfection, with fervent faith and superior faculties, can attain liberation within six months by properly performing the complete practice including the preparation, main part, and conclusion.

The *Indestructible Tent Tantra* also says, "Practicing six months with unwavering faith and conviction, the fruit of vajradhara[6] is attainable."

The *Tantra of the Array of Commitments* says, "With confident faith and veneration, one will attain the fruit of vajradhara within six months."

As mentioned in chapter 2, faith is the crucial faculty for a Vajrayana practitioner. Many lineage masters such as Jamyang Khyentse Wangpo (1820–1892) have asserted the importance of faith in Vajrayana practice, citing tantric texts and their personal practical experience. Through the history of Nyingma lineage, many faithful Vajrayana practitioners have attained realization.

For instance, one hundred years ago thirteen disciples of the great Nyingma master Dudjom Lingpa (1835–1904) attained rainbow body by faithfully practicing the Great Perfection. This happened right in the Larung Gar valley, now the site of the Larung Gar Five Sciences Buddhist Academy.

More recently, I personally witnessed auspicious signs of accomplishment at the time of their death in several lineage disciples of my own guru the great Jigme Phuntsok Rinpoche.

As Jigme Phuntsok Rinpoche said in *The Song of Victory*, a practitioner with the most superior faculties and the most fervent faith can attain realization in as few as six months through practicing the Great Perfection. The tantras say that those with medium faculties can attain liberation in the bardo, the intermediate stage between death and rebirth. Those with lower faculties will encounter their vajra gurus and Vajrayana teachings in the next life, before they reach twenty-five years old. They will then attain liberation after practicing the Great Perfection. Therefore, if you encounter your vajra guru and Vajrayana before age twenty-five, it is mostly due to affinity from your past lives.

The Great Perfection texts such as the *Heart Essence of Chetsun (Chetsun Nyingtik)*, the *Heart Essence of Infinite Expanse (Longchen Nyingtik)*, and the *Heart Essence of Vimalamitra (Vima Nyingtik)* suggest different lengths of time required for realization—three, six, or seven years—with practitioners' differing faith and diligence primarily accounting for the time differences. Your encountering the Great Perfection results from merits accumulated through many previous lives. Longchenpa made two inferences about this in his *Treasury of the Supreme Vehicle*:

First, since we have encountered the supreme Vajrayana in this life, we must have made offerings and attended to infinite numbers of buddhas in our past lives, and have also been among their followers;

Second, since we have encountered the supreme Vajrayana, we will definitely accomplish realization in this present life, during the bardo, or in the next life.

As Jigme Phuntsok Rinpoche mentioned in his vajra song, those who have received the empowerment, transmission, and teachings of the Great Perfection share similar circumstances with Buddha Samantabhadra who, in one split second, attained self-realization and liberation because of this transcendental tantric Dharma.

As stated in *The Great Perfection of Wisdom Sutra* (*Mahaprajnaparamita Sutra*), someone lost and wandering aimlessly in the wild knows he is close to a village and on the right track home, when he sees a cattle herder. In a parallel way, now that we have encountered qualified teachers and the Vajrayana teachings, we are also close to liberation, like a fish that has been hooked and will surely be pulled onto shore.

Jigme Phuntsok Rinpoche has said that the Great Perfection, though appearing quite simple, is extremely profound. If practitioners have no faith in their root guru and in the teachings, and no great compassion toward sentient beings, no matter how hard they try they cannot attain realization. It is just like the case of a person born blind: no matter how bright the sunshine, that person is incapable of seeing it.

If a practitioner has fervent devotion and faith in the supreme Vajrayana and in the guru, the view of the Great Perfection may appear easy—there is nothing difficult to understand, so the practitioner simply has to practice diligently to recognize the true nature of the mind.

THE FIVE-STEP PROCESS OF VAJRAYANA PRACTICE

The practice of Vajrayana, the Great Perfection included, requires a proper sequential order. You shouldn't immediately ask for instructions for the highest Dharma practice whenever you meet a guru. You should approach the practice from the bottom up, instead of from the top down. This is similar to our progress through worldly education. We start from first grade of elementary school instead of from the third year of university, and move upward sequentially.

Of course, some gurus, out of their compassion, may early on offer you an oral transmission of the highest teachings such as *Lama Yangtik*, or the *Innermost Heart Drop of the Guru*. If you attain realization upon hearing this transmission, I sincerely rejoice. As long as a guru's actions benefit beings, that guru may not require all disciples to start from scratch. But for most practitioners, attaining realization is a profound journey, so it's better to follow the legacy of eminent masters and take a gradual approach. This approach prepares a practitioner, so that when it's time to perform the

Vajrayana main practice, the practitioners can more efficiently and effectively transform their afflictions into enlightenment.

Nowadays many Vajrayana practitioners insist on hastily performing the twofold practice of the Great Perfection—*trekchö* (cutting through) and *tögal* (direct crossing)—hoping to quickly realize the primordial purity and spontaneous presence that are the nature of all phenomena. This sense of urgency is not good for their practice. I don't encourage such hasty attempts to practice the Great Perfection. An ordinary practitioner intending to take the tantric path should start with the preliminary practices. Once the preliminaries are done, the practitioner can receive empowerment from the guru, then proceed to the main practice.

When people follow this process, their experience and realization will exceed those of people who dodge the preliminaries. Therefore, sequential stages of practice are essential, and this has been emphasized by lineage masters including Longchenpa, Mipham Rinpoche, and Jigme Phuntsok Rinpoche.

Some gurus instruct their disciples with a top-down approach, starting with the Great Perfection, perhaps for some special reason. But disciples who take this approach may never establish solid foundations for their Vajrayana practice. It is as if they start to paint a mural on a wall when that wall's foundation is still fragile. After a while the wall will likely collapse. Therefore, it's safer to build solid foundations before painting murals.

According to Rongzompa (1012–1088), one of the most important masters of the Nyingma lineage, a Vajrayana practitioner should follow a five-stage process: relying on a guru, receiving empowerment, upholding tantric vows (samaya), hearing and contemplating Vajrayana teachings, and practicing in a quiet place. I often pay attention to the state of Dharma beginners. Some are about to step onto the Vajrayana path, some have just started, some have gone on and off, and the majority are still indecisive. If you want to get real benefits from Vajrayana practice, it's best to follow this five-step process.

Step 1: Relying on a Guru

In the context of Vajrayana, we should consider a spiritual teacher as a *vajra guru*. Relying on such a guru is essential for Vajrayana practice, and students should examine the vajra guru *before* taking empowerment with them, lest they jump in hastily and later find themselves in an awkward position.

Characteristics of a qualified teacher are explained in chapter 7. Below are the specific qualities of a vajra guru, according to Patrul Rinpoche's *The Words of My Perfect Teacher*:

► The vajra guru should have been brought to maturity by a stream of ripening empowerments, flowing down through a continuous unbroken lineage.

► The vajra guru should not have transgressed samayas and vows taken at the time of empowerment. Different tantras require different vows, such as the fourteen root downfalls,[7] or the five root vows[8] in the *Guhyagarbha Tantra*.

► The vajra guru should be calm and disciplined, with few disturbing negative emotions and thoughts. A person trapped in mental afflictions and conceptual thoughts is not qualified to be a vajra guru.

► The vajra guru should have mastered the entire meaning of the ground, path, and result tantras in Vajrayana. Otherwise, how can the guru deliver appropriate tantric teachings to disciples?

► The vajra guru should have attained all the signs of success in the generation and completion stages of the practice, such as seeing visions of the *yidam*, or tantric deity. The guru should at least have seen the yidam in dreams or inner experience, even if these visions haven't yet been directly seen. Moreover, the guru needs to have perfected mantra practice, particularly the mantra of the yidam and its inner experience.

► The vajra guru should have experienced the nature of reality and attained liberation.

► The well-being of others should be the vajra guru's sole concern, with a heart full of compassion.

► The vajra guru should have few preoccupations, having given up clinging to the "ordinary things" of this life. Gurus utilize such things to propagate the Dharma and benefit beings. Biographies of renowned masters show they didn't avoid ordinary things that were indispensable to the masters' Dharma activities.

► The vajra guru practices diligently for future lives, having generated renunciation through practicing the four thoughts that turn the mind.

► Seeing samsara as suffering, the vajra guru should feel great sadness, and should encourage the same feeling in others. For example, realized masters such as Longchenpa, Patrul Rinpoche, and Mipham Rinpoche shared their feelings and reflections on the meaninglessness of samsara with others, once they had achieved certain levels of realization.

▸ The vajra guru should be skilled at caring for disciples and should use appropriate teachings for each of them.

▸ The vajra guru should fulfill all his or her teacher's commands and thus be able to hold the blessings of the lineage, in order to retain the exceptional power of the Dharma teachings.

Step 2: Receiving Empowerment

An empowerment is a ceremony that gives recipients formal authorization to proceed on the Vajrayana path. As previously mentioned, the "why" of empowerment can be explained through an analogy of watering seeds planted in the soil. Once those seeds have been watered, they have an opportunity to sprout. Similarly, once we have received an empowerment, our buddha-nature has an opportunity to be revealed. Therefore, empowerment is needed to formally proceed on the Vajrayana path, just like one needs a visa to enter a foreign country.

Whether or not someone fully receives the transmission of an empowerment is a far deeper issue than ritual formalities. Fully receiving an empowerment depends on the two causes[9] and four conditions.[10] Some of these causes and conditions are related to the guru who bestows the empowerment, for example, whether the guru has completed reciting the relevant mantras, has attained all the signs of success in the practice, is qualified to bestow empowerment, and more. The other aspect has to do with the disciple, whether the person receiving the empowerment has sufficient faith, intelligence, and other qualities.

After receiving an empowerment, a disciple's work has just started: they have simply received the authorization to hear, study, and practice the Vajrayana teachings that pertain to that empowerment. Now the disciple must proceed on this path.

Step 3: Uphold Samaya Vows

After receiving an empowerment, the disciple is obliged to uphold the tantric precepts of samaya, the set of vows and commitments that are given as part of the empowerment. Upholding precepts generates higher mind, which then generates higher wisdom. This reasoning comes from canonical texts related to the threefold training of precepts, meditation, and wisdom. The threefold training starts with precepts as the precondition for the other two. Precepts are the root of merits, and are essential on the path to awakening.

Very often, I hear people complain about the Buddhist precepts. "There are too many precepts," they say. "I don't think I can uphold them." The precepts offer guidelines for cultivating positive actions. To practice Vajrayana, you must uphold samaya vows; for example, you should avoid the fourteen root downfalls, or you should uphold the five root vows in the *Guhyagarbha Tantra*. Just as you need moral discipline to be a good person, upholding precepts is not constraining. Instead, it guards your Dharma practice.

It is very dangerous to receive empowerments without knowing the samaya that must be upheld. It would be similar to the situation of a novice monk who took ordination, or a householder who received refuge, but didn't know what precepts to uphold. Once Buddhists receive an empowerment, they then become vajra students—a more advanced type of student of Buddhism. Maintaining this higher precept standard is essential for practicing Vajrayana teachings. Those who fail to uphold tantric precepts may lose authorization to hear, study, and practice Vajrayana.

Step 4: Hear and Study the Vajrayana Teachings

Now that you've relied on a guru, received an empowerment, and are upholding samaya vows, you are authorized to practice Vajrayana. But to practice properly you first must hear and study the teachings. Unfortunately many Buddhists nowadays do not really hear and study the teachings. The practice of some Buddhists, even including those who took refuge ten or twenty years ago, just includes offering incense at a shrine table, prostrating in front of a Buddha statue, or performing Buddhist recitations. They rarely study the Dharma in a formal and systematic way.

Even if such people have the opportunity to study the Dharma, initially they may study day and night while putting everything else aside, but over time they become less motivated, and thus make little progress. Some people consider Vajrayana practice similar to yoga training or even qigong practice. Because such practitioners lack understanding of Vajrayana's meaning and system, their entrance into the practice is superficial and they're likely to regress. Therefore, it is very important to thoroughly hear and study Vajrayana teachings.

Study of Vajrayana teachings involves two stages. The first stage involves teachings on preliminary practices from texts including *The Words of My Perfect Teacher*, the first eight chapters of *Finding Rest in the Nature of the Mind*, and the *Great Treatise on the Stages of the Path to Enlightenment*. After this come teachings on the main practice, including the *Great Exposition of Secret Mantra* of the Gelukpa lineage, the *Path Including Its Result* (*Lamdre*) of the Sakya lineage, and Nyingma texts on the Great Perfection including the *Seven Treasuries*, *Trilogy of Natural Freedom*, the *Four Parts of the Heart Essence* (*Nyingtik Yabshyi*), and more.

Step 5: Put Teachings of Vajrayana into Practice

It is not sufficient to hear and study the teachings. A Vajrayana practitioner must apply them and live them. Even if practitioners can speak eloquently on Vajrayana theories and attract big audiences, without personal practice, those practitioners cannot eradicate their own mental afflictions. Failing to properly apply the teachings deviates from the primary purpose of Buddhism: to relinquish suffering and to eventually awaken.

Vajrayana practitioners should strictly follow a sequential order of practice. Nyingma practitioners start with the four common preliminaries, which are the four contemplations on the precious human life, impermanence and death, the cause and effect of karma, and the defects of samsara. Next come the five uncommon preliminaries, which are taking refuge, arousing bodhichitta, recitation and meditation on Vajrasattva, mandala offerings, and guru yoga. The last part of the preliminaries is phowa, the practice for directing the transference of consciousness at the time of death.

After completing the preliminaries, a practitioner can proceed to the main practice, including the generation stage, the completion stage, and the ultimate Great Perfection. If this sequential process is followed, the practitioner will purify deluded mind and recognize the nature of mind.

COMMON QUESTIONS ABOUT VAJRAYANA

Why Choose the Vajrayana Path?

Today's practitioners, especially householders, are so busy with work and family, there is little time left for them to study, contemplate, and meditate on the Dharma. It is difficult, if not impossible, for them to free time for systematic study of Sutrayana teachings such as the Five Great Treatises. Take the Geluk monastic curriculum, for example: it can take twenty-five years to finish the whole course of study, starting from the foundational topics in Sutrayana. While a comprehensive Sutrayana study can greatly help establish right views, it is very demanding for many busy householders.

Many eminent masters have asserted that Sutrayana alone may not be sufficient to quickly bring realization to some practitioners, so Vajrayana knowledge, empowerments, and pith instructions are much needed for them. Vajrayana can very efficiently subdue mental afflictions, which is a powerful practicality that attracts Buddhists from both the East and the West.

Fast-paced modern life drives sincere spiritual practitioners to find the quickest possible routes to enlightenment. Throughout my trips to North America and Europe, I noticed that many Dharma practitioners were not interested in studying complex Buddhist doctrines. They didn't have time for study, so they could not understand the teachings in depth. Yet, these people were fully aware that mental afflictions are the root of their sufferings. They were looking for the most direct and efficient solution, and Vajrayana was the best choice.

During his own Dharma tours around the world, my root guru the great Jigme Phuntsok Rinpoche often bestowed upon Western practitioners the teachings, transmissions, and empowerment of the *Manjushri Great Perfection*, a mind *terma* or hidden treasure that he revealed during his morning meditation break in the Asura Cave of Mount Wutai in China in 1987. Jigme Phuntsok Rinpoche said Vajrayana practice is very "simple" because it incorporates the quintessence of the Buddha's teachings and lays out a direct path for practitioners. When we grasp the views and practices of Vajrayana, we'll easily generate a panoramic understanding of all the Buddha's teachings.

Of course, we can't assert that all beings today are ideal candidates for Vajrayana practices. In fact, many people don't need to practice Vajrayana;

they can attain rebirth in the Pure Land by following the Pure Land Buddhism,[11] or recognize the nature of mind through practicing Chan Buddhism.

Many people acknowledge similarities between Vajrayana and Chan Buddhism, and biographies of enlightened Chan masters show how effective that tradition is. However, owing to their lack of knowledge on the fundamentals of Buddha's teachings, some modern Chan practitioners are prone to the pitfall of becoming nihilists if they don't practice correctly, which means they may fail to act virtuously and will instead simply remain in a state of mental blankness. Let me explain why this is the case.

There were debates between Chan Buddhism and Tibetan Buddhism in history, the most famous of which took place between Heshang Moheyan (eighth century), representing a path of sudden enlightenment of Chan Buddhism, and Kamalashila (c. 740–795), representing a gradual path to enlightenment. According to Tibetan accounts, Heshang Moheyan lost the debate. Nevertheless, the sudden path of enlightenment continues to have a place among practitioners. In fact, there is no such distinction between "gradual" and "sudden" within Chan Buddhism. Huineng, the Sixth Patriarch, stated: "There is no sudden or gradual in the Dharma, but among people who are keen or dull. The dull is recommended to take the gradual path, and the keen the sudden path. Once enlightened, there is no distinction between these two methods from the outset."

Heshang Moheyan advocated the sudden path and promoted the rejection of all mental engagement and virtuous/non-virtuous actions, which, according to Longchenpa, shares similar features with the highest teachings of the Great Perfection. According to the sudden path advocated by Heshang Moheyan, enlightenment comes about through meditation, a path of non-thought. I've encountered beginning practitioners who immediately choose to "just sit" in a state of conscious awareness, without first discerning virtues and vices. For a practitioner with sharp faculties, this is an extraordinary practice, which possibly brings sudden realization. However, the same practice can be very risky to those with less developed faculties: they may become nihilists.

Here is another phenomenon worth addressing. Nowadays some practitioners, especially those in the East, hold only partial views about Vajrayana. Owing to their lack of systematic Dharma studies, these practitioners think it is permissible, for instance, for a vajra teacher to know only the Avalokiteshvara mantra. As another example, they consider someone a

Vajrayana veteran if they've only read *A History of Tibet*,[12] *White Annals*,[13] or *Red Annals*,[14] or if they've only studied the transmissions, liturgies, and basic commentaries of one or two Tibetan masters. To understand Vajrayana, practitioners should comprehensively study its history, tradition, beliefs, and practices. By doing so, practitioners will realize that while Vajrayana may offer the "fast track" to enlightenment, it still involves vigorous, systematic Dharma studies and practices.

In addition, many profound definitive teachings are only clearly and directly covered in Vajrayana, but not in Sutrayana. While doubts often arise while one studies Sutrayana, they are naturally clarified after one systematically studies Vajrayana. In my case, I began my monastic life at Larung Gar over thirty years ago, and until now I have spent half of my time on Sutrayana and the other half on Vajrayana. I primarily practice Vajrayana for daily meditation because many Sutrayana teachings lack corresponding liturgies and practice instructions. For example, it is unclear how to practice major Sutrayana texts like the *Four Hundred Verses on the Middle Way*, or the *Fundamental Wisdom of the Middle Way*. Therefore, it happens often that a Sutrayana practitioner has to search Vajrayana liturgies to find equivalent Sutrayana practices. While Sutrayana studies play an important role in helping me build a solid Dharma foundation, most of the extraordinary experiences and blessings I have been receiving come from my Vajrayana practice.

Why Maintain Secrecy in Vajrayana?

Another name for Vajrayana is "secret mantra," because the intent is that it must be taught and practiced in secrecy. While Vajrayana is extremely precious to us tantric practitioners, it may not necessarily be of benefit to unqualified recipients who could misunderstand or even slander it. For example, a non-Buddhist or a novice Buddhist may not be able to assimilate and accept the tantric view that the innate nature of our mind is the Buddha. As such, the secrecy in Vajrayana is not for the sake of hiding something hideous, but for the sake of benefiting tantric practitioners and avoiding harm to others. Therefore, Vajrayana students should keep tantric teachings they've received "hidden," and Vajrayana gurus should remain exceptionally cautious when bestowing empowerments and giving pith instructions.

Even some aspects of Sutrayana need to be kept secret from certain groups of people. For example, the precepts for monks (bhikshus) and nuns (bhikshuni) must be hidden from male novices (*samaneras*), female novices (*shramaneri*), and householders. In addition, some precepts for male and female novices must also be kept hidden from householders.

Another example is with regard to the teachings of emptiness: Aryadeva says in *Four Hundred Stanzas on the Middle Way*:

> For the unreceptive, conceptions of a self are the best;
> To teach them selflessness is not.
> They would go to bad rebirths,
> While the extraordinary attain peace.

Aryadeva says it is good to teach unreceptive beings that there is a self, because their attachment to the self will help them give up unwholesome behaviors, making it easier for them to have a good rebirth; it is not good to teach them emptiness because they cannot accept the notion of selflessness and will further denigrate it, so the teaching should remain secrecy to them.

Is Union Practice a Part of Buddha's Teachings?

Union practice involves a form of sexual union with a physical consort as part of advanced Vajrayana practices. It is also known as "yoga of bliss," "consort practice," "sexual yoga," or in Sanskrit, *karmamudra*.

Up to today, the idea that all Vajrayana practices involve sexuality remains a widespread misconception in the West and East. While some charlatans may have used union practice as an excuse to engage in sexual harassment and abuse, the practice itself is a profound skillful means for advanced tantric practitioners.

A beginning Buddhist, who is overwhelmed by confusing opinions on this issue, may wonder: "What is the stand on sexuality in Buddhism at large?" From the perspective of Sutrayana, there are certain occasions that sexual activities are considered virtuous. Here is a relevant story Patrul Rinpoche put in *The Words of My Perfect Teacher*, and a similar one exists in *The Great Jewel Heap Sutra*[15]:

There was a Brahmin named Lover of the Stars who lived in the forest for many years, keeping the vow of chastity. One day he went begging in a village. A young Brahmin woman fell so hopelessly in love with him that she was about to kill herself. Moved by compassion toward her, he married her, which brought him merit that he would otherwise have to accumulate in the next forty thousand kalpas.

According to the vows of individual liberation, a monk breaching vows of chastity will be reborn in a hell realm. However, the Brahmin monk did so with a bodhichitta motivation and no trace of personal desire, so instead he accumulated a vast amount of merit.

Thus, it shows that under certain circumstances, sexual practices are allowed and beneficial, if guided by bodhichitta and if afflictions can be transformed into wisdom.

A verse in the *Mahayana Secret Adornment Sutra* talks about Vajrayana's union practice of karmamudra:

> Together with consorts,
> Often pursuing pleasures without desire.
> Such a practice,
> Is the state of a bodhisattva.

This means that the practice of union with consorts does not originate from ordinary self-gratifying sexual desire, but instead requires a bodhisattva's high level of realization. Thus, it is very obvious the practice is not for ordinary people.

The union practice resonates with the tantric view that affliction is bodhi, or enlightenment, if skillfully utilized through Vajrayana practice. To understand this, let us consider the three poisons of desire, anger, and ignorance.

From the Common Vehicle's standpoint, the three poisons are the primary causes keeping sentient beings trapped in samsara and away from attaining enlightenment. In comparison, Vajrayana practitioners recognize the true nature of the three poisons and transform them swiftly into enlightenment. This view is well elaborated in Longchenpa's *Finding Rest in the Nature of the Mind*.

That said, in any monastery upholding the heritage of Tibetan Buddhism, sangha members are not allowed to directly engage in the union practice. But, it is mentioned in tantras that practitioners are allowed to practice karmamudra if they have reached a certain high level of realization.

While the union practice can be a skillful means for advanced Vajrayana practitioners, the practice isn't suitable or mandatory for every tantric practitioner. Milarepa demonstrated an example in this regard. Despite being one of Tibet's most legendary realized yogis, Milarepa spurned a suggestion that he practice karmamudra like his own guru Marpa.

"My guru is a fully realized yogi," Milarepa said. "I don't have his level of realization. A lion can easily leap over a big gorge, but if a rabbit tries to jump over the same gorge, it will surely die."

Despite Milarepa's extraordinary state of realization, he considered himself so far less accomplished than Marpa that he refrained from union practice. If Milarepa considered himself unqualified to engage in the union practice, what does this say about ordinary practitioners like us? Furthermore, if a "master" proposes a "union practice" with you, you must ponder whether this master's level of realization has exceeded Milarepa's, before saying yes to the proposal.

It is very important that people outside the Vajrayana tradition—before they acquire knowledge and experience of Vajrayana—do not generate wrong views about the profound skillful means of union practice. It is understandable that someone may find it difficult to accept union imagery[16] or hear about union practice, but please be cautious not to slander it for lack of understanding.

Some may protest, "Isn't it true that Buddhism calls for the eradication of lust? If union practice is a part of Buddhist teachings, I don't see how it really differs from the Shaktism in Hinduism since they both engage in sexual practices!" Alas! Whoever scattered this wrong view is truly pitiful. If you think union practice is hideous and wrongful, then how to explain the verse in the *Mahayana Secret Adornment Sutra* that I just quoted?

How to Take in the Idea of "Seeing the Guru as the Buddha"

A Vajrayana practitioner shouldn't reject seeing the guru as the Buddha. Some people dispute the Vajrayana idea of seeing the guru as the Buddha, contending this is contrary to the first of the four reliances "to rely on the Dharma, not the teacher." While the first reliance suggests Buddhists should rely on the genuine teachings of a teacher, not that teacher's persona, it doesn't conflict with the central role of the guru in Vajrayana.

It's easy for practitioners without a solid Dharma foundation to misinterpret the first reliance and to conclude the guru principle makes no sense. If this happens, the guru's blessings cannot reach them. As a result it will be extremely difficult for them to recognize the nature of mind, when relying solely on their own intellectual understanding of the Dharma. As you may know, Vajrayana contains many skillful means that can help practitioners attain realization. Sometimes, through the blessing of a realized guru, students like yourselves can realize the nature of mind after hearing just a few words or seeing a symbolic gesture.

With this realization, you will see the true nature of everything, either from the aspect of emptiness or the aspect of luminosity. At that time, even if all the sages of the world gather around and refute you in chorus, arguing the true nature is something else, you won't budge at all.

The practical guidance of "seeing the guru as the Buddha" is only covered in the tantras, not in the sutras. When practicing guru yoga—the practice of merging your mind with the wisdom of the guru—you are asked to see the guru as the Buddha. As Khenpo Ngawang Pelzang explained in *A Guide to the Words of My Perfect Teacher*, in the tradition of the Great Perfection, seeing the guru as the Buddha is to see the guru as the *dharmakaya* Buddha. In fact, when you engage in such a practice, you not only see the guru as the Buddha but also all sentient beings, yourself included, as buddhas. The guru yoga practice is very profound, so normally you need to go through a gradual process before attaining accomplishment. As Jigme Lingpa said, the notion of seeing the guru as the Buddha pertains to the ultimate state, when our own mind and the guru's wisdom merge to become one.

As mentioned in chapter 7, as a beginner Buddhist you should simply start by seeing the guru as a nice person. Then gradually, after you have been following the guru for a long while—say, eight or ten years—through systematic study of the Dharma you will become deeply impressed by their words and deeds, and your faith in the guru will continue to grow. Eventually, you'll reach the state that you want to receive the guru's empowerment and finally get it, and there won't be the slightest trace of suspicion in your mind about any teaching expounded by the guru.

At this point you have developed the real, unwavering, and unconstrained faith in the guru, and you truly see the guru as the Buddha. As such, you have the capability of merging your mind with the guru's mind, the latter of which is inseparable from the Buddha's wisdom.

You must still place great importance on hearing, contemplation, and meditation. Only after studying and practicing the Dharma for a certain time can you truly understand how to follow a spiritual teacher, as well as whether you have fully merged your mind with the teacher's wisdom mind. Then the practice of guru yoga alone is enough to bring you to enlightenment. But it is the highest level of practice and state of realization, and it normally takes us time to finally get there.

THE CRUCIAL IMPORTANCE OF PRELIMINARY PRACTICES

Without preliminary practices, a Vajrayana practitioner is building castles in the air. Great enlightened masters persistently emphasized the value of preliminary practices for their spiritual journey and that of other practitioners. For example, Dilgo Khyentse Rinpoche wrote in *The Excellent Path to Enlightenment*:

> Do not think that the ngöndro is a sort of simple beginner's practice, or that it is not as profound as Mahamudra, the Great Seal, or Atiyoga — the Great Perfection. In fact, the preliminary practice comes at the beginning precisely because it is of such crucial importance and is the very basis of all other practices. If we were to go straight to the so-called main practice without the preparation of ngöndro, it would not help us at all. Our minds would be unprepared and untamed. It would be like building a beautiful house on the surface of a frozen lake—it simply would not last.[17]

Yukhok Chöying Rangdrol (1872–1952), was a renowned master in Sertar county of the Tibetan region for his years of steady practice in solitude. His disciples wouldn't be given higher teachings for the first two or three years under his guidance, but practiced preliminaries day after day. This strict focus on the preliminaries laid a solid foundation for those disciples. During the terror of the Cultural Revolution, many Buddhists' devotion and faith degenerated, and some even defamed the Dharma. But in contrast Lama Yukhok's disciples persevered despite hardships, and none of them reneged on their dedication to the Three Jewels.

In the Tibetan Buddhist tradition, generally speaking, it is only after a practitioner has completed the preliminaries that a qualified guru will then offer that practitioner the teachings of highest yoga tantra. Some gurus, however, for specific reasons may immediately offer beginning students the highest teachings.

In the past I've met practitioners who told me they had received the highest teachings from certain gurus. When I ask if they have finished preliminary practices, they respond that the guru didn't require that, saying something like, "because I already have pretty decent faculties as a tantric practitioner." Many people haven't even received empowerment, yet they ask for the Great Perfection teachings. Alas!

Practitioners who don't understand the importance of preliminary practices may underestimate the effort needed, and may eventually blame everyone and everything for their failing of realization. Those who downplay the preliminaries sometimes generate wrong views toward the guru and the Dharma, and their practice fails miserably. Therefore, if your aspiration is to attain realization, I hope you will wholeheartedly follow the traditional practice sequence transmitted from the lineage masters during all stages of your own practice.

AN OVERVIEW OF THE PRELIMINARY PRACTICES

Many Buddhists ask, "Why must we practice the preliminaries, instead of something else?"

First, let's consider the four common preliminary practices that are undertaken as a foundation for the main practices of Vajrayana. We need to contemplate the "preciousness of human life." Otherwise, we won't make the best use of our human life. While we may be fully aware that the human life is precious, without contemplating "impermanence and death" we won't be motivated to practice diligently. Next, through contemplating "the principle of cause and effect" we come to understand rebirth, and how our virtues will bring us to the three higher realms and our vices to the three lower realms. Finally, we need to contemplate "the defects of samsara" and thus realize that whether we are reborn in a lower or a higher realm we are still trapped in the mire of samsara. Instead of settling for entrapment, we should aim for liberation from cyclic existence.

As Lama Tsongkhapa said in *Three Principal Aspects of the Path*,

When, through growing accustomed to thinking in this way,
Hope for the pleasures of samsara no longer arises even for an
   instant,
And throughout both day and night you long for liberation,
Then, at that time, true renunciation has been born.[18]

So after realizing the four common preliminaries, a practitioner will sever attachment to this life and future lives and will generate genuine renunciation.

Next we proceed to practicing the uncommon preliminaries, 100,000 repetitions of each: recitation of the verses on taking refuge and arousing bodhichitta, recitation of the one-hundred-syllable mantra of Vajrasattva and meditation on that yidam, mandala offerings, and guru yoga. "Taking refuge" reflects the fact that we've embarked on the Buddha's path. "Arousing bodhichitta" distinguishes between the Common Vehicle and Mahayana, so we understand we practice to liberate not just ourselves but all sentient beings. "The recitation and meditation of Vajrasattva" purifies all wrongdoings and downfalls since beginningless time. "Mandala offering" accumulates the extensive merit and wisdom that move us toward enlightenment. "Guru yoga" frees us from all obscurations, so we can realize the true nature of mind.

Please do practice the preliminaries steadily and seriously. Without practicing the preliminaries, our mind is like uncultivated land, in which the ordinary seeds of virtue will not grow, let alone the seeds of the highest Vajrayana teachings.

Without real practice the teachings generate no substantial meaning, no matter how eloquently you can delineate them. As a result, whenever you encounter negative life events including sickness, old age, and death, you cannot cope with and transform those adversities. You will suffer passively. By contrast, if the Dharma has deeply merged with your mind through practice, you will remain calm and at great ease even when you face challenges, including death.

To achieve higher states of wisdom, we must first tame our minds. To tame the mind we must complete the preliminary practices. After accomplishing the common and uncommon preliminaries, we become qualified for Vajrayana's main practice, and can then proceed further on the path to enlightenment.

Conclusion

Eventually we can achieve nirvana—our final goal as stated in the fourth Dharma seal. We awaken to the true nature of our mind—our buddha-nature. There is no nirvana apart from buddhahood—the awakened state when we fully bring forth our innate buddha-nature, as Arya Maitreya says in the *Uttaratantra Shastra*:

> It is the dharmakaya. It is the tathagata. It is the highest truth.
> It is the ultimately true nirvana.
> Like the sun and its rays, these aspects are inseparable:
> So there is no nirvana apart from buddhahood itself.

This is the last stanza of the Buddhist scripture my root guru the great Jigme Phuntsok Rinpoche conferred on us disciples.

Jigme Phuntsok Rinpoche's health began to worsen in late 2003, while he was teaching us the *Mahayana Uttaratantra Shastra* at Larung Gar by following Dölpopa Sherap Gyeltsen's (1292–1361) commentary. Yielding to our requests, he agreed to pause the teaching and to leave for medical treatment in Chengdu, a city nearly four hundred miles away.

I had accompanied him on almost all his trips around the world, so I asked to come along to look after him. Jigme Phuntsok Rinpoche declined, saying, "This time, you don't have to go."

On the day of his departure, sangha members gathered along the road to see him off. Fellow disciple Khenpo Chimey Rinchen and I walked to the end of the very long line of people, waiting for Jigme Phuntsok Rinpoche. This scene is still vivid in my mind. The crowd seemed so far away from where we were standing. Snow was lightly falling, enclosing both of us in a thin, mist-like blanket of white. When his car finally drove by us, Jigme

Phuntsok Rinpoche lowered the window and waved goodbye, before his car slowly dwindled out of sight toward Chengdu.

That was the last time I saw my guru the great Jigme Phuntsok Rinpoche alive.

My peerless guru had spent his entire life bestowing on us the authentic Dharma. On a fierce winter day in early 2004, he left his earthly frame and passed into parinirvana. His teaching of Buddhist scriptures ended with this very stanza: *there is no nirvana apart from buddhahood itself.*

The great Jigme Phuntsok Rinpoche was a true guru. He introduced buddha-nature to us, and taught us to recognize our own buddha-nature.

Like all other true gurus, he is not just a teacher, he is the teachings, the precious vessel holding the unbroken lineage of key instructions and practices. His life is the path, revealed in his words, his gestures, even his silence. His mastery is service: an unswerving commitment to liberate all sentient beings from suffering. Through his vast wisdom and effortless skill, he awakens deeper insights and experiences in the mind-streams of his disciples, and opens the door of liberation to others, according to their capacities.

Often a true guru's most profound lessons are transmitted so subtly that we don't immediately recognize them. His words or behaviors often carry a secret, hidden meaning—a skillful means of indirectly prodding us toward further development and deeper understanding. Therefore, when relying on a guru, it's important to remember there is always a secret, hidden meaning.

Then what is the secret meaning of this stanza being the last Dharma teaching of Jigme Phuntsok Rinpoche? I rarely pondered on this until I began to translate and teach Dölpopa's commentary in recent years. Then thoughts started to surface: through this stanza, perhaps my peerless guru was telling us his high level of realization—that he is the Buddha.

Through this stanza, perhaps he blesses each and every one of his disciples to recognize buddha nature, that this very mind is and has always been that of the Buddha.

Perhaps all those years of training, assimilating teachings, honing our minds through hearing, contemplation, and meditation, cultivating respect for our lineage and both the capacity and willingness to preserve it, my peerless guru was preparing us, through this stanza, for his departure from this world when he left his legacy in our care.

I may not yet have gotten all the secret meaning my peerless guru wanted to tell us through the stanza. But one thing I know for certain is that this stanza carries his great blessings, which are beyond time and space.

So, at the end of this book I solemnly share this precious verse with you:

There is no nirvana apart from buddhahood itself.

I sincerely wish this verse will signal the dawn of your enlightenment. I wish that you truly come to see what is, and has always been, within; that you truly see that everything, every being, every state of mind, including samsara and nirvana, is buddha-nature.

May the sun of wisdom and the moon of compassion arise in you!

May the immaculate wisdom and compassion of Dharma pervade everything and everyone that the moon and the sun shine upon!

APPENDIX:
HOW TO PREPARE FOR DEATH

MANY PEOPLE fear death. How can we overcome this fear and have a "good death" from a Buddhist perspective?

In recent years, hospice care has become more accessible to terminally ill people. A pioneer in this was Ram Dass, an American spiritual teacher who previously was a clinical psychologist. In the 1980s Ram Dass cofounded the Dying Center, the first residential hospice in the United States, where people went to die consciously.

Once Ram Dass guided the death process of a patient named Bruce by reading instructions for navigating the bardo, the intermediate state between lifetimes, from *The Tibetan Book of the Dead*. Following the instruction, Ram Dass guided Bruce to remain calm and peaceful, and recognize the primordial clarity of mind. Gradually Bruce's agonized expression disappeared, and he passed away very peacefully.

Such bardo instructions are utterly important to the dying person because an overwhelming fear of death will surely impede liberation. Some Chinese Buddhist masters equate the dying process to being freed from jail, graduating from school, moving to a new place, or changing an outfit. With this attitude we will overcome death anxiety and greet death with calm and peace.

What must we do to die well?

Ordinary people preparing for death need deathbed recitations and a practice called transference of consciousness in addition to daily practice including chanting mantras or the name of Amitabha. These significantly increase our chance of attaining liberation at death, reflected by the Tibetan saying, "No amount of wealth can compete with a single *mani* mantra at death."

As a person dies, the four primary elements of earth, water, fire, and air dissolve, and consciousness becomes unclear and disordered, so it is very difficult for the dying person to make the perilous journey alone. Even if a dying person has practiced the Dharma well in this life, he or she will find it hard to continue the practice at death. Hence it's crucial to have others offer guiding prayers by the deathbed.

Master Yinguang taught, "Reciting mantras for a dying person is like helping a weak person climb a mountain."

How can you help a dying person at his or her deathbed? Buddhist teachings say the dying person should lie on his or her right side in the "sleeping lion" position, the Buddha's posture when he passed into parinirvana. Guru Rinpoche Padmasambhava said, "Humans, and even animals, will not fall into the lower realms if they die in the posture of sleeping lion."

But if the dying person changes posture because of physical pain, there is no need to force him or her. Simply let that person stay in any comfortable position.

Next, place a prayer wheel near the person's pillow, and visualize all the buddhas throughout the ten directions radiating the light of blessings. Family and friends should gather around the dying person's head, not the feet, and softly chant "NAMO AMITABHA" or "OM MANI PADME HUM." If this cannot be done, play recordings of chanting, so the dying person can constantly hear the names of buddhas.

If possible, place Buddha Amitabha's picture, a Buddhist scripture, and a stupa above the head of the dying person. It's good to light seven butter lamps, or at least one, to provide light and warmth as the person enters the dark and treacherous bardo stage.

During the process of dying make sure nobody moves or touches the person's body, especially from the waist down. After the person dies leave the corpse untouched for at least twenty-four hours. It's best to not cremate the body until three days have passed.

During the dying process, family members should devotedly chant mantras or the Buddha's name, or if capable recite a sadhana such as the "Liturgy for the Recitation at the Time of Death." In addition, for forty-nine days after death family members should perform daily virtuous deeds on behalf of the deceased including releasing captured animals, adopting vegetarian diets, offering butter lamps, and reciting scriptures.

Family and friends must not cry and wail next to the corpse. The *Sutra of the Right Mindfulness of Dharma* says: "Perturbed by the whine of sorrow,

HOW TO PREPARE FOR DEATH — 221

the bardo being is blown by his karmic wind and falls into an unfortunate realm."

The dying person could have had a good birth. However, after hearing loved ones crying, the person becomes attached to them and loses mindfulness. In the end, the person takes a bad rebirth.

In her *Journeys to the Bardo*, renowned Tibetan dakini Lingsa Chökyi described the detrimental effect of her family's crying as she was dying. She floated out of her body, and saw her corpse lying on the bed. When she talked to family members, nobody could see or hear her. While her children were crying, she felt as if she was being hit by a hailstorm of blood and pus all over her body, causing her excruciating pain.

Luckily she then arrived in front of a Dharma master who was doing phowa practice for her. The master was resting his mind in its luminous nature, which made her so blissful.

Therefore, at the deathbeds of family or friends, we must know what will help or harm them. According to Buddhism, crying only exacerbates the sufferings of the deceased. The best choice is to replace crying with chanting the names of buddhas.

NOTES

TRANSLATORS' NOTE

1. Mipham Rinpoche's *The Way of Living: The Precious Jewel That Attracts Divinity and Excellence*.
2. Gyalse Tokme Zangpo's *Thirty-Seven Practices of a Bodhisattva*.
3. Jigme Phuntsok Rinpoche's *The Song of Victory*.

PREFACE

1. As a gesture of veneration, Tibetan disciples rarely call the guru by their real name. Instead, they use an honorific name. The great Jigme Phuntsok Rinpoche's disciples, including Khenpo Sodargye, and Tibetans at large, normally call him "The Dharma King of Wish-Fulfilling Jewel." For the sake of clarity for readers, the translation team decided to use "Jigme Phuntsok Rinpoche" throughout this book.
2. In 1980 the great Jigme Phuntsok Rinpoche founded Larung Gar Five Sciences Buddhist Academy in the Larung valley near the town of Sertar, Garze Prefecture, Sichuan Province.

CHAPTER 1: THE FOUR DHARMA SEALS

1. In Sanskrit, it means "instant" or "moment," the shortest possible span of time.
2. Longchenpa, *Finding Rest in the Nature of the Mind*, trans. the Padmakara Translation Group (Boulder, CO: Shambahala, 2017), chap. 2, v. 7.
3. Āryadeva and Geshe Sonam Rinchen, *Āryadeva's Four Hundred Stanzas on the Middle Way: With Commentary by Gyel-Tsap*, trans. Ruth Sonam (Ithaca, NY: Snow Lion Publications, 2008), chap. 2, v. 33.
4. Jamgön Mipham, *Gateway to Knowledge*, vol. 4, ed. Kathy Morris, trans. Erik Pema Kunsang (Hong Kong: Rangjung Yeshe Publications, 2012), 23.
5. Jamgön Mipham, 21.

6. Jamgön Mipham, 23.

7. Shantideva, *The Way of the Bodhisattva*, trans. the Padmakara Translation Group, 2nd rev. ed. (Boston: Shambhala, 2006), chap. 6, v. 10.

8. Jamgön Mipham, *Individual Selflessness,* trans. Adam Pearcey, Lotsawa House, 2008, https://www.lotsawahouse.org/tibetan-masters/mipham/individual -selflessness.

9. J. M. Twenge and W. K. Campbell, *The Narcissism Epidemic: Living in the Age of Entitlement* (New York: Free Press, 2009).

10. Jamgön Mipham, *Ascertaining the Two Kinds of Selflessness,* trans. Adam Pearcey, Lotsawa House, 2016, https://www.lotsawahouse.org/tibetan-masters /mipham/two-kinds-of-selflessness.

11. Wisdom (Skt. *prajna*; Tib. *sherab*) is identified as "the recognition during the formal meditation session that all phenomena are empty, and the knowledge during the post-meditation phase that all phenomena are unreal, like a magical illusion or a dream" by Patrul Rinpoche in *The Words of My Perfect Teacher* (New Haven, CT: Yale University Press, 2011).

12. Matthew A. Killingsworth and Daniel T. Gilbert, "A Wandering Mind Is an Unhappy Mind," *Science* 330 (6006), November 20, 2010, 932; DOI: 10.1126/science.1192439.

13. The first five are related to our experience of the phenomenal world: the eye, ear, nose, tongue, and body consciousness. The sixth is mental consciousness, which assembles the input of the first five into a coherent whole. The seventh is the *klesha* or deluded consciousness—our afflicted mental consciousness. The eighth is *alaya* consciousness—the universal basis of all our mental activity and the storehouse of our "karmic seeds."

14. Jamgön Mipham, *Ascertaining the Two Kinds of Selflessness,* trans. Adam Pearcey.

15. A shravaka (Tib. *nyantö*) is a follower of the Common Vehicle who strives to attain the level of an arhat.

16. The four great logical arguments of the Middle Way are:

   ▸ The investigation of the cause: the Diamond Splinters
   ▸ The investigation of the result: refuting existent or nonexistent results
   ▸ The investigation of the essential identity: neither one nor many
   ▸ The investigation of all: the Great Interdependence

Chapter 2: Faith in Buddhism

1. The Four Reliances are:

   ▸ rely on the message of the teacher, not on the teacher's personality;
   ▸ rely on the meaning, not just on the words;
   ▸ rely on the real meaning, not on the provisional one; and
   ▸ rely on your wisdom mind, not on your ordinary, judgmental mind.

2. The translation of the verse is based on the corresponding content in Narada's *The Buddha and His Teachings* (Mumbai: Jaico Publishing House, 2006).

3. Dakini Muntso Rinpoche, niece of the great Jigme Phuntsok Rinpoche, was born on the 2nd day of the 12th Tibetan month in 1966 (the Year of the Fire Horse) in Sertar, Sichuan Province. She is an embodiment of many bodhisattvas and is recognized as the emanation of Dakini Yeshe Tsogyal by accomplished masters. In 1999, as the reincarnation of the great female accomplisher Minling Mingyur Paldon, Dakini Muntso was enthroned at Mindrolling Monastery, one of the principal Nyingma monasteries. In the Tibetan year of the Wood Monkey (2004), after the parinirvana of Jigme Phuntsok Rinpoche, Dakini Muntso Rinpoche was elected as the leader of Larung Gar Five Sciences Buddhist Academy by the sangha there.

4. *Tirthika* is a general term referring to heretics or non-Buddhists.

5. Such as Vasubandhu's (c. fourth–fifth century) commentary on the *Treasury of the Abhidharma* and Rongzom Chökyi Zangpo's (1012–1088) *Entering the Way of the Great Vehicle*.

6. *Bhagavant* means "fortunate," "illustrious," and "sublime." Thus it applied to the Buddha and his predecessors.

7. Patrul Rinpoche, *The Words of My Perfect Teacher*, 175–76.

8. The degenerate age, or Kali Yuga (Skt. *kaliyuga*; Tib. *tsöden gyi dü*), is a period when there are five degenerations: life span (beings' life expectancy declines); afflictions (ignorance, desire, anger, jealousy, pride and other delusions become stronger); sentient beings (it's hard to subdue and help them); time (wars and famines proliferate); and views (false beliefs become prevalent).

9. The translation of the verse is from *The Words of My Perfect Teacher*, 172.

10. Sunakshatra, Shakyamuni Buddha's cousin, spent many years following the Buddha. He could learn many of the Buddha's teachings by heart, but still developed wrong views toward the Buddha. He was later reborn as a hungry ghost.

11. Devadatta was Shakyamuni Buddha's cousin, who made three attempts to kill the Buddha.

12. Kalandaka is a wealthy Indian man who is said to have donated a bamboo grove to Shakyamuni Buddha.

13. A *samanera* is a novice male monastic in a Buddhist context.

14. *Naga* is a Sanskrit word that refers to a serpent or snake.

15. A shastra (Tib. *tenchö*) is a treatise or commentary on the words of the Buddha.

16. Amitabha, meaning "infinite light," is the principal buddha in Pure Land Buddhism.

17. Patrul Rinpoche, *The Words of My Perfect Teacher*, 173.

18. *Kalpa* is a Sanskrit word meaning an aeon, or a relatively long period of time (by human calculation) in Hindu and Buddhist cosmology. Generally speaking, a kalpa is the period of time between the creation and recreation of a world or universe.

19. A rakshasa is a demonic being from Hindu mythology that was later incorporated into Buddhism.

20. The story of Asanga appears in *The Words of My Perfect Teacher*, 211–12.

21. Dhomang Monastery was built in the eighteenth century during the reign of Emperor Qianlong of the Qing Dynasty. Since its establishment, Dhomang Monastery has supported thirteen great practitioners who attained the rainbow body. Patrul Rinpoche, author of *The Words of My Perfect Teacher*, also practiced at Dhomang Monastery.

22. Patrul Rinpoche, *The Words of My Perfect Teacher*, 173.

23. The quote first appeared in H. Tuke, *Le corps et l'esprit: Action du moral et de l'imagination sur le physique* (Paris, 1886), translated by C. A. Herter in H. Bernheim's *Suggestive Therapeutics* (New York: G. P. Putnam's Sons, 1889).

24. The translation of the verse is adopted from *The Changeless Nature: The Ultimate Mahayana Treatise on the Changeless Continuity of the True Nature*, trans. Ken and Katia Holmes, 2nd ed. (Eskadalemuir, Scotland: Karma Drubgyud Darjay Ling, 1985).

25. In the Karma Kagyu tradition, the head lama is Gyalwa Karmapa and the mantra is KARMAPA CHENNO. It is believed that sounds of this mantra are directly connected with the enlightened mind of Karmapa and carry its enlightened qualities, bringing help when it is most necessary for the benefit of others.

26. Avalokiteshvara is a bodhisattva who embodies the compassion of all buddhas. In Tibet the bodhisattva is known as Chenrezik.

27. Manjushri is a bodhisattva associated with wisdom in Mahayana Buddhism. In Tibetan Buddhism he is also a *yidam*, or meditational deity.

CHAPTER 3: BODHICHITTA

1. Shantideva, *The Way of the Bodhisattva*, chap. 1, v. 7.

2. Jigme Phuntsok Rinpoche specifically refers to the realization of the Great Perfection.

3. *Pandita* was a title in Indian Buddhism awarded to scholars who have mastered the five sciences, including the science of language, the science of logic, the science of medicine, the science of fine arts and crafts, and the inner science of spirituality.

4. Patrul Rinpoche, *The Words of My Perfect Teacher*, 7.

5. *Pratyekabuddhas*, meaning "solitary realizers," are followers of the Common Vehicle who attain the level of a pratyekabuddha arhat by themselves, in solitude.

6. Shantideva, *The Way of the Bodhisattva*, chap. 1, v. 15–16.

7. Patrul Rinpoche, *The Words of My Perfect Teacher*, 259.

8. The Sanskrit *bhumi* (Tib. *sa*) means stage or level but literally translates as "ground."

9. Shantideva, *The Way of the Bodhisattva*, chap. 5, v. 47.

10. Patrul Rinpoche, *The Words of My Perfect Teacher*, 221.
11. Shantideva, *The Way of the Bodhisattva*, chap. 5, v. 131.
12. Ibid., chap. 5, v. 136.
13. Ibid., chap. 5, v. 129.
14. Ibid., chap. 3, v. 13–14.

CHAPTER 4: THE THREE SUPREME METHODS

1. Patrul Rinpoche, *The Words of My Perfect Teacher*, 8.
2. The translation of this verse is adopted from *A Guide to The Words of My Perfect Teacher*, trans. the Padmakara Translation Group (Boston: Shambhlala Publications, 2004).
3. On this matter, Longchenpa taught the following: "The learned masters of the past have debated whether the Shravakas and Pratyekabuddhas realize the no-self of phenomena. In our tradition, we find many opinions expressed on this matter—just as even among the Shravaka School there were those that accepted and those that denied the existence of the personal self. Now, there can certainly be no success in the achievement of arhatship without the realization of the no-self of the aggregates. Yet, according to the teaching of the sutras, their realization of the phenomenal no-self is incomplete and of small account, like the hole gnawed by an insect in a mustard seed." The English translation of this quote is from *The Adornment of the Middle Way: Shantarakshita's Madhyamakalankara with Commentary by Jamgön Mipham*, trans. the Padmakara Translation Group (Boston: Shambhala Publications, 2010).
4. *Maha Prajnaparamita Sastra*, trans. Gelongma Karma Migme Chödrön, Wisdom Library, 2019, https://www.wisdomlib.org/buddhism/book/maha-prajna paramita-sastra/d/doc225241.html.
5. Heaven of the Thirty-Three (Skt. *trayastrimsa*; Tib. *sum chu tsa sum*) is the second heaven of the desire realm, situated on the summit of Mount Meru and presided over by thirty-three gods.
6. A struggle session was a sort of public humiliation and torture that was used particularly during the Cultural Revolution to shape public opinion and humiliate, persecute, or execute political rivals.

CHAPTER 5: THE TWO TRUTHS

1. *Relative truth* is also translated as "conventional truth," "all-concealing truth," or "concealer truth." *Ultimate truth* is also translated as "absolute truth."
2. Nagarjuna's *Root Stanzas of the Middle Way* is considered the foundational text of the Middle Way (Madhyamaka) tradition. In Tibetan Buddhist scholarship, there exists a distinction between the Autonomy School (Svatantrika) and the Consequence School (Prasangika) to the Middle Way reasoning, and the latter

of which represents the final and true thought of the Buddha. Masters like the supreme scholar Butön said that the distinction was entirely a Tibetan invention, and was not used among Indian Middle Way scholars, so Nagarjuna's *Root Stanzas* doesn't belong to either of the two sub-schools. Mipham Rinpoche believed that although the terms of Autonomy School and Consequence School attributed to Tibetans, the viewpoints of the two sub-schools originated from India.

3. Nagarjuna, *The Root Stanzas of the Middle Way*, trans. the Padmakara Translation Group (Boulder, CO: Shambhala, 2016), chap. 24, v. 9.

4. Literally, *sutrayana* means "the vehicle (*yana*) based on sutras." It means "all non-Vajrayana Buddhism," and is known as the "Causal Vehicle."

5. The Sanskrit word *kaya* literally means "body" but can also signify dimension, field, or basis. This term designates the different manifestations or dimensions of a buddha.

6. Shantideva, *The Way of the Bodhisattva*, chap. 9, v. 2.

7. The translation is taken from Chandrakirti, *Introduction to the Middle Way*, trans. the Padmakara Translation Group (Boston: Shambhala Publications, 2005). In Dzongsar Jamyang Khyentse Rinpoche's commentary, the verse is translated as "All entities can be seen truly or deceptively, so whatever there is has two natures: the domain of perfect seeing is suchness; false seeing has been termed all-concealing truth [by the Buddha]."

8. This definition is adopted from *In Praise of Dharmadhatu*, by Nāgārjuna and Rangjung Dorje, trans. Karl Brunnhölzl (Ithaca, NY: Snow Lion Publications, 2007).

9. This refers to the class of Buddhist literature primarily discovered by Nagarjuna in the second century. Its central topic is emptiness.

10. Nagarjuna, *The Root Stanzas of the Middle Way*, chap. 24, v. 10.

11. The verse is translated from Khenpo Sodargye's Tibetan-Chinese translation.

12. Ultimate truth can be the actual ultimate truth—the refutation of four extremes and eight fabrications of conceptual elaboration in the domain of nonconceptual wisdom posited by the Consequence School (Prasangika), or the approximate ultimate truth—the above-mentioned emptiness but as an object of mind in the domain of conceptual consciousness posited by the Autonomy School (Svatantrika).

13. Nagarjuna, *The Root Stanzas of the Middle Way*, opening verse.

14. Ibid., chap. 15, v. 10.

15. Mark Siderits and Shoryu Katsura, *Nāgārjuna's Middle Way: Mulamadhyamakakarika*.

16. *Adornment of the Middle Way*, v. 1.

17. The outer Vajrayana refers to the action tantra, the conduct tantra, and the yoga tantra; the inner Vajrayana refers to Mahayoga, Anuyoga, and Atiyoga.

18. Chandrakirti, *Introduction to the Middle Way*, chap. 5, v. 27.

19. The translation is from Ibid., 198–99.
20. *Adornment of the Middle Way*, v. 96–97.
21. *Adornment of the Middle Way*, v. 93.

CHAPTER 6: REBIRTH AND KARMA

1. A normal school is an institution created to train high school graduates to be teachers by educating them in the norms of pedagogy and curriculum. Most of these schools, where they still exist, are now called "teacher-training colleges" or "teachers' colleges."
2. Padmasambhava's teachings state that we go through four bardos from birth to death, and then rebirth: the bardo from conception to death; the bardo of the moment of death; the bardo of the absolute nature; and the bardo of coming into the next existence.
3. *The Diamond Sutra*, translated by the Chung Tai Translation Committee in 2009, from the Chinese translation by Tripitaka master Kumrajiva (fifth century).
4. This view corresponds to philosophical materialism, which holds the view that matter is the fundamental substance in nature, and all phenomena, including consciousness, are results of material interactions.
5. However, this doesn't mean all karmas are immutable. For example, Vajrasattva practice, if done properly, can purify negative karmas.
6. Chandrakirti, *Introduction to the Middle Way*, chap. 6, v. 37.
7. The Buddhist logic on rebirth comprises a comprehensive system of inferential methods that are hard for beginners to quickly digest. If you prefer to validate truth through logical reasoning, you should also study Sakya Pandita's *Treasury of Valid Knowledge and Reasoning* and the classical works of the Middle Way as mentioned in chapter 5 of this book. In doing so, you will eventually understand why beings' minds will never discontinue for no reason.
8. From a Buddhist perspective, all non-Buddhist philosophies are considered to fall into one of the two extremes: "eternalism," believing in the existence or permanence of something, or "nihilism," believing in nonexistence. Emptiness, the true nature of all phenomena, goes beyond both of these extremes, which was explained by the Buddha in the sutra of the second turning of the wheel of Dharma, and further elaborated upon by masters such as Nagarjuna and Chandrakirti.
9. L. Feuillet, H. Dufour, and J. Pelletier, "Brain of a White-Collar Worker," *The Lancet* 370 (July 21, 2007): 262.
10. R. Lewin, "Is Your Brain Really Necessary?" *Science* 210, issue 4475 (1980): 1232–34.
11. *Geshe* is a Tibetan Buddhist academic degree for monks and nuns used primarily in the Geluk lineage.

12. Khenpo Tsultrim Lodrö, a close Dharma brother of Khenpo Sodargye who joined Larung Gar in 1984, also published a book on past-life and present-life, titled the *Truth of Life*. Using scientific evidence and Buddhist logical reasoning, he provides very convincing arguments for the existence of rebirth. Impressed by his work, Khenpo Sodargye translated the book from Tibetan to Chinese, and gave the teachings to Chinese sangha members at Larung Gar.

Chapter 7: The Spiritual Teacher

1. Patrul Rinpoche, *The Words of My Perfect Teacher*, 137.
2. The nine attitudes are that which is like the dutiful child, a diamond, the earth, the foothills, a worldly servant, a sweeper, a foundation, a dog, and a ferry, respectively. For detailed explanations, refer to pages 77–80 of the *Great Treatise on the Stages of The Path to Enlightenment*, vol. 1, by Tsong-kha-pa.
3. Sachen Kunga Nyingpo, *Parting from the Four Attachments*, trans. Rigpa Translations, Lotsawa House, 2011, https://www.lotsawahouse.org/topics/parting-from-four-attachments/.
4. The eight worldly preoccupations are hope for happiness and fear of suffering, hope for fame and fear of insignificance, hope for praise and fear of blame, hope for gain and fear of loss.
5. Patrul Rinpoche, *The Words of My Perfect Teacher*, 137.
6. Ibid., 152.
7. *Mahasiddha* is a term for someone who embodies and cultivates the "*siddhi* of perfection" through spiritual practices. Specifically, siddhis are spiritual, paranormal, supernatural, or otherwise magical powers, abilities, and attainments.
8. The "meat" here refers to the flesh of a living animal that was slaughtered for food to serve to the teacher. It is not in the form of "pure meat"—the meat of an animal that died because of old age, sickness, or other natural causes that were results of its own past actions.
9. The translation of the verse is from *The Words of My Perfect Teacher*, 141.
10. Name of the clan or tribe in which the Buddha was born.
11. An *upasaka* is a male Buddhist layperson, who has taken refuge in the Three Jewels and undertaken the five precepts.
12. An *upasika* is a female Buddhist layperson, who has taken refuge in the Three Jewels and undertaken the five precepts.
13. The three higher trainings are the trainings in discipline, meditation, and wisdom. Because they actually lead to liberation and omniscience, they are called "higher" trainings.
14. According to the *Flower Ornament Sutra*, encouraged by Bodhisattva Manjushri, Sudhana visited and studied with fifty-three spiritual teachers and became equal to the buddhas in one lifetime. Among the fifty-three teachers, were a bodhisattva, king, perfumer, laywoman, old man, earth goddess, goldsmith, and so on.

15. The translation of Sunaksatra's conversation to the Buddha was taken from *The Words of My Perfect Teacher*, 147.

16. These texts include *The Words of My Perfect Teacher*, *Finding Rest in the Nature of the Mind*, *The Wish-Fulfilling Treasury*, *Treasury of Precious Qualities*, *The Great Treatise on the Stages of the Path to Enlightenment*, and *The Fifty Verses of Guru Devotion*.

17. In *The Words of My Perfect Teacher*, Patrul Rinpoche urges tantric practitioners to cultivate pure perception. For example, one can see the guru and one's vajra peers as Padmasambhava and his twenty-five disciples, or as Amitabha and the assembly of bodhisattvas, and so forth.

18. Jigme Phuntsok Rinpoche, *The Swift Bestowal of Blessings: A Guru Yoga*, trans. Adam Pearcey, Lotsawa House, 2018, https://www.lotsawahouse.org/tibetan -masters/khenpo-jigme-phuntsok/guru-yoga-swift-bestowal-of-blessings.

19. Jigme Phuntsok Rinpoche, *A Yogi's Song of Happiness*, trans. Adam Pearcey, Lotsawa House, 2018, www.lotsawahouse.org/tibetan-masters/khenpo-jigme -phuntsok/yogis-song-of-happiness.

CHAPTER 8: HEARING, CONTEMPLATION, AND MEDITATION

1. The Five Great Treatises form the basis of Buddhist philosophical studies, including *vinaya* (precept), *abhidharma* (superior knowledge of phenomena), *pramanavartika* (the valid cognition), Madhyamaka (the Middle Way), and *prajnaparamita* (the perfection of transcendent wisdom).

2. An example of such texts is *A Guide to The Words of My Perfect Teacher* by Khenpo Ngawang Pelzang (1879–1941).

3. Patrul Rinpoche, *The Words of My Perfect Teacher*, 35.

4. Dzogchen practitioners should refer to Mipham Rinpoche's suggestion in *Beacon of Certainty* that if one wants to realize the primordial purity in the ultimate Great Perfection, they have to master the unique tenets of the Consequence School (Prasangika); if one hasn't realized emptiness that is free from all extremes and elaborations, one cannot cut through to primordial purity.

5. This is the *Jewel Rain Sutra* (*Ratnamegha Sutra*) in the Chinese Tripitaka. The title is also translated as the *Jewel Cloud Sutra*.

6. *Letter to a Friend*, v. 107.

7. You may find the first 92 practical guidances belonging to the preliminary practices online at https://khenposodargye.org/

8. Establish an outer retreat by being away from attachment and anger.
Establish an inner retreat by not amassing wealth.
Establish a secret retreat by being free of dualistic perception.
Establish an upper retreat by not hoping for something good.
Establish a lower retreat by not fearing something bad.
Establish a peripheral retreat by avoiding being caught up in plans and actions.
If you establish these six types of retreat, obstacles cannot possibly arise.

9. *Siddhis* are spiritual, paranormal, supernatural, or otherwise magical powers, abilities, and attainments.
10. Patrul Rinpoche, *The Words of My Perfect Teacher*, 261.

CHAPTER 9: THE GREAT PERFECTION

1. The Three Vehicles refer to the three primary branches of Buddhism, including Theravada or "Common Vehicle," Mahayana or "Great Vehicle," and Vajrayana or "Diamond Vehicle."
2. The translation of this verse is from *The Words of My Perfect Teacher*, 9.
3. Five wisdoms are the five aspects of primordial wisdom. They are wisdom of *dharmadhatu*, mirrorlike wisdom, wisdom of equality, wisdom of discernment, and all-accomplishing wisdom.
4. The five buddha families are buddha family, vajra family, jewel family, lotus family, and action family.
5. The eight major practice lineages refer to the traditions that transported the Buddhist teachings from India to Tibet. They are Nyingma, Kadampa, Sakya, Marpa Kagyu, Shangpa Kagyu, Shije and Chö, Jodruk, and Nyendrub lineage.
6. *Vajradhara* means the "vajra holder," the primordial buddha. It is also an honorific title reserved for the senior-most masters.
7. The fourteen root downfalls refer to: (1) disrespecting the vajra master; (2) transgressing the words of the buddhas; (3) insulting one's vajra brothers and sisters: (4) abandoning love for sentient beings; (5) abandoning the bodhicitta in aspiration or application; (6) criticizing the teachings of the sutras and tantras; (7) revealing secrets to those who are unworthy; (8) mistreating one's body; (9) abandoning emptiness; (10) keeping bad company; (11) failing to reflect on emptiness; (12) upsetting those who have faith in the teachings; (13) failing to observe the samaya commitments; (14) denigrating women.
8. The five root vows are: (1) to venerate the guru; (2) not to abandon the unsurpassed [vehicle]; (3) not to interrupt the [practice of] mantra and mudra; (4) to have loving-kindness for those who enter the genuine path; (5) not to divulge the secret truths to others.
9. The two causes refer to the associated cause, which is the presence of the buddha nature, and the cooperative cause, which is the use of various substances during the empowerment, such as the vase, image cards, and so forth.
10. The Four Conditions are:

    1. the causal condition is the disciple who has faith and intelligence;
    2. the dominant condition is the teacher who is fully qualified;
    3. the objective condition is the teacher's knowledge of the empowerment, deities, mantras, and samadhi; and
    4. the immediate condition is the previous phase or empowerment, since each phase prepares the student for what follows, and that is why empowerments must be given in the proper sequence. (Source: rigpawiki.org)

11. Some faithful elderly practitioners, despite little knowledge of Buddhist doctrine, still attain rebirth in the Pure Land exclusively through reciting the name of Amitabha.

12. *A History of Tibet* is a historical work written by Ngawang Lobsang Gyatso, the fifth Dalai Lama, who ruled Tibet from 1617 to 1682.

13. *White Annals* is an unfinished work on the early history of Tibet by Gendün Chöpel.

14. *Red Annals* was written by Tsalpa Kunga Dorje in 1346, and mainly focuses on Tibetan history, both political and religious, as well as on some local events.

15. In a similar story in the *Great Jewel Heap Sutra* (*Maharatnakuta Sutra*) the Brahmin monk's name is Lifter of the Trees. In the beginning, the monk refused the young Brahmin woman's earnest request to live together, in order to uphold his vow of chastity. However, when knowing the young woman would rather die if she couldn't live with him, the monk generated great compassion and decided to give up his robes and marry her. They lived together as husband and wife for twelve years, before he was ordained as a monk again at a proper time. It says in the sutra that his dropping of chastity liberated him from the sufferings of many kalpas.

16. It is also called *yab-yum* in Tibetan ("father-mother"), which represents the primordial union of wisdom and compassion, depicted as a male deity in union with his female consort. The male figure represents compassion and the female partner represents wisdom.

17. Dilgo Khyentse Rinpoche, *The Excellent Path to Enlightenment*, trans. the Padmakara Translation Group (Ithaca, NY: Snow Lion, 1996), 24.

18. Je Tsongkhapa Lobzang Drakpa, *Three Principal Aspects of the Path*, trans. Adam Pearcy, Lotsawa House, 2006, https://www.lotsawahouse.org/tibetan-masters/tsongkhapa/three-principal-aspects.

Selected Bibliography

Āryadeva and Geshe Sonam Rinchen. *Āryadeva's Four Hundred Stanzas on the Middle Way: With Commentary by Gyel-Tsap.* Translated by Ruth Sonam. Ithaca, NY: Snow Lion Publications, 2008.

Blum, Mark L., trans. *The Nirvana Sutra.* Berkeley, CA: BDK America, 2014.

Chandrakirti. *Introduction to the Middle Way: Chandrakirti's Madhyamakavatara with Commentary by Jamgön Mipham.* Translated by the Padmakara Translation Group. Boston: Shambhala, 2005.

Choying Dorje. *The Complete Nyingma Tradition from Sutra to Tantra, Books 1 to 10: Foundations of the Buddhist Path.* Translated by Ngawang Zangpo. Boulder, CO: Snow Lion, 2015.

The Chung Tai Translation Committee, trans. *The Diamond of Perfect Wisdom Sutra.* 2009. www.chuatulam.net/a206/the-diamond-of-perfect-widsom-sutra.

Cleary, Thomas, trans. *The Flower Ornament Scripture: A Translation of the Avatamsaka Sutra.* Rev. ed. Boston: Shambhala, 1993.

Dilgo Khyentse Rinpoche. *The Excellent Path to Enlightenment.* Translated by the Padmakara Translation Group. Ithaca, NY: Snow Lion, 1996.

Easwaran, Eknath, trans. *The Dhammapada.* 2nd ed. Tomales, CA: Nilgiri Press, 2009.

Feuillet, Lionel, Henry Dufour and Jean Pelletier. "Brain of a White-Collar Worker." *The Lancet* 21 (July 2007): 262.

Gendün Chöphel. *In the Forest of Faded Wisdom: 104 Poems by Gendun Chopel.* Translated by Donald S. Lopez Jr. University of Chicago Press, 2009.

Jamgön Mipham. *Gateway to Knowledge*, vol. 4. Edited by Kathy Morris, translated by Erik Pema Kunsang. Hong Kong: Rangjung Yeshe Publications, 2012.

———. *Ascertaining the Two Kinds of Selflessness.* Translated by. Adam Pearcey. Lotsawa House, 2016. https://www.lotsawahouse.org.

Jigme Lingpa. *Treasury of Precious Qualities.* Translated by the Padmakara Translation Group. Boston: Shambhala, 2010.

Khenpo Ngawang Pelzang. *A Guide to the Words of My Perfect Teacher.* Translated by the Padmakara Translation Group. Boulder, CO: Shambhala, 2004.

Longchenpa. *Finding Rest in the Nature of the Mind.* Translated by the Padmakara Translation Group. Boulder, CO: Shambahala, 2017.

Lorber, John. "Is Your Brain Really Necessary?" *Science* 12 (December 1980): 1232–34.

Nagarjuna. *Nāgārjuna's Letter to a Friend: With Commentary by Kangyur Rinpoche.* Translated by the Padmakara Translation Group. Boulder, CO: Snow Lion, 2013.

———. *The Root Stanzas of the Middle Way.* Translated by the Padmakara Translation Group. Boulder, CO: Shambhala, 2016).

Nāgārjuna and Rangjung Dorje. *In Praise of Dharmadhatu: Nāgārjuna and Rangjung Dorje on Buddha Nature.* Translated by Karl Brunnhölzl. Boulder, CO: Snow Lion, 2021.

Nyoshul Khenpo Jamyang Dorjé. *A Marvelous Garland of Rare Gems: Biographies of Masters of Awareness in the Dzogchen Lineage.* Translated by Richard Barron. Padma Publishing, 2005.

Patrul Rinpoche. *The Words of My Perfect Teacher.* New Haven, CT: Yale University Press, 2011.

Shantarakshita and Jamgön Mipham. *The Adornment of the Middle Way: Shantarakshita's Madhyamakalankara with Commentary by Jamgön Mipham.* Translated by the Padmakara Translation Group. Boston: Shambhala, 2010.

Shantideva. *The Way of the Bodhisattva.* Translated by the Padmakara Translation Group. 2nd rev. ed. Boston: Shambhala, 2006.

Siderits, Mark and Shoryu Katsura, trans. *Nāgārjuna's Middle Way: Mulamadhyamakakarika.* Boston: Wisdom Publications, 2013.

Soma Thera, trans. *Kamala Sutta: The Buddha's Charter of Free Inquiry.* Access to Insight, 1994. www.accesstoinsight.org/lib/authors/soma/wheel008.html.

Thurman, Robert F., trans. *The Holy Teaching of Vimalakīrti: A Mahāyāna Scripture.* Reprint edition. University Park: Penn State University Press, 2001.

Tsong-kha-pa. *The Great Treatise on the Stages of the Path to Enlightenment* (Vol. 1). Translated by the Lamrim Chenmo Translation Committee. Edited by Joshua W. C. Cutler and Guy Newland. Boston: Snow Lion, 2014.

ABOUT THE AUTHOR

KHENPO SODARGYE was born in 1962 into a nomadic family in a small valley of the Tibetan region of Kham. He was ordained in 1985 and went on to become a lineage holder of the Great Perfection (Dzogchen) tradition, as well as a preeminent practitioner and scholar at Larung Gar Five Sciences Buddhist Academy in Sertar. Khenpo Sodargye was the great Jigme Phuntsok Rinpoche's chief Tibetan-to-Chinese translator. He has traveled extensively in North America, Europe, Africa, and Asia to offer teachings at Dharma centers and universities.